Feeding Frenzy

Attack Journalism and American Politics

A NEW LANAHAN EDITION IN POLITICAL SCIENCE

Other Books by Larry J. Sabato

Peepshow
(with Mark Stencel and Robert Lichter)

American Government:
Continuity and Change, Fourth Edition
(with Karen O'Connor)

Toward the Millennium: The Election of 1996

Dirty Little Secrets:
The Persistence of Corruption in American Politics
(with Glenn Simpson)

Campaigns and Elections

Paying for Elections

The Party's Just Begun:
Shaping Political Parties for America's Future

PAC Power:
Inside the World of Political Action Committees

Goodbye to Good-Time Charlie:
The American Governorship Transformed, Second Edition

The Rise of Political Consultants:
New Ways of Winning Elections

The Democratic Party Primary:
Tantamount to Election No Longer

Feeding Frenzy

Attack Journalism and American Politics

A NEW LANAHAN EDITION IN POLITICAL SCIENCE

Larry J. Sabato

Robert Kent Gooch Professor
Director, The Center for Governmental Studies
University of Virginia

LANAHAN PUBLISHERS, INC.

Baltimore

This book was composed in a typeface called Bembo.
Composition by Bytheway Publishing Services, Norwich, New York.
Manufacturing by Victor Graphics, Inc., Baltimore, Maryland.

ISBN 0-9652687-8-0

LANAHAN PUBLISHERS, INC.
324 Hawthorne Road
Baltimore, MD 21210

4   5   6   7   8   9   0

Contents

Preface

WITH THE ORIGINAL publication of *Feeding Frenzy* (and its follow-up version: Free Press, 1991, 1993), my goal was threefold. First, I wanted to present the phenomenon of "attack journalism." I called this phenomenon "feeding frenzy," and the phrase stuck. Thanks in part to the media itself, "feeding frenzy" is now fixed in the political vocabulary of our time. In describing "attack journalism," I wanted to expose through many cases and interviews the harm done by the media to politicians of all stripes, and in doing so, expose the harm done to the journalistic profession itself. I sought to examine the origins of feeding frenzies; how politicians would err in reacting to them; how journalists would stretch professional standards, and how feeding frenzies literally took on a life of their own.

Second, there was a history here, and I wanted to make it coherent. The Watergate Scandal of the 1970s seemed to be a pivotal point. Before that, journalists were content to keep within their own circle such items as President Franklin D. Roosevelt's debilitating medical condition and President John F. Kennedy's scandalous behavior with women. But this all changed in the aftermath of Watergate. Going through this history helped us to see what is with us today.

Third, I proffered some lessons in the original version of *Feeding Frenzy*—some recommendations of what the media might or might not change considering the harmful consequences of feeding frenzies. The lessons were not learned: The past decade has brought with it feeding frenzies in greater numbers, and if possible, frenzies of even greater intensities.

Last summer, college publisher Donald Fusting of LANAHAN PUBLISHERS, INC. inquired about the fate of *Feeding Frenzy*. I told him it was out of print. But he seemed to think that my original model of feeding frenzies was still current and that many of the original cases and interviews remained compelling. He proposed an alternative version of *Feeding Frenzy* for inclusion in a new series of books, THE NEW LANAHAN EDITIONS IN POLITICAL SCIENCE. The idea would be to prepare a much briefer manuscript based on the original book that would offer the essence of my model, as well as including many of the cases and interviews. This volume is the result: a concise and inexpensive book that can be assigned in college courses where our hopes for future change lie—with our students.

Preparing such a manuscript for the THE NEW LANAHAN EDITIONS series was not an easy task. Here I must, and am most pleased to, acknowledge the work of Ann G. Serow, Ph.D., experienced high school and college teacher and editor of the successful *LANAHAN READINGS in the American Polity*. Taking on the manuscript, Dr. Serow immediately comprehended my ideas, deleted what time has clearly passed, re-organized what needed coherence, and provided a more concise and readable manuscript. Special thanks go to the Kingswood-Oxford team of on-vacation proofreaders: Molly Albano, Sara Chase, Matt Ritter, Molly Shima, Laura Spinella, and Ryan Vautour, and to Debra Makay for her careful copyediting of the manuscript.

Larry J. Sabato
Robert Kent Gooch Professor
Director, Center for Governmental Studies
University of Virginia
November, 1999

Preface to the 1991 Edition

IN THE COURSE of my research for this volume, the feisty Texas journalist Sarah McClendon, a member of the White House press corps, made an observation to one of my student assistants that is worth citing at the outset:

You know, it's foolish the way all these professors write these books about something they've never experienced. You can tell him I said that. . . . What the hell is he [doing]? He knows nothing about the subject. Why doesn't he leave it to people who do know something about it? He has to come to us to get information to write his book.

In truth, any academic writing about the press is on the outside looking in, dependent on the journalistic guild for cooperation and insight. Fortunately for this professor, about 150 broadcast and print reporters plus several dozen candidates, political consultants, and campaign staffers, were willing to be helpful (including the redoubtable Ms. McClendon). Most were exceptionally frank, with relatively few exercising the close-mouthed discretion of master Republican operative Stuart Spencer, who — when asked to reveal a few of his presidential campaign secrets — perhaps wisely replied, "If I had terminal cancer, I'd tell you." I am deeply indebted to all those who so generously shared their time and memories, and, following Ms. McClendon's advice, I have tried to let those who "know something" about the subject share that knowledge by means of this book.

A few notes about the 208 interviews conducted for this volume: All quotations in the text are taken from on-the-record interviews unless otherwise noted. Minor grammatical and structural errors were corrected, and when an interviewee specifically asked me to do so during the course of an interview, off-color language was sanitized. With the main exception of interviewees who requested that their sessions not be recorded, all interviews were taped and the tapes have been preserved. A handful of interviewees (fewer than two dozen) agreed to talk only on deep background: No tapes were made, their names appear nowhere in this volume, and no direct anonymous quotations have been drawn from their sessions.

Those selected — sometimes serendipitously — for interviews comprise a reasonably diverse group of print and broadcast journalists, but no claim is made either for the representativeness or comprehensiveness of the chosen scribes and broadcasters. The vast majority are either veterans in senior positions who have had the opportunity to view their profession from a number of perspectives during lengthy careers or more-junior reporters who had covered one or more of the specific case studies surveyed for this book. Only about a dozen interviews that were requested were denied. A complete listing of on-the-record interviews appears in the Appendix.

I have come away from these sessions with many of journalism's best, with genuine respect and admiration for what their life's work has produced, as well as a greater appreciation for the difficulties they face in undertaking it. From the outside it is easy to romanticize journalism and equally easy to be hypercritical of it. I hope I have avoided both extremes, though I have not been shy in making observations and in second-guessing my interviewees. As a member of the only two groups of professionals — academics and authors — thinner-skinned than journalists, I can appreciate the reactions of some reporters and editors to this volume. I can only ask their forbearance if not their forgiveness for any hurtful comments it contains.

Not incidentally, I have been faced with some of the same agonizing decisions reporters and editors confront every day: Which conflicting version of events is closer to the truth? Which memories are more accurate? Which interpretations are more fair and balanced? What should be included and what excluded about the foibles of those making (and reporting) the news? Concerning accuracy, I have done my best to separate wheat from chaff, but undoubtedly I have not always succeeded. The full truth about many past political controversies seems destined to remain elusive. In my decisions about what to publish, I have tried to err on the side of caution, deleting surnames where unnecessary embarrassment would accrue and being only specific enough to make my point. On the other hand, where sources permitted and details were required to prove a significant allegation or assertion, I have not hesitated to do so.

In two and a half years of research for this book, I have benefited from the efforts, support, and guidance of many. Generous financial backing was provided by the Faculty of Arts and Sciences of the University of Virginia and the Center for the Humanities of the Virginia Foundation for the Humanities and Public Policy. For this essential help I would like to thank my departmental chairman, Clifton McCleskey; University of Virginia Provost Hugh P. Kelly; Dean of the Faculty of Arts and Sciences Raymond J. Nelson; and Virginia Foundation Executive Director Robert C. Vaughan and his staff. I also wish to acknowledge a travel grant from the Gerald R. Ford Foundation for research at the Ford presidential library.

Few investigators have ever been blessed with such remarkable student assistants. My University of Virginia group called themselves the Piranhas and adopted the slogan, "We Feed on Frenzies." Their enthusiasm and hard work thrilled and delighted me. Three were especially dedicated: Leslie Greenwald, whose meticulous administrative abilities were a godsend; Katie Dunn, who expertly supervised the manuscript in its later stages; and Mark Stencel, a very talented budding journalist whose keen interviewing skills were superbly applied to this project. The other splendid Piranhas were Christopher Barbuto, Jonathan Blank, Aaron Book, Mark Brazeal, Lewis Brissman, Ned Lilly, Miguel Monteverde, Richard Strulson, and Richard Winston. I salute them all.

Many others deserve acknowledgment as well, including a number of my University of Virginia faculty colleagues, Henry J. Abraham, Michael Cornfield, Martha Derthick, Steven E. Finkel, J. J. Murray, and David O'Brien; Scott M. Matheson, Jr., for his wise legal counsel; colleagues at other institutions, Timothy E. Cook of Williams College, Robert M. Entman of Duke University, and Charles O. Jones of the University of Wisconsin at Madison; Alan Ehrenhalt, Marcus D. Rosenbaum, and Sandra Stencel, all of Congressional Quarterly, Inc.; Rossita Thomas of the Congressional Research Service; friends Jill Abramson, Wyatt G. Andrews, E. J. Dionne, Jerald terHorst, and Kent Jenkins; Glenn Simpson of Roll Call; Bruce Nichols of Macmillan, Inc.; Barry Jackson of the Center for Public Service, University of Virginia, who designed Figure 4.1; my patient, long-suffering secretary, Nancy Rae; champion transcriber Linda Miller and her associate Regina Rae; skilled typist Debbie

LaMori; Steven Johnson and Steven Teles, who professionally scripted background papers on many of the case studies cited in this book; University of Virginia students Tao Bernstein, Greg Golladay, Charles Kromkowski, John Kirincich, and C. Gray Wheeler; Weldon and Mildred Cooper, for their usual sustenance; Jo McCleskey and Nancy Bowles for their friendship; and last but certainly not least, Erwin Glikes, president and publisher, and Peter Dougherty, senior editor, The Free Press, whose suggestions, encouragement, and belief in the importance of this project have been instrumental in its completion, and Edith Lewis of The Free Press for her superb shepherding of the manuscript to publication.

My thanks to all for helping me find some news and commentary that is fit to print. The remaining errors unfit for publication but in cold print nonetheless are my responsibility alone.

Charlottesville, Virginia
January, 1991

Preface to the 1993 Paperback Edition

Your book saved me. —GEORGE STEPHANOPOULOS, Clinton campaign and (later) White House communications director, referring to his use of *Feeding Frenzy* during Clinton's Gennifer Flowers crisis

Thanks for going after the sleaze-mongers. —MARVIN BUSH, son of George and Barbara, in a comment concerning the author's criticism of 1992 press reports about President Bush's supposed "mistress"

TIMING IS EVERYTHING in sex, politics, and publishing, and the first edition of this book was badly timed. As chance would have it, the book's release date was August 19, 1991, and its elaborate multimedia promotional launching collapsed under the weight of that day's attempted Russian coup aimed at ousting Mikhail Gorbachev from power. *Feeding Frenzy* might well have sunk without a trace, an innocent victim of a massive international frenzy—save for the American press.

The news media's behavior in the 1992 campaign revived the book and its central arguments, and made the phrase "feeding frenzy" a vital part of the political lexicon. From Bill Clinton's Gennifer Flowers to George Bush's "other Jennifer," and a dozen other episodes, too, the

airwaves and the headlines hummed and bristled with press excesses from
start to finish in 1992. And for all of it I am perversely grateful to my
friends in the media, for they have made this updated paperback edition
possible. Yet I still hope for the time when this book can be classified as
history and not current events, perhaps after some of the modest press
reforms proposed in these pages are finally adopted.

The first edition had its intended effect of provoking discussion among
journalists about declining standards in political coverage. I have benefited
enormously from the reactions of dozens of newspersons and other citizens
to my recommendations, and I appreciate the time many took to write
or call with their thoughts. Of course, some in the press reacted favorably
while others expressed disagreement or even anger. To the latter group,
at least, I managed to prove that, just as journalists are the politician's
burden, so also can academics be the journalist's burden.

Along the way to this second edition I was fortunate to have the
services of yet another superb research assistant, Michael J. Ard, a graduate
student in government and foreign affairs at the University of Virginia.
He was ever resourceful, dependable, and industrious, and I hereby declare
him to be an official Piranha. Mike joins me in thanking Mark Stencel
for his continuing research help to this project. One of the original band
of Piranhas, Mark has since gone on to greater things on the staff of the
Washington Post, and it is a source of pride and relief to me that his
association with a news critic did not make him a pariah as well as a
Piranha in his newsroom.

The staff members of The Free Press have truly been a delight to
work with over the past two years, and I sincerely thank them all—
especially Suzanne Herz. I have been fortunate to have had two fine Free
Press editors: first Peter Dougherty, and now Bruce Nichols, a friend
whose prodigious talents have been applied to several of my earlier projects
and, lately, to this one. May this edition be equal to the result of the
remarkable effort that the Free Press's staff put into the original.

Charlottesville, Virginia
March, 1993

Feeding Frenzy

Attack Journalism and American Politics

A NEW LANAHAN EDITION IN POLITICAL SCIENCE

CHAPTER ONE

Inquisition, American Style

Attack Journalism and Feeding Frenzies

I would never have comprehended the anguish visited by the "death watch" of the media. To have people surrounding our home with a real carnival atmosphere, shouting questions at you with a boom microphone and long-lens cameras, it makes one feel like a hunted animal driven to his lair.
— JIM WRIGHT, former Speaker of the House[1]

This is guilt by press. We might as well have hanging by the press. We [shouldn't] have Gestapo tactics by the media in this country.
— ROGER AILES, media consultant to the 1988 Bush/Quayle campaign, commenting on the coverage of Dan Quayle[2]

IT HAS BECOME a spectacle without equal in modern American politics: The news media, print and broadcast, go after a wounded politician like sharks in a feeding frenzy. The wounds may have been self-inflicted, and the politician may richly deserve his or her fate, but the journalists now take center stage in the process, creating the news as much as reporting it, changing both the shape of election-year politics and the contours of government. Having replaced the political parties as the screening committee for candidates and officeholders, the media propel some politicians toward power and unceremoniously eliminate others. Unavoidably, this enormously influential role — and the news practices employed in exercising it — has provided rich fodder for a multitude of press critics.

These critics' charges against the press cascade down with the fury of rain in a summer squall. Public officials and many other observers see journalists as rude, arrogant, and cynical, given to exaggeration, harassment, sensationalism, and gross insensitivity. From the conservative perspective, their reporting is, more often than not, viewed as evidence of blatant liberal bias, with the facts being fitted to preconceived notions. At the same time, the left indicts the media for being too hesitant to find fault with the status quo and too close to the very establishment they are supposed to check. Moreover, critics of all stripes see journalists as hypercritical of others yet vengeful when criticized themselves, quick to accuse yet slow to correct error, willing to violate the constitutional values of due process and fair trial in the Fifth and Sixth Amendments by acting as judge and jury, yet insistent on wrapping themselves in the First Amendment when challenged on virtually anything. Especially in the post-Watergate era of institutionalized investigative reporting and "star journalism," the press is perceived as being far more interested in finding sleaze and achieving fame and fortune than in serving as an honest broker of information between citizens and government.

In the wake of recent elections and political scandals, feelings about the news media are running particularly strong. This intensity shows in the kinds of modifiers that were added to the word *journalism* during the course of research and interviewing for this study:

blood-sport	peek-a-boo
character cop	Peeping Tom
cheap-shot	skinhead
food-fight	soap opera
gotcha	tabloid
hit-and-run	totalitarian
jugular	trash
keyhole	voyeur
paparazzi	

Some of these insulting adjectives came from a suspect class: politicians speared by the pens of scribes. All losing candidates naturally blame the press — politicians are never responsible for their own defeats — and surprisingly few winners have much good to say about the profession that they believe made victory more difficult. Such universal condemnation by politicians may ironically be taken as welcome proof that the press is doing its job.

Less reassuring, however, is another chorus of critics of modern journalism. A host of the most senior, respected, and experienced news professionals are themselves becoming equivocal about, embarrassed over, even repulsed by the conduct of some of their colleagues. While disagreeing with many of the criticisms leveled at reporters from outside the profession, they are nonetheless concerned about the media's growing distortion of the political process and deeply disturbed that legitimate press inquiry sometimes gets quickly and completely out of hand. And they fear a rising tide of antipress sentiment if the excesses are left unchecked. Already, several public opinion studies have revealed a dramatic decline in citizens' confidence in, and respect for, the news media: Most Americans no longer believe that the press generally "gets the facts straight," and they rate journalism among the professions with the "lowest ethical standards." Fully 78 percent in one study agreed that "the media spend too much time focusing on [campaign] things that are irrelevant, like candidates' personal lives" rather than centering their coverage on "the most important issues."[3] The evidence also suggests that recent controversies have weakened public support for First Amendment press freedoms.

These thoughtful and credible practitioners, many of them interviewed for this book, are less worried about the press's obsession with scandal — a staple of news in virtually every free society and certainly for the whole of American history — than with the *kinds* of scandals now considered reportable and the *manner* in which they are investigated and reported. First of all, scandal coverage is no longer restricted to misuse of public office, incompetence in the exercise of public responsibilities, or some other inadequacy or malfeasance in a *public* role; it extends to purely *private* misbehavior, even offenses, some of them trivial, committed long before an individual's emergence into public life. No wise politician today dares utter St. Augustine's legendary prayer: "Give me chastity and continency, but not just yet." Even a college student contemplating a political career had best think twice about youthful indulgences, given degenerating press standards. When *New York Times* columnist William Safire wrote the following words in protest just after Gary Hart's 1987 presidential withdrawal, they seemed alarmist:

If we do not turn the tables on the titillaters, we will load future news conferences with such significant policy questions as: "Sir, there are widespread reports of your impotence; when was the last time you and your wife had sexual relations?" "Madam, how do you deal with the persistent rumors that your national security adviser is a herpes victim?" "Have you or any member of your family ever taken illegal drugs?" "Some say that you once saw a psychiatrist — exactly what was your problem?"[4]

Since Safire's predictions appeared, variations of the latter two questions have already been asked of candidates, and one wonders only half whimsically whether fellow *Times* columnist Russell Baker's vision of "adultery disclosure forms" to be filed before the New Hampshire primary will also come to pass someday.[5] Soon no public figure may be too unimportant for close scrutiny. Editors and reporters at several major publications are seriously considering expanding their circle of legitimate targets for private life investigations to include top aides to candidates and even people uninvolved in politics who are "in the news" prominently. Similarly, no offense may be too minor to ignore in this "bare-all" age. Journalist Timothy Noah, while at *Newsweek*, was called with a scandal tip about Republican presidential candidate Alexander Haig: He was observed parking in a spot reserved for the handicapped in a supermarket parking lot. At this rate it seems almost inevitable that a candidate will be exposed for using an express checkout lane when purchasing more than the ten-item limit.[6]

Press invasion of privacy is leading to the gradual erasure of the line protecting a public person's purely private life. This makes the price of public life enormously higher, serving as an even greater deterrent for those not absolutely obsessed with holding power — the kind of people we ought least to want in office. Rather than recognizing this unfortunate consequence, many in journalism prefer to relish their newly assumed role of "gatekeeper," which, as mentioned earlier, enables them to substitute for party leaders in deciding which characters are virtuous enough to merit consideration for high office. As ABC News correspondent Brit Hume self-critically suggests:

We don't see ourselves institutionally, collectively anymore as a bunch of journalists out there faithfully reporting what's happening day by day. . . . We have a much grander view of ourselves: we are the Horatio at the national bridge. We are the people who want to prevent the bad characters from crossing over into public office.

Hume's veteran ABC colleague Sander Vanocur agrees, detecting "among some young reporters a quality of the avenging angel: they are going to sanitize American politics."[7] More and more, the news media seem determined to show that would-be emperors have no clothes, and if necessary to prove the point, they personally will strip the candidates naked on the campaign trail. The sheer number of journalists participating in these public denudings guarantees riotous behavior, and the "full-court press" almost always presents itself as a snarling, unruly mob more bent on killing kings than making them. Not surprisingly, potential candidates deeply fear the power of an inquisitorial press, and in deciding whether to seek office, they often consult journalists as much as party leaders, even sharing private vulnerabilities with newsmen to gauge reaction. The *Los*

Angeles Times's Washington bureau chief, Jack Nelson, had such an encounter before the 1988 campaign season, when a prospective presidential candidate "literally asked me how long I thought the statute of limitations was" for marital infidelity. "I told him I didn't know, but I didn't think [the limit] had been reached in his case!" For whatever reasons, the individual chose not to run.

As the reader will see later, able members of the news corps offer impressive defenses for all the practices mentioned thus far, not the least of which is that the press has become more aggressive to combat the legions of image makers, political consultants, spin doctors, and handlers who surround modern candidates like a nearly impenetrable shield. Yet upon reflection, most news veterans recognize that press excesses are not an acceptable antidote for consultant or candidate evils. In fact, not one of the interviewed journalists even attempted to justify an increasingly frequent occurrence in news organizations: the publication of gossip and rumor *without convincing proof*. Gossip has always been the drug of choice for journalists as well as the rest of the political community, but as the threshold for publication of information about private lives has been lowered, journalists sometimes cover politics as *Entertainment Tonight* reporters cover Hollywood. A bitter Gary Hart observed: "Rumor and gossip have become the coins of the political realm,"[8] and the *New York Times's* Michael Oreskes seemed to agree: "1988 was a pretty sorry year when the *National Enquirer* was the most important publication in American journalism." With all the stories and innuendo about personal vice, campaigns appear to be little more than a stream of talegates (or in the case of sexual misadventures, tailgates).

The sorry standard set on the campaign trail is spilling over into coverage of governmental battles. Ever since Watergate, government scandals have paraded across the television set in a roll call so lengthy and numbing that they are inseparable in the public consciousness, all joined at the Achilles' heel. Some lynchings, such as John Tower's failure to be confirmed as secretary of defense, rival any spectacle produced by colonial Salem. At the same time more vital and revealing information is ignored or crowded off the agenda. *Real* scandals, such as the savings-and-loan heist or the influence peddling at the Department of Housing and Urban Development in the 1980s, go undetected for years. The sad conclusion is inescapable: The press has become obsessed with gossip rather than governance; it prefers to employ titillation rather than scrutiny; as a result, its political coverage produces trivialization rather than enlightenment.

And the dynamic mechanism propelling and demonstrating this decline in news standards is the "feeding frenzy."

Like Sharks in a Feeding Frenzy

I feel like bait rather than a senior member of Congress. [The press are] investigative sharks.

—U.S. Congressman JACK BROOKS (D., Texas)[9]

The term *frenzy* suggests some kind of disorderly, compulsive, or agitated activity that is muscular and instinctive, not cerebral and thoughtful.[10] In the animal world, no activity is more classically frenzied than the feeding of sharks, piranhas, or bluefish when they encounter a wounded prey. These attack-fish with extraordinarily acute senses first search out weak, ill, or injured targets. On locating them, each hunter moves in quickly to gain a share of the kill, feeding not just off the victim but also off its fellow hunters' agitation. The excitement and drama of the violent encounter build to a crescendo, sometimes overwhelming the creatures' usual inhibitions. The frenzy can spread, with the delirious attackers wildly striking any object that moves in the water, even each other. Veteran reporters will recognize more press behavior in this passage than they might wish to acknowledge. This reverse anthropomorphism can be carried too far, but the similarity of piranha in the water and press on the campaign trail can be summed up in a shared goal: If it bleeds, try to kill it.

The kingdom of politics and not of nature is the subject of this volume, so for our purposes, a feeding frenzy is defined as the press coverage attending any political event or circumstance where a critical mass of journalists leap to cover the same embarrassing or scandalous subject and pursue it intensely, often excessively, and sometimes uncontrollably. No precise number of journalists can be attached to the term *critical mass*, but in the video age, we truly know it when we see it; the forest of cameras, lights, microphones, and adrenaline-choked reporters surrounding a Gary Hart, Dan Quayle, or Geraldine Ferraro is unmistakable. Table 1.1 contains a list of thirty-eight events from 1952 to 1992 that surely qualify as frenzies. They are occasions of sin for the press as well as the politicians, and thus ideal research sites: Several of them will serve as case studies for this book. A majority (twenty-three) are drawn from presidential politics, while seven examples come from the state and local levels, with the remaining eight focused on government scandals or personal peccadilloes of nationally recognized political figures. What follows is a brief case-by-case historical account of certain selected frenzies.

TABLE 1.1   MAJOR FEEDING FRENZIES: 1952 –1992

From Presidential Politics

1952	Richard Nixon's "secret fund"
1968	George Romney's "brainwashing" about Vietnam
1968	Spiro Agnew's "fat Jap" flap
1969	Ted Kennedy's Chappaquiddick
1972	Edmund Muskie's New Hampshire cry
1972	Thomas Eagleton's mental health
1976	Jimmy Carter's "lust in the heart" *Playboy* interview
1976	Gerald Ford's "free Poland" gaffe
1979	Jimmy Carter's "killer rabbit"
1980	Billygate (Billy Carter and Libya)
1983	Debategate (Reagan's use of Carter's debate briefing books)
1984	Gary Hart's age, name, and signature changes
1984	Jesse Jackson's "Hymietown" remark
1984	Geraldine Ferraro's family finances
1985–86	Jack Kemp's purported homosexuality
1987	Gary Hart and Donna Rice
1987	Joseph Biden's plagiarism and Michael Dukakis's "attack video"
1987	Pat Robertson's exaggerated résumé and shotgun marriage
1988	Dukakis's mental health
1988	Dan Quayle (National Guard service, Paula Parkinson, academic record, rumors such as plagiarism and drugs)
1988	George Bush's alleged mistress
1992	Bill Clinton and Gennifer Flowers, marijuana use, and draft evasion
1992	Ross Perot's alleged transgressions

From the State and Local Levels

1987–88	Governor Evan Mecham on the impeachment trail (Arizona)
1987–88	Chuck Robb and the cocaine parties (Virginia)
1983–90	Mayor Marion Barry's escapades (District of Columbia)
1987	Governor Dick Celeste's womanizing (Ohio)
1988	Mayor Henry Cisneros's extramarital affair (San Antonio, Texas)
1989–90	Governor Gaston Caperton's "soap opera" divorce (West Virginia)
1990	Texas governor's election: drugs, rape, and "honey hunts"

Noncampaign Examples

1973–74	The Watergate scandals
1974	Congressman Wilbur Mills and stripper Fanne Foxe
1986–87	The Iran-Contra affair
1987	Supreme Court nominee Douglas Ginsburg's marijuana use (and campaign repercussions)
1989	John Tower's losing fight to become secretary of defense
1989	Speaker Jim Wright's fall from power
1989	Tom Foley's rocky rise to the Speakership
1989–90	Barney Frank and the male prostitute

Feeding Frenzies: Capsule Summaries of Selected Case Studies

Richard Nixon's "Secret Fund" (1952):

Nixon, then a U.S. senator from California and the Republican vice presidential nominee, was accused of maintaining a hidden political fund of about eighteen thousand dollars collected from home-state supporters. The Democratic-leaning *New York Post* carried the first reports of the fund — somewhat sensationalized accounts that, in Nixon's words, "let [him] have it with both barrels." An avalanche of coverage followed, and soon the "secret fund" was the central issue of the presidential campaign. Though legal, the previously undisclosed nest egg caused such a stir that Nixon was nearly forced from Dwight Eisenhower's ticket. Some of Eisenhower's staff and key party elders wanted Nixon to step down; former GOP presidential nominee and New York Governor Thomas E. Dewey personally urged Nixon to resign. Nixon saved himself with a dramatic if maudlin television appeal that became known as the "Checkers speech," so named because of a black-and-white cocker spaniel a supporter had given to Nixon's young daughters, which Nixon swore never to give up, come what might in the political wars.

Spiro Agnew's "Fat Jap" Flap (1968):

Shortly after characterizing Polish Americans as "Polacks," Agnew, the Greek-American Republican candidate for vice president, referred to Gene Oishi, a Japanese-American campaign reporter from the *Baltimore Sun*, as "the fat Jap." Agnew had known the journalist for years and claimed the remark was in jest, but others saw the quip as more evidence of Agnew's ethnic insensitivity. After some initial hesitation due in part to Oishi's reluctance to go public, the *Washington Post* eventually broke the story, forcing a flustered Agnew to offer excuses and then apologies.

Ted Kennedy's Chappaquiddick (1969):

On the evening of July 19, 1969, Senator Edward M. Kennedy of Massachusetts drove his Oldsmobile off a wooden bridge on Chappaquiddick Island, drowning his passenger, a young campaign worker named Mary Jo Kopechne. The senator left the scene of the accident, did not report it to the police for many hours, and according to some accounts, considered concocting an alibi for himself in the interim. At the time, Kennedy managed to escape severe legal and political consequences for his actions thanks to his family's connections (which helped to contain the inquest and grand jury) as well as a nationally televised "Checkers"-

like speech a week after the accident. But virtually no journalist who has closely examined the evidence fully believes Kennedy's story, and more than twenty years later, the tragedy still trails the senator, with aggressive press investigations revived in five-year-anniversary intervals. Probably more than any other single factor, Chappaquiddick — a frenzy without end — has ensured that Ted Kennedy will not follow his brother John to the White House.

Edmund Muskie's New Hampshire "Cry" (1972):

Angered by *Manchester Union-Leader* publisher William Loeb's attacks on his wife and himself, Muskie — the early favorite for the Democratic presidential nod — raged against Loeb in front of the newspaper's building during a late February snowstorm. The *Washington Post's* David Broder, among many others, reported that Muskie had "tears streaming down his face," though in retrospect Broder and his colleagues acknowledge that the "tears" could have been melting snow. Whatever the truth, these dispatches about Muskie's lack of composure damaged his stable, steady image and contributed to Muskie's poorer-than-expected showing in the New Hampshire primary. Muskie's "cry" was a signal event in his surprising decline and eventual collapse as a credible front-runner.

Thomas Eagleton's Mental Health (1972):

Democratic nominee George McGovern's presidential hopes virtually evaporated when it was revealed shortly after the party convention that his newly chosen vice presidential running mate, Missouri Senator Eagleton, had been hospitalized on three occasions for depression and had undergone electroshock therapy. Eagleton had withheld the explosive information from McGovern at the convention, but too many Missouri politicians and others knew his secret for it to be kept under wraps. An anonymous tip to the *Detroit Free Press* about Eagleton's past began the chain of events that eventually brought the Democrat's sad episodes to public view. The least responsible coverage of the ensuing frenzy was provided by columnist Jack Anderson, who — based on a questionable and unverified tip — falsely reported a half dozen Eagleton "arrests" for drunk driving and other traffic offenses. Anderson's gross breach of journalistic ethics in printing unproved gossip generated some sympathy for Eagleton, but it could not save him. Under pressure from McGovern and many senior Democrats, Eagleton withdrew from the ticket, but not before McGovern had swallowed a suicide pill by declaring himself to be "1,000 percent" behind his doomed partner.

Jimmy Carter's "Lust in the Heart" Playboy Interview (1976):

Carter admitted in an unsolicited comment to two *Playboy* freelance writers that he had "looked on a lot of women with lust" and had "committed adultery in my heart many times," strange revelations all the more damaging because they appeared in a soft-porn magazine. A separate *New York Times Magazine* interview with Norman Mailer, also published during the general election campaign, added fuel to the frenzy's fire thanks to Carter's impolitic remark, "I don't care if people say 'fuck'." The press had a field day with Carter's oddball offerings, but some journalists correctly saw the controversy as a warning sign of the future direction of American politics. As the *New York Times* editorialized, the erosion of "the legitimate boundaries of [politicians'] private lives and intimate feelings" had begun.

Gerald Ford's "Free Poland" Gaffe (1976):

During a critical debate with Jimmy Carter a month before the presidential election, Ford declared in response to a question from Max Frankel of the *New York Times*, "There is no Soviet dominance of Eastern Europe." While the statement was prophetic given events a decade later, it seemed absurd to reporters at the time — so much so that Ford's chances of being elected president in his own right were diminished considerably. The press pounced on this passage of the debate and talked of little else for days afterward, so much so that a public initially convinced that Ford had won the debate soon turned overwhelmingly against him.

Jimmy Carter's "Killer Rabbit" (1979):

While home fishing in Georgia during a summer when his popularity was at low tide, Carter's small boat was "attacked" by a mysterious swimming rabbit, which the president warded off with a paddle. Once leaked into print by Brooks Jackson of the Associated Press, the bizarre story captured the press's and the public's imagination, becoming a metaphor for Carter's hapless, enfeebled presidency. The incident encouraged Senator Edward Kennedy's primary challenge to Carter's renomination, and it became a symbolic preamble to Carter's landslide loss in November 1980.

Gary Hart(pence) (1984):

With an upset victory over Walter Mondale in the New Hampshire Democratic primary, Hart became the wonder boy of 1984 politics, causing reporters and voters to ask, "Who is Gary Hart?" Some of the answers were perplexing: Hart had shortened his name (from Hartpence), shaved a year off his age, and changed his signature several times. Hart compounded his problems by offering vague or misleading explanations for the alterations, leaving the truth to be discovered piecemeal by investigative reporters for a dozen newspapers and magazines. The disclosures gave many voters pause, taking some of the luster off his rising star.

Jesse Jackson's "Hymietown" Remark (1984):

Jackson referred to Jews as "Hymies" and to New York City as "Hymietown" in January 1984 during a conversation with a black *Washington Post* reporter, Milton Coleman. Jackson had assumed the references would not be printed because of his racial bond with Coleman, but several weeks later Coleman permitted the slurs to be included far down in an article by another *Post* reporter on Jackson's rocky relations with American Jews. A storm of protest erupted, and Jackson at first denied the remarks, then accused Jews of conspiring to defeat him. The Nation of Islam's radical leader, Louis Farrakhan, an aggressive anti-Semite and old Jackson ally, made a difficult situation worse by threatening Coleman in a radio broadcast and issuing a public warning — in Jackson's presence — to Jews: "If you harm this brother [Jackson], it will be the last one you harm." Finally, Jackson doused the fires in late February with an emotional speech admitting guilt and seeking atonement before national Jewish leaders in a Manchester, New Hampshire, synagogue. Yet Jackson refused to denounce Farrakhan, and lingering, deep-rooted Jewish suspicions guaranteed an enduring split between Jackson and the Jews. The frenzy also heightened tensions between Jackson and the "white" establishment press.

Geraldine Ferraro's Family Finances (1984):

The first woman nominated for vice president by a major party, Ferraro was Walter Mondale's last best hope for an upset victory against Ronald Reagan. That hope was extinguished when the finances of Ferraro and her husband, John Zaccaro, became the dominant issue of the pre–Labor Day campaign. Charges of suspect real estate deals and unethical campaign funding filled the airwaves and newsprint for two weeks. Some publications, especially the *Wall Street Journal*, also pursued Zaccaro's purported, extremely tenuous Mafia connections — so intensely, in fact, that many observers perceived anti-Italian prejudice in the quest. Finally Ferraro held a cathartic late-August press conference before an audience of 150 journalists and three dozen television cameras to clear the air, and the campaign was then able to move on to other issues.

Jack Kemp's Purported Homosexuality (1985–86):

Kemp has suffered harm from a sordid rumor that keeps turning up like the proverbial bad penny. As an aide to California Governor Ronald Reagan in 1967, Kemp was indirectly and unfairly linked to a "homosexual ring" that existed within the Reagan circle. Kemp's immediate boss was one of the group, and Kemp had had some financial dealings with him that included the purchase of a lodge where, completely unknown to Kemp, gay parties were held. (Kemp had never even visited the lodge.) These flimsy connections allowed the rumor to follow him, however, and he has been forced to fight the recurrent gossip over nearly a quarter-century. Repeatedly the rumors have arisen, been debunked, and come alive again after the passage of a few years. In 1985 and 1986, preparing to campaign for the 1988 Republican presidential nomination, Kemp ran the gauntlet of investigation first by one news outfit, then another, then another, with unanimous findings of innocence but no final vindication. Occasionally, as with NBC's *Today* show, a media organization would use the earlier inquiries not as a reason to abjure further investigation but as a pretext to pursue the same tired subject.

Gary Hart and Donna Rice (1987):

In the public's mind, probably no event from the 1988 campaign proved more memorable than the undoing of Democratic candidate Hart. Long plagued by rumors of "womanizing," the front-running Hart watched his chances for the presidential nomination evaporate in May, when the *Miami Herald* reported that Hart had spent the night with an attractive young model named Donna Rice. Acting on an anonymous tip, the *Herald* had staked out Hart's Washington town house, and though the surveillance was flawed (it was not continuous, and both house entrances were not always covered), the circumstances were suspicious enough to generate a massive media frenzy. Hart fought back, but his damage-control operation collapsed in the face of other real or threatened disclosures, such as the revelation that Hart and Rice had earlier taken an overnight cruise to Bimini on the aptly christened yacht *Monkey Business*. The denouement came after a *Washington Post* reporter asked Hart, "Have you ever committed adultery?" Hart refused to answer the question at the time, but the meaning of the query soon became clear. The *Post* had identified another woman with whom Hart had had a long-standing relationship. Faced with that potential disclosure and caught up in an overwhelming media maelstrom, Hart went home to Colorado, withdrawing from the presidential race in a bitter farewell speech on May 8.

Joseph Biden's Plagiarism; Michael Dukakis's "Attack Video" (1987):

Democratic presidential candidate Biden, a U.S. senator from Delaware, was driven from the nomination battle after delivering, without attribution, passages from a speech by British Labour party leader Neil Kinnock. A barrage of subsequent press revelations also contributed to Biden's withdrawal: a plagiarism incident during his law school years; the senator's boastful exaggerations of his academic record at a New Hampshire campaign event; and the discovery of other quotations in Biden's speeches, these pilfered from past Democratic politicians. The controversy became two frenzies in one when it was disclosed that the Dukakis campaign had earlier secretly distributed to several news media outlets an "attack video" juxtaposing the Biden and Kinnock speeches and revealing Biden's word theft. The Dukakis campaign at first stonewalled and denied any part in the tape's distribution, but when the truth emerged Dukakis was forced to fire his campaign manager, John Sasso, who had orchestrated the maneuver, as well as his political director, Paul Tully, a less involved but knowing participant. Dukakis himself insisted he had no prior knowledge of their actions, and though wounded by it, his candidacy survived the incident.

Dukakis's Mental Health (1988):

Rantings by the Lyndon LaRouche cult about Michael Dukakis's supposed visits to a psychiatrist became an especially sordid chapter of the 1988 presidential campaign. Followers of the extremist LaRouche circulated leaflets containing unsubstantiated claims about Dukakis's mental health at the Democratic National Convention. Within weeks the allegations found their way into print, assisted by Dukakis's refusal to release his full medical records as well as rampant speculation on the subject in a few media outlets (especially the *Washington Times*). A "joking" reference to the matter by President Reagan triggered full-blown press disclosure of the rumor. The president quickly apologized for his crude remark ("I'm not going to pick on an invalid"), and the incident faded with no evidence at all emerging to confirm the baseless gossip.

Quayle Season (1988):

George Bush's selection of little-known Indiana Senator Dan Quayle as his Republican running mate proved to be one of the most controversial vice presidential choices in history. In fact, most major news organizations devoted far more resources to investigating rumors about Quayle than they did to covering the two presidential candidates. Within hours of

Bush's announcement, Quayle was embroiled in a melee with the media about his Vietnam War service in the National Guard. The intense inquiry into whether Quayle's wealthy family had pulled strings to help him avoid combat by gaining him admission to the guard nearly provoked a press riot at times. Other mini-"scandals," some related to the guard issue and some not, erupted as well, including Quayle's poor academic record, his admission to law school despite his college grades, and a golf trip to Florida whose other participants included the lobbyist-seductress Paula Parkinson. Rumors of purported Quayle wrongdoing—from youthful drug use to college plagiarism—also occasionally reached print without a shred of supporting evidence.

Mayor Marion Barry's Escapades (1983–90):

Few public officials — with the possible exceptions of Louisiana Governor Huey Long and Boston Mayor James Curley — have ever survived politically so many flagrant run-ins with the law and polite society for so long as did Washington, D.C.'s Mayor Marion Barry. The nation's capital had been abuzz with reports of the mayor's possible use of illegal drugs and numerous extramarital affairs for years before a January 1990 FBI sting aimed at Barry finally revealed the truth for all to see. While the police operation seemed like entrapment to some, Barry was arrested at the Vista International Hotel after he indisputably bought and smoked crack cocaine with a longtime paramour-turned-informant. The FBI usefully filmed the incident to convince doubting Thomases, not to mention a federal grand jury, which indicted the mayor on a cluster of cocaine and perjury charges. Despite the admission by Barry's own lawyer that the mayor had used drugs, a deeply divided, racially mixed jury deadlocked on most of the counts in August 1990, convicting Barry of a single misdemeanor charge of cocaine possession. The judge and the voters of D.C. were less sympathetic: Barry was sentenced to a jail term, a relatively harsh penalty for a first drug conviction, and then the beleaguered mayor lost his bid for a city council seat in the fall. Barry retained the support of about a quarter of his city, however, and his case badly strained race relations. Many local African Americans directed their ire not just at white prosecutors but also at white-owned media, especially the *Washington Post*, which had been strongly critical of Barry.

Watergate (1973–74):

The grandest scandal of modern times, Watergate led to the resignation of President Nixon and the convictions of many White House aides—

even two U.S. attorneys general — on various charges. The scandal began with the bugging of Democratic National Committee headquarters in Washington's Watergate office-apartment complex by officials of the Committee to Reelect the President on June 17, 1972. A cover-up of White House links to the burglary ensued, orchestrated by Nixon's closest staffers with the president's participation. The nation then endured two years of damaging revelations by Congress and the press — especially the *Washington Post* team of Bob Woodward and Carl Bernstein. After forced resignations, indictments galore, and a tissue of presidential lies, Nixon's defenses collapsed with the Supreme Court–mandated release of the tapes of his White House meetings about Watergate. Ironically, these tapes had been made secretly by Nixon himself, and they contained a "smoking gun" — clear proof of Nixon's involvement in the cover-up. Faced with near-certain impeachment in the House and conviction in the Senate, Nixon became the only president ever to resign, on August 9, 1974. In an unrelated but coordinate scandal, Vice President Spiro Agnew had resigned his office earlier (in October 1973) after a bribery and corruption probe. His resignation was part of a plea bargain that included no contest to a charge of income tax evasion. In many ways Watergate transformed journalism, not least by elevating the practitioners of investigative reporting to hero status.

Barney Frank and the Male Prostitute (1989):

This story was broken by the conservative *Washington Times*, which trumpeted every juicy morsel with front-page hype. It turned out that Congressman Frank had had a lengthy relationship with a male hooker who ran a bisexual prostitution service out of Frank's apartment. Though Frank was apparently ignorant of some of the prostitute's activities, his indiscretion had been so great that his standing in the House was greatly damaged. His home district in Massachusetts was more forgiving, reelecting him easily in 1990 despite a House reprimand of Frank passed overwhelmingly in July of that year.

Cumulatively, these capsule summaries yield several insights about feeding frenzies. First, there has been a far greater concentration of frenzies in recent years, the reasons for which will be examined later. Second, the classic American scandal centering on financial impropriety (the "Teapot Dome" genus) has been overtaken by new types appropriate to our culture in the media age — gaffes, "character" issues, and personal lifestyle questions. Third, all frenzies are not equal. Some are extended and monumentally important megafrenzies (such as Watergate), others blessedly brief and less damaging all around ("frenziettes," if you will). Some are simple one-ring media circuses, others the complex, three-ring variety. Some are triggered by a major, real event (such as Ted Kennedy's deadly Chappaquiddick accident), while others are press-sustained or -exaggerated "medialities," political scientist Michael J. Robinson's term for "events, developments, or situations to which the media have given importance by . . . featuring them in such a way that their real significance has been modified, distorted, or obscured."[11] These differences acknowledged, all case-study events nevertheless have in common the kind of press coverage contained in the definition of feeding frenzy.

Several cautions are in order. By no means are the chosen cases meant to be an exhaustive list of modern feeding frenzies. However, while not comprehensive, the list is representative of the phenomenon, and the conclusions reached later are applicable to many other examples. Nor is press treatment of special feeding frenzy events necessarily indicative of day-to-day coverage of politics and government, though one suspects it is becoming more so. After all, the potential for coverage to spin out of control is always present, and the standards and excesses observed during frenzies inevitably affect everyday journalism. Finally, it should be emphasized that not all consequences of frenzies are bad. To the contrary, some questionable candidacies and some regrettable governmental practices have been ended as a result, and intense coverage has attracted the public's attention to certain abuses as nothing else could have. Yet the means chosen by the media certainly do not always justify even the most golden ends.

Throughout this book, the reader may wish to consider the weighty obligations that should accompany the press's exceptional privileges. No group in America life is as constitutionally protected as is the press; no profession is afforded such wide latitude for unfettered enterprise as is journalism; no individuals are so entrusted with enormous yet nearly unchecked influence as are newspersons. In exchange for this position of privilege, the press has a special and coordinate obligation to be extraordinarily painstaking and eminently fair in exercising its freedoms. The abuses painfully visible during feeding frenzies damage the political fabric of America by cheapening public discourse, trivializing the campaign agenda, breeding cynicism, and discouraging able people from seeking public office. Just as important for the press, journalism's excesses undermine the very credibility of the news profession. This serious threat to the press's most valuable asset inevitably menaces press freedom and, therefore, the democratic system that relies greatly on the check provided by the news media.

The stakes are high, then, not just for the press but for the rest of us. The future quality of American democracy and its politics depends in good measure on reversing the deterioration in journalistic standards — a decline that will be documented in this book.

CHAPTER TWO

The Press of Yesteryear

From Canard to Cover-up to Exposé

The journalists of the United States [possess] a vulgar turn of mind. The characteristics of the American journalist consist in an open and coarse appeal to the passions of his readers; he abandons principles to assail the characters of individuals, to track them into private life and disclose all their weaknesses and vices. Nothing can be more deplorable than this abuse of the powers of thought.

IT WAS NOT Gary Hart or any modern political figure who uttered these words, though it is easy to imagine it so. Rather, Alexis de Tocqueville penned these lines in 1835,[1] proving beyond question that some of the press abuses of the present day have a long and distinguished history. It is that history which will be examined in this chapter, with particular emphasis on the latter half of the twentieth century.

The press has played many roles and assumed many postures in U.S. history. Moreover, like every other American institution, its power, promise, and performance have varied greatly from era to era. Just in the modern age — from World War II to the present — the breadth, depth, and influence of the news media have expanded enormously, as political journalism has passed through three successive phases in its recent development:

From about 1941 to 1966, journalists engaged in what I would call "lapdog" journalism — reporting that served and reinforced the political establishment. In this period, mainstream journalists rarely challenged prevailing orthodoxy, accepted at face value much of what those in power told them, and protected politicians by revealing little about their non-official lives, even when private vices affected their public performance.

Wartime necessities encouraged the "lapdog" mentality that had already become well established in Franklin Roosevelt's earlier administrations. But lapdog journalism perhaps reached its zenith under another Democratic president, John F. Kennedy.

From about 1966 to 1974 was a period of "watchdog" journalism, when reporters scrutinized and checked the behavior of political elites by undertaking independent investigations into statements made by public officials. The Vietnam War and the Watergate scandals stimulated this kind of journalism. In the later years of this period, the first discussions of private lives appeared, though usually only in the context of public performance.

Since about 1974, political reporters have engaged in what I would term "junkyard dog" journalism — political reporting that is often harsh, aggressive, and intrusive, where feeding frenzies flourish, and gossip reaches print. Every aspect of private life potentially becomes fair game for scrutiny as a new, almost "anything goes" philosophy takes hold.

Press Past as Press Prologue

Journalism — the process and profession of collecting and disseminating new information about subjects of public interest (i.e., the news) — has been with us in some form since the dawn of civilization. Yet its practice has often been remarkably uncivilized, and far more so at the beginning of the American Republic than today.

A hint of future directions appeared in the very first newspaper published in America in 1690, which carried a report that the king of France "used to lie with" his son's wife.[2] George Washington escaped most press scrutiny of his private life, but he detested journalists nonetheless; his battle tactics in the Revolutionary War had been much criticized in print, and an early draft of his "Farewell Address to the Nation" at the end of his presidency contained a condemnation of the press described as "savage."[3] Thomas Jefferson was treated especially harshly by elements of the early American press. Jefferson, normally a defender of a free press, commented, "even the least informed of the people have learned that nothing in a newspaper is to be believed."

Jefferson probably did not intend that statement to be taken literally, since he himself was instrumental in establishing the *National Gazette*, the newspaper of his political faction and viewpoint. The *Gazette* was created to compete with a similar paper founded earlier by Alexander Hamilton and his anti-Jefferson Federalists. The era of party newspapers extended from Washington's tenure through Andrew Jackson's presidency. The editor of Jackson's party paper, the *Globe*, was included in the president's influential if informal Kitchen Cabinet, and all of Jackson's appointees with annual salaries greater than one thousand dollars were required to buy a subscription. Incidentally, from George Washington through James Buchanan, all government printing contracts were awarded to the newspaper associated with the incumbent administration.[4]

The partisan press eventually gave way to the "penny press." In 1833 Benjamin Day founded the *New York Sun*, costing a penny at the newsstand. Politically a more independent publication, not inextricably tied to one party, it was the forerunner of the modern press built on mass circulation and commercial advertising to produce profit. By 1861 the penny press had so supplanted its partisan predecessor that President Abraham Lincoln announced his administration would have no favored or sponsored newspaper.

The press thus became markedly less partisan but not necessarily more respectable. Mass-circulation dailies sought wide readership, and readers were clearly attracted by the sensational and the scandalous. The sordid side of politics became the entertainment of the times. One of the best-known examples occurred in the presidential campaign of 1884, when the *Buffalo Evening Telegraph* headlined "A Terrible Tale" about Democratic nominee Grover Cleveland. In 1871, while sheriff of Buffalo, the bachelor Cleveland had allegedly fathered an illegitimate child. Even though the woman in question had been seeing other men too, Cleveland willingly accepted responsibility since all the other men were married, and he had dutifully paid child support for years. Cleveland won the election.

The era of the intrusive press was in full flower. First "yellow journalism" and then "muckraking" were in fashion. Pioneered by such prominent publishers as William Randolph Hearst and Joseph Pulitzer, yellow journalism featured pictures, comics, and color designed to capture a share of the burgeoning immigrant population. The front-page "editorial crusade" became common, the motto for which frequently seemed to be Damn the Truth, Full Speed Ahead. The muckrakers—so named by President Theodore Roosevelt after a special rake designed to collect manure[5]—took charge after the turn of the century. Such journalists as Upton Sinclair and David Graham Phillips searched out and exposed real and apparent misconduct by government, business, and politicians in order to stimulate reform.[6] There was no shortage of corruption to reveal, of course, and much good came from their efforts. But an unfortunate side effect of the emphasis on crusades and investigations was increasing violation of legitimate privacy rights. The current controversy about press intrusiveness is in some ways an echo of the one that raged a century ago, when Louis D. Brandeis — later to become a distinguished Supreme Court justice — and his law partner Samuel D. Warren published these all-too-familiar thoughts about journalistic excesses:

The press is overstepping in every direction the obvious bounds of propriety and of decency. Gossip is no longer the resource of the idle and of the vicious, but has become a trade, which is pursued with industry as well as effrontery. To satisfy a prurient taste the details of sexual relations are spread broadcast in the columns of the daily papers. To occupy the indolent, column upon column is filled with idle gossip, which can only be procured by intrusion upon the domestic circle.[7]

News Rules for New Times

As the news business grew, its focus gradually shifted from passionate opinion to corporate profit. Newspapers hoping to maximize profit were more careful not to alienate the advertisers and readers who produced their revenues, and the result was less harsh, more "objective" reporting. Meanwhile, media barons became pillars of the establishment, no longer the antiestablishment insurgents of yore, and in some cases they were perhaps less willing to give offense to fellow elites who occupied public office. World War I also seemed to change the rules of engagement for many journalists, as patriotism made victory a common cause for newsmen and politicians alike. After the war, real scandal — the massive Teapot Dome uproar of Warren Harding's administration — occupied those still in the muckraking tradition, as did the 1927 revelations about Harding's White House mistress, Nan Britton, and their illegitimate child. The press was apparently unaware of Harding's torrid affair with Britton, which was sometimes consummated in a closet near the Oval Office. The truth came out only after the deaths of President and Mrs. Harding, when Britton published a best-selling account.[8]

As in so many other areas of American life, Franklin D. Roosevelt's presidency rewrote the rules of engagement for the relationship between the press and the politicians they covered. That relationship became more "correct," in diplomatic parlance, with the tone of press coverage increasingly sedate. Perhaps it was partially the crisis atmosphere and sobering effect of the Great Depression, whose dire consequences for most Americans even the end of Prohibition in 1933 could not lighten. Then, too, most working reporters were probably strong personal supporters of Roosevelt who rooted for him to succeed, and those who did not still recognized his overwhelming popularity. Later, World War II had its effects; reporters practiced self-censorship and refused to publish any information about America's leader that might give aid and comfort to the Axis powers.

Whatever the precise combination of causes, Roosevelt was protected by the press in ways that would have amazed some of his harassed predecessors. Roosevelt, a polio victim, was wheelchair-bound, but of 35,000 press photographs of FDR, only two showed his wheelchair.[9] When the president occasionally fell in public, photographers would take no pictures and live radio broadcasters would make no mention of the fact.[10] In 1944, as a desperately ill Roosevelt sought a fourth term, publishers such as Henry Luce — a GOP supporter, incidentally — refused to print photos hinting at FDR's poor state of health. And many supporters knew of or strongly suspected the president's estrangement from his wife, Eleanor, while others were clearly aware of Roosevelt's relationship with Lucy Mercer, who resided in the White House at times and was with FDR in Warm Springs at his death. Not a word of any of it reached print.

The Rooseveltian rule of thumb for press coverage of politicians was simple, and it endured for forty years: The private life of a public figure should stay private and undisclosed unless it seriously impinged on his or her public performance. (In many cases even *serious* infringement did not warrant publication, as we shall see.) The rule's variations and practical applications were many. Politicians could earn special absolution for sins committed on the road, for example, as the *Washington Post*'s David Broder recalls:

The first campaign I covered was 1960 and I remember being formally initiated on the press bus by Bill Lawrence of the *New York Times* into something he called the "West of the Potomac" rule, which was basically that anything that happened west of the Potomac, you didn't talk about east of the Potomac. And it was a protective rule both for what was then substantially an all-male press corps and also for the candidates. We gave them kind of a license to live whatever way they wanted to live on the road.

The post-Roosevelt Washington press corps, according to veteran journalist Paul Duke, was "rather sleepy" and "content to report from handouts and routine news briefings. There wasn't a hell of a lot of penetrating coverage back then." The press and the pols were frequently pals, socializing together extensively and assisting one another in various ways.

The Media's Camelot: JFK and the Press

The most taboo topic of all in the 1950s and 1960s was sex, of course. The Roosevelt example notwithstanding, John F. Kennedy's presidency provided the most severe test ever of the rule. Kennedy's reputation, and the press's, would be shaped by the outcome.

By many credible accounts, John F. Kennedy was not King Arthur but Sir Lancelot in the Camelot of his presidency. Even thirty years later, it is not the large number of his sexual dalliances so much as his sheer recklessness in pursuing them that stuns. Garry Wills, author of *The Kennedy Imprisonment*, has written of "the calculated regimen of John Kennedy, the daily dose of sex taken, as it were, for muscle tone."[11] And indeed, Kennedy put Warren Harding, Franklin Roosevelt, and his other adulterous predecessors to shame with a "regimen" that included, over the years, many dozens of liaisons. Marilyn Monroe, Jayne Mansfield, Angie Dickinson, and stripper Blaze Starr are only a few of the better-known paramours with whom JFK has been linked, not to mention a healthy dose of anonymous airline stewardesses, secretaries, and aides. There was apparently no slackening of Kennedy's sexual pursuits after his election. To the contrary, the presidency facilitated his desires, with fre-quent travel, time away from his wife, guaranteed privacy courtesy of the ever-discreet Secret Service, and the alluring aphrodisiac of his supremely powerful office.

It is now well established that one of Kennedy's principal mistresses was Judith Campbell (née Immoor, later Exner), a striking brunette intro-duced to Kennedy by Frank Sinatra in Las Vegas in early 1960. Shortly thereafter Sinatra played matchmaker for Campbell again, this time to Sam Giancana, the notorious Chicago mob boss and successor to Al Capone as head of a billion-dollar crime syndicate. Campbell was close to both men over much of the same period, and the evidence is strong that each man was fully aware of the other. Campbell appears to have acted as a courier, and there was no lack of business to be conducted between these scions of politics and crime. Giancana assisted Kennedy's presidential campaign with a substantial financial contribution before the crucial West Virginia primary and later in Cook County, Illinois, where a squeaker election was won for Kennedy, possibly corruptly. More impor-tant, Giancana had been recruited by the CIA for a Mafia–U.S. govern-ment collaborative effort: the assassination of Cuban Premier Fidel Castro, to be attempted sometime during the early 1960s. The motives for cooper-ation were different but complementary. The United States wanted to rid itself of a Communist dictatorship just ninety miles from its shores, while the Mafia bosses intended to avenge Castro's shutdown of all their Cuban casinos as well as curry favor with American politicians who had the power to prosecute them.

These extraordinary revelations came to light not because of a persis-tent, inquisitive press but indirectly by means of a governmental inquiry. A dozen years after Kennedy's assassination, the U.S. Senate Select Intelligence Committee was investigating the CIA's plans to kill foreign leaders when Campbell's role was uncovered. The committee, headed by Idaho Democratic Senator, and Kennedy family friend, Frank Church, down-played the JFK-Campbell relationship, and its report cited only an un-named, genderless "friend" of the president when referring to Campbell.

Did an aggressive, post-Watergate press leap to uncover the whole truth? Hardly. The initial story was leaked exclusively to Watergate's lead attack dog, the *Washington Post*, whose editors chose to minimize and bury it deep inside the November 16, 1975, edition. The bylined reporter, Lawrence Stern, and his *Post* colleague George Lardner both thought it was a front-page story because it was a scoop and Stern was able to provide many details about the incident, including Campbell's name.[12]

There the matter rested for a month, with no widespread interest expressed by the news media, until a report surfaced that Senate committee staffers were being ordered to swear they were not the source of the earlier leak to the *Post*. This sparked *New York Times* columnist William Safire to launch a virtual one-man crusade against an attempted cover-up by Senator Church, who was at that time also a presidential aspirant. Among Safire's observations in his first column on the subject was this compelling justification for his examination of Kennedy's private life even under terms of the Rooseveltian rule of coverage: "The private life of any public figure is nobody's business but his own. . . . But when the nation's Chief Executive receives even a few calls from the *home telephone* of the leader of the Mafia in Chicago, that crosses the line into the public's business."[13]

Safire's agitation opened the sluice, and the JFK-Campbell relationship became fair game for extensive review in virtually all major publications. Some went further. *Time* magazine, for instance, used the opportunity to discuss Kennedy's long-protected wild side; backdoor tales of JFK's White House trysts and the names of many of his flames first achieved respectable print there. While controversial at first — the strong reaction to the *Time* piece demonstrated that many preferred not to hear of Kennedy's foibles — the truth about the private JFK has gradually emerged since that time. Judith Campbell Exner herself, well paid to do so by publishers and magazines, told sordid tales of White House intrigue.[14] For those who care to see, the presidential knight's once-shining armor has been tarnished badly.

The most pressing question left to answer is why the press did not see anything worth reporting about the president's shocking behavior *at the time*. There surely can be no doubt of the seriousness of Kennedy's offenses; these were indiscretions that mattered. Consider the elements:

- The possibilities for blackmail of the president were many and substantial. Kennedy was reportedly quite casual about his flings, once openly discussing his need for frequent sex with British Prime Minister Harold Macmillan and Macmillan's foreign secretary. Unfriendly as well as friendly intelligence services might well have known of the president's entangling alliances. Inside the U.S. government there is evidence that one official used his knowledge of JFK's compromised private life to his personal advantage. FBI Director J. Edgar Hoover learned of the Campbell love triangle, and at a private luncheon with the president in March 1962 laid out his findings. It would logically follow that Hoover's tacit or overt threat to expose Kennedy's philandering with a mob moll made Hoover virtually untouchable by the normal chain of command control. Indeed, the autocratic FBI chief seemed to have carte blanche authority to do as he wanted in many sensitive areas.

- Public funds, facilities, and personnel were involved in JFK's illicit affairs with Campbell and others. From the White House to *Air Force One* to hotels around the country, some aides and security men must have scheduled and facilitated Kennedy's meetings with women. Some have claimed that members of the Secret Service actually procured "appropriate" women for the president, especially at non-Washington sites in advance of his trips.[15]

- The president's recklessness had potentially grave consequences bearing directly on his public responsibilities. On occasion Kennedy reportedly shook his guards and the military aide carrying the nuclear code "football" to seek more privacy with a sexual partner. This was at the height of the Cold War era, when a president might have only a few minutes' response time before a Russian missile attack.[16]

- Exner and others have told of JFK's intermittent use of marijuana and amphetamines.[17] Mind-altering drugs affect anyone's judgment, and in the nuclear age such a presidential transgression would be exceptionally foolhardy.

White House reporters during the Kennedy administration were not aware of all of this, of course. Some may have known nothing at all, but virtually every major journalist had heard and suspected plenty. As columnist Mary McGrory puts it, "The classic question has become, 'What did you know about John Kennedy's private life and when did you know it?'" For many newsmen of the time, the answer can only be a confessional. Granted, as Jack Germond cautions, "After the fact, reporters always claim they knew." But the abundance of proof available to reporters before and during Kennedy's presidency is indisputable.

Why did none of the incidents ever reach print or air during Kennedy's lifetime? According to Robert Pierpoint, this was a subject of active debate among some journalists at the time:

There was quite a bit of discussion in the White House press corps about how we should handle this. It was an ethical problem of concern to us in part because he was fairly blatant about it. But overall the basic feeling was that we shouldn't touch it because it wasn't our business or the public's business.

This adherence to the Rooseveltian "rule," which benefited the press as well as politicians, was indisputably part of the explanation. David Broder suggests as much:

The reason we didn't follow up [on the womanizing rumors] is clearly because of that "gentleman's understanding" that boys will be boys — and it was all boys. Nobody wanted to spoil the fun for anybody else, and besides, the attitude back then was, what the hell difference does it make? . . . The hypocrisy was evident, was acknowledged, and indeed was institutionalized. But I would argue that it was as much self-protective of the press corps as it was protective of the candidate. What people said was, "Well, shit, if you're going to whistle on this guy . . . are we going to go back and start telling about each other? Is that the next step?"

This "institutionalized hypocrisy" would be less offensive in retrospect if the media had been a bit more reluctant (if not guilt-ridden) while participating. Yet in some cases adherence to the rule seemed downright enthusiastic. As the *Wall Street Journal*'s Brooks Jackson sums up the problem, here was a case where "reporters got too close to their source." Many journalists liked Kennedy, agreed with his politics, and revelled in their acceptance by, and association with, the glamorous, dashing, wealthy, jet-setting Kennedys. Kennedy also had a disarming ability to charm journalists by taking them into his confidence, soliciting their views, and making them "part of the action." Broder again:

One of Kennedy's techniques for dealing with the press was to say things that were so goddamn candid — to some about sexual things but even his political comments — so that you knew if you printed it, you would be ending your intimate relationship: that is, the president would say, "you couldn't have thought that I would say something like that on the record." It was a way of co-opting us.

Using this device and others, says Howell Raines of the *New York Times*, "Kennedy was alarmingly successful at turning journalists into cheer-leaders."

It is also true that the press may have been doing what much of the public wanted. People cherish their myths and heroes; while they love gossip, many also shrink from a painful or shocking truth, and in retrospect they would prefer not to know. When JFK's secret life became public in the mid-1970s — long after emotions about Camelot had had a chance to cool — some publications were inundated with letters denouncing them for "destroying" Kennedy's reputation and "assassinating" him anew. In the heyday of the Kennedy era, playing the role of skunk at the garden party was considerably less appealing. Longtime *Detroit News* White House correspondent Jerald F. terHorst, later President Ford's first press secretary, explains, "No paper wanted to look like it was going out of its way to find something nasty about this very popular president." TerHorst also pointed out that Kennedy was president before the courts weakened the libel laws, so the threat of legal action alone served as a deterrent to publication of anything but an airtight case.

Lyndon Johnson, Richard Nixon, and the Media

Kennedy's two successors as president, Lyndon B. Johnson and Richard M. Nixon, are often viewed today as having endured an unremittingly hostile and critical press, by contrast to the kid-gloves treatment accorded JFK. While that may have been true on some policy matters, especially Vietnam for Johnson and Watergate for Nixon, the reality was quite different in the area of private life. Both LBJ and Nixon benefited from the liberal expansion of the Rooseveltian rule under Kennedy; while suffering the bark and bite of the newly developed "watchdog" journalism — engendered in good part because of press opposition to the Vietnam War (and the governmental lying attending the war) — these presidents still enjoyed the full private-life protections more typical of journalism's "lapdog" era.

Naturally enough, it was Johnson, the vulgar Texan, far more than the uptight Nixon, who pushed the rule to its limits. Johnson's lack of couth was legendary and for the most part went unreported. When presented with a prize bull by Tennessee's governor one day, Johnson punched a male reporter in the ribs and in earshot of the entire press corps, including women, he is said to have asked, "Hey, how'd you like to be hung like that?" Even in more formal settings, Johnson could exhibit foul-mouthed coarseness that made Nixon sound like a piker when he cursed in the taped privacy of the Oval Office. When asked a tough question by a persistent reporter during an impromptu press conference in Texas, an irritated Johnson replied, "What are you trying to do, fuck me?"[18] The physically unappealing Johnson was almost certainly less successful with women than Kennedy, but it was not for want of trying — and again, the press knew about some of his attempts. A White House

secretary and friend of Douglas Kiker (then of the *Atlanta Constitution*)
told him how Johnson "used to chase her around and around his desk.
She would have to crawl through it just to get away from him." Jerry
terHorst, in his book on *Air Force One*, told an eye-opening tale about Vice
President LBJ's pursuit of Nancy Dickerson (then Nancy Hanschman)
of NBC News.[19] Conducted over a radio telephone line accessible to
eavesdropping by any radio operator sweeping the airwaves, Johnson,
flying over the Atlantic toward Europe, pleaded with Dickerson, then in
Vienna, to meet him for dinner in Paris. As terHorst phrased it, Johnson's
interest in Dickerson "was something other than fatherly," and his attempts
to corral Dickerson and many other women were no secret in the White
House press corps.

Of greater fascination for an observer in the 1990s is the press's lack
of concern about Johnson's occasional drinking bouts. Long before he
became president, LBJ was known as a hard drinker. Robert Novak recalls
a National Press Club party when Johnson, then Senate majority leader,
was "drunk as a skunk. He was just raving. A friend and I shepherded
him into the elevator and then his limousine. The next day at his regular
morning press conference, Johnson said, 'Oh, Novak—had a little too
much to drink last night, did you?'" Everybody in the know laughed,
and no one reported a word.

It will surprise many—probably no one more than the press-loathing
Richard Nixon—to learn that Nixon also benefited from the news media's
reluctance to discuss private matters. In both the 1960 and 1968 campaigns,
journalists refrained from making public some information about the
Republican presidential candidate's consultations with a New York psy-
chotherapist in the 1950s and possibly later. (Columnist Drew Pearson
disclosed the matter in a 1968 National Press Club speech only *after* the
November election.) Even during the height of the Watergate scandals,
when damaging revelations about Nixon tumbled forth with great regular-
ity and eager acceptance, the press considered certain matters to be off-
limits. Several high-ranking White House correspondents received anonymous but seemingly authoritative telephone calls claiming the beleaguered
president was having a homosexual affair with his close friend Charles
("Bebe") Rebozo. (The calls were made during Nixon's weekend visits
with Rebozo on Key Biscayne, Florida.) The charge appeared ridiculous
on its face—and no evidence whatsoever has been unearthed to support
it in the years since—yet many ludicrous allegations were thoroughly
investigated and sometimes printed or aired in the highly charged atmosphere of Watergate. But this particular indictment was simply too personal for the times. Said one newsman on the receiving end of the calls:

"I didn't think it was my role to look into it. If he was having an affair with Rebozo, fine. Maybe he needed it; he was under a lot of strain."

Nixon was one of the last presidential politicians not to be challenged on a major private matter, and in his case it may partly have been a reluctance to pile on since he was already sinking under the weight of Watergate. By the 1970s the standards were changing rapidly, and the Rooseveltian rule was being sharply revised. Some of the causes, such as relaxation of libel laws, predated Watergate. But the seminal event, the apocalypse that spawned both a major feeding frenzy and the "character issue," was Ted Kennedy's accident at Chappaquiddick.

Edward Kennedy and Chappaquiddick: The Personal Turns Public

For years Senator Edward Kennedy, like his brother Jack, had enjoyed an adoring press. During his first campaign for the Senate in 1962, the *Boston Globe* broke the bombshell story of Ted's undergraduate expulsion from Harvard for cheating under the subdued and kindly headline TED KENNEDY TELLS ABOUT HARVARD EXAMINATION INCIDENT with the text presented as Kennedy's admirable, straightforward attempt "to set the record straight."[20] After JFK's assassination the press, perhaps partly out of grief and partly in hopes of one day recapturing the glory of Camelot, was even more protective of Ted and hid the truth of the excessive drinking, compulsive womanizing, and erratic behavior so obvious to newspeople who covered him.[21] Then came Chappaquiddick, and the press never looked the other way again. Kennedy has been too flagrant, his actions too costly for one young woman, and his excuses too flimsy and insulting to the many perceptive minds in the press corps. Good reporters were ashamed of, and the press as a whole was severely criticized for, the process of concealing Kennedy's manifest vices that had preceded the senator's own cover-up of the facts surrounding the accident.

With Chappaquiddick, many journalists began to believe that private life and individual character traits had such profound effects on politics and public policy that politicians' personal lives could no longer be ignored. This attitude was reinforced and extended by two other political upheavals that occurred in rapid succession: the dumping of Senator Thomas Eagleton from the 1972 Democratic ticket on account of his previously hidden psychiatric problems, and the Watergate revelations — not just about corruption but about Nixon's personality, tendencies, and frame of mind. From this "unholy trinity" of Chappaquiddick, Eagleton, and Watergate was created a new godhead to replace the Rooseveltian one. The new rule of political coverage was as open as its predecessor had been closed:

Since any aspect of private life is potentially relevant to an official's public performance, the reasoning went, everything is fair game — personal relationships, private behavior, and any matter exhibiting an official's "character" or "judgment." Furthermore, literally anything that affects the political players and outcome — including unproved rumor and innuendo — can be made public in the process.

This new "anything goes" rule has evolved along with the "junkyard dog" journalism it encourages. The new rule has also been gradually broadened over the two decades of its development, as new circumstances and fresh frenzies have pushed the frontiers of acceptable scrutiny ever forward. For instance, Nixon's possible psychotherapy was not an issue in 1968, but after the 1972 Eagleton frenzy, a mere hint — false as it turned out — that a stressed Gerald Ford had also been a patient of Nixon's presumed psychiatrist became one of the major issues investigated in his Senate confirmation as vice president in 1973.

Just as sex and alcohol (and later drugs) were firmly established as legitimate subjects for journalistic inquiry, other aspects of the campaign and the candidate have come to be dissected with a heretofore-unknown precision. For instance, every phrase, quip, and gaffe has become grist for the character mill. Spiro Agnew's "fat Jap" remark, Jimmy Carter's "lust in the heart" admission, and Jesse Jackson's "Hymietown" slur were presented as mirrors into their souls, the contents of their characters. Edmund Muskie's alleged "cry" in the New Hampshire snow and Gary Hart's change of name, age, and signature led to press psychoanalysis of their supposedly derivative personalities and personal inadequacies. Ground once off-limits has been converted into territory worth fighting for. Jerry terHorst characterizes the press corps of the 1950s and 1960s this way: "We stayed a hundred yards away from anything that had a sexual overtone." By contrast, an ambitious reporter today would do almost anything to get to a political sex scandal first. The standards of financial propriety for legislators have become much stricter; yesterday's accepted norm for private enrichment is today's career-threatening conflict of interest. In today's environment the private lives of aides, even those not on the public payroll, are sometimes as closely scrutinized as those of the elected representatives they serve. "Anything goes" coverage extends to the state and local levels as well, with similar effects.

This discussion has traced the path of American journalism from its partisan origins to the current day, with particular emphasis on the evolution from "lapdog" to "watchdog" to "junkyard dog" in the years since Franklin Roosevelt's presidency. As it has happened, the abandonment of "lapdog" journalism and the press's desire to check the policy excesses of government are praiseworthy. So, too, is the press's newfound determination to reveal the personal excesses of those running the government when the vices affect their public performance. But along the way, legitimate "watchdog" journalism has spun out of control and has developed the nasty demeanor and side effects of the "junkyard dog" variety.

The Changing Media Scene

Paradoxically and simultaneously, the news media have expanded in some ways and contracted in others, dramatically changing the ways in which they cover politics. The growth of the political press corps is obvious to anyone familiar with government or campaigns. The number of print (newspaper and magazine) reporters accredited at the U.S. Capitol has jumped greatly. Similarly, the gain for broadcast (television and radio) journalists is equally impressive and proportionately larger. On the campaign trail a similar phenomenon has been occurring. In the early primaries in the 1960s, a presidential candidate would attract a press entourage of at most a couple of dozen, but by the 1980s, a hundred or more print and broadcast journalists could be seen tagging along with a front-runner. A politician's every public utterance is thus made and intensively scrutinized in a media pressure-cooker.

At the same time, more journalists are not necessarily attracting a larger audience, at least on the print side. Partly, of course, newspapers have been losing their audience to television. At the dawn of the 1960s a substantial majority of Americans reported that they got most of their news from newspapers, but by the latter half of the 1980s television was the people's choice by almost two to one. Moreover, by a 55 to 21 percent margin, Americans now say they are inclined to believe television over newspapers when conflicting reports about the same story arise. Of course, most individuals still rely on *both* print and broadcast sources, but there can be little question that television news is increasingly important, that despite its many drawbacks (simplicity, brevity, entertainment orientation, and so on) it is "news that matters."[22] While not eclipsing newspapers, television frequently overshadows them, even as it often takes its agenda and lead stories from the headlines produced by print reporters (especially those working for the "print elite," such as the *New York Times*, the *Washington Post*, the *Wall Street Journal*, AP, UPI, *Time, Newsweek*, and *U.S. News & World Report*).

The television news industry differs from its print cousin in a variety of ways. For one, the number of outlets has been increasing, not declining as with newspapers. The three networks now receive broadcast competition from CNN, C-SPAN, Fox and PBS. While the audiences of all the alternate shows are relatively small compared to the networks, they are growing while the networks' market shares contract. The potential for further cable expansion is still large. In addition, the national TV news corps is often outnumbered on the campaign trail by local television reporters. Satellite technology has offered any of the thirteen hundred local stations willing to invest in the hardware an opportunity to beam back reports from the field.

The decline of the networks' market shares and the local stations' decreasing reliance on the networks for news — coupled with stringent belt-tightening ordered by the networks' corporate managers — resulted in severe news staff cutbacks at NBC, CBS, and ABC during the 1980s. These "economy measures" had an obvious impact on the morale of television journalists.

More important, the cutbacks have affected the quality of broadcast journalism. Many senior correspondents bemoan the loss of many desk assistants and junior reporters who did much of the legwork necessary to get less superficial, more in-depth pieces on the air. "Even critical interviews sometimes just don't get done," one network newsman noted. As a consequence, campaign stories requiring extensive research are often discarded in favor of the simplistic, eye-catching, sexy items that frequently form the core of a feeding frenzy incident.

CHAPTER THREE

The Boys in the Bush

The Attack Mentality within the News Media

As you look into press coverage of various things, you discover there's no rational explanation to it. There just isn't.
—journalist PAUL DUKE

ANYONE WHO HAS ever worked in the news media, or studied the subject dispassionately, knows full well that the conspiracy theorists are wrong. "The media" constitute no monolith, and news organizations are too disorganized and too competitive for much plotting to occur, much less succeed. Feeding frenzies are certainly not the result of intentionally coordinated action, and the chaos surrounding press coverage of most of them surely proves it. Rather, frenzies are a product of other conditions and forces both internal and external to the media, some that have fermented for many years, some of relatively recent vintage. Paul Duke is unquestionably correct in his assessment of the often nonsensical basis of much press coverage, yet academics by nature are inclined to search out the method in the madness.

Growing Intensity and Declining Civility in Coverage

Conditions are always ripe for the spawning of a frenzy in the brave new world of omnipresent journalism. Advances in media technology have revolutionized campaign coverage. Handheld miniature cameras (minicams) and satellite broadcasting have enabled television to go live anywhere, anytime, with ease. Instantaneous transmission (by broadcast and fax) to all corners of the country has dramatically increased the velocity of campaign developments today, accelerating events to their conclusion at breakneck speed. Gary Hart, for example, went from front-runner to ex-candidate in less than a week in May 1987. Continuous public-affairs programming, such as C-SPAN and CNN, helps put more of a politician's utterances on the record, as Senator Joseph Biden discovered to his chagrin when C-SPAN unobtrusively taped Biden's exaggeration of his résumé at a New Hampshire kaffeeklatsch in 1987. (This became a contributing piece of the frenzy that brought Biden down.) C-SPAN, CNN, and satellite broadcasting capability also contribute to the phenomenon called "the news cycle without end," which creates a voracious news appetite demanding to be fed constantly, increasing the pressure to include marginal bits of information and gossip and producing novel if distorting "angles" on the same news to differentiate one report from another. The extraordinary number of local stations covering national politics today — up to several hundred at major political events — creates an echo chamber producing seemingly endless repetitions of essentially the same news stories. This local contingent also swells the corps traveling the campaign trail. Reporters not infrequently outnumber participants at meetings and whistlestops.

In such situations any development is almost inevitably magnified and overscrutinized; the crush of cameras, microphones, and people combined with the pressure of instant deadlines and live broadcasts hype events and make it difficult to keep them in perspective. When a frenzy begins to gather, the intensity grows exponentially. Major newspapers assign teams of crack reporters and researchers to the frenzy's victim. When Democratic vice presidential candidate Geraldine Ferraro was the focus of an investigation concerning her family finances in August 1984, for example, the *Philadelphia Inquirer* assigned a dozen employees to the story full-time, and the *Washington Post* and the *New York Times* five each. Television news time is virtually turned over to the subject of the frenzy. Republican vice presidential nominee Dan Quayle was the subject of ninety-three network evening news stories over the twelve days of his frenzy in August 1988 — more coverage than twelve of the thirteen presidential candidates had received during all the primaries combined. Much like the vice presidential candidates who had preceded him as frenzy victims (Eagleton and Ferraro), Quayle alone garnered three-quarters of all the evening network time devoted to the presidential campaign during his August dog-days tribulations. By comparison, the Reagan-Gorbachev summit meeting in December 1987 registered considerably less network news interest.

Oddly enough, just as the coverage of major political events is expanding with the increased number of media outlets on the campaign trail, the quality is simultaneously declining. Superficial "horserace" reporting — a focus on who's ahead, who's behind, and who's gaining — is now the norm. Of seven thousand print news stories surveyed between Labor Day and Election Day 1988, 57 percent were horserace items and only 10 percent concentrated on real policy issues.[1] On television network news shows during the 1988 primary campaign, two and a half times more horserace pieces aired than did policy-issue ones.[2] Reporters love the horserace and not policy for many different reasons. Most journalists are generalists, unfamiliar with the nuances and complexities of many issues and therefore unprepared to produce stories on them. Then, too, the horserace fits many reporters' rather cynical view of politics: Elections are but a game, not a contest of the power of competing ideas. And a focus on the horserace is partisanly unbiased, far more "objective" and disinterested than is the construction of an issue agenda for coverage. The length of modern campaigns also plays a part; reporters may be trying to stave off boredom. Tom Rosenstiel of the *Los Angeles Times* compares American elections not to a horserace but a football game where "we play about forty-seven quarters before any of the fans have come into the stadium. The players are on the field and the press is in the press box, and we have played for months before anybody cares or watches." The boredom is such that the press from time to time stops analyzing the game and concentrates attention on individual players — the source of more than one feeding frenzy over the years. Moreover, this gamesmanship coverage of politics aids in developing frenzies by discouraging sober discussion of policy choices while fostering personal conflict, controversy, and confrontation.

Competitive Pressures

The first lady of Ohio had a succinct explanation for the Cleveland *Plain Dealer*'s front-page focus on her husband, Governor Richard Celeste, and his alleged extramarital affairs. "They're not in the business to promote Dick Celeste. They're in the business to sell papers. And this sells papers."[3] Scandal and sex do indeed sell well — a great deal better than dispassionate discussion of policy issues. Some of *Nightline*'s highest ratings ever were achieved for shows featuring scandal-ridden Christian broadcasters Jim and Tammy Faye Bakker. ABC News's Peter Jennings admitted that he and his cohorts "deliberately exploited them for the sheer prurient entertainment value." The same could be said of the media's handling of Donna Rice in Gary Hart's travails or Barney Frank and his male prostitute. The *Miami Herald*'s Tom Fielder conceded that the Hart/Rice story had embedded in it "a salaciousness that attracted the tabloid press . . . and accounted for a great deal of the feeding frenzy in that incident." The more tantalizing the offense, or the more it breaks new ground, or the more volatile the mix of vices, the more irresistible the subject is for the news media.

While it has ever been so, today there are added inducements for scandal coverage. First and foremost, contemporary corporate managers of broadcast and print media are closely attuned to the contribution each outlet makes to the overall profit or loss of the company. Ratings and circulation increasingly matter, and executives are not unaware of the experiences of newspapers such as the *Washington Times*, where screaming front-page headlines about Barney Frank and an unrelated homosexual "call boy" scandal boosted newsstand sales by 25 percent in the summer of 1989. Nor are individual reporters oblivious to the reward system in the age of "star journalism." Fame and fortune are the gold waiting at scandal's end for some in journalism today, as columnist Robert Novak explains: "There are very high rewards in both money and in fame, much more than when I started. A lot of very bright young men and women want the rewards, and they know damn well that carefully covering Fairfax County [Virginia] is not going to do it for them."

The competitive philosophy governing this new generation of go-getters can be summed up by their fevered adherence to journalism's two ultimate imperatives: "Don't get beaten to a story by another media outlet," and "If we don't break this, someone else will." Both axioms, and especially the second one, serve to encourage bad judgment and premature decisions to publish or air stories. As the *Washington Post's* managing editor, Len Downie, concedes, "A lot of half-baked things get into newspapers including ours because people begin writing too much before they have enough facts." Some of the worst situations occur when competing media outlets become dueling entrepreneurs.

Competitive pressures also propel each newspaper and network to try to make a contribution, no matter how small and insignificant, to the unfolding frenzy. Each new fact merits a new story, complete with a recapitulation of the entire saga. This press pile-on by means of minor, "wiggle" disclosures is an ordeal akin to water torture (drip, drip, drip, day after day after day) and well known to many frenzy victims. Every newly uncovered, unattributed quotation borrowed by a Biden speech-writer became a news item. "Every day there is another story about another building," sighed an exasperated Geraldine Ferraro in her time of trial over family finances in 1984.[4] Wiggle disclosures extend and intensify a feeding frenzy, while stretching the available news thin and reiterating it excessively.

Good judgment can be impaired and high standards lowered in the heat of competitive battle. What is becoming more common, and more disturbing, is the domino effect of a kind of "lowest-common-denominator" journalism: If one newspaper prints or one broadcaster airs a story, however questionable or poorly documented it may be, other media outlets will then publish or broadcast the news without independently verifying it. This abdication of journalistic responsibility encourages the purveyors of campaign smut to search out the weak media link. Many newsmen cited experiences similar to those of ABC News's Hal Bruno, who received a series of telephone calls in the summer of 1987 about a major presidential campaign rumor:

I got calls from people saying, "The *New York Times* is gonna break the story on the weekend." And every week it would be a different news organization you were told had pictures and was gonna break the story. At one time a person called me and said he understood that ABC is gonna break this story. And I said to this person, "You're talking to ABC," and the person said, "Oh, I meant NBC," and hung up.

"All you need anymore is to get to the right reporter and the right paper, which is to say the wrong reporter and the wrong paper, to get a rumor published," notes the *Washington Post's* Benjamin Weiser. Some journalists, such as the *New York Times's* Michael Oreskes, bemoan the loss of vigilant gatekeeping by many in the media:

When we refuse to publish it, someone else publishes it. Then the fact that they published it becomes a story, so it still gets into our paper even though we originally decided it wasn't worth publishing. So you really lose control over your role as the gatekeeper. . . . On account of this some people begin to weaken their standards and say, "Well, it's going to get published anyway, so I'll go ahead and publish it first."

In good part then, a feeding frenzy is a manifestation of an adrenaline-charged news competition, with the initial contest won by the outlet breaking the story, the middle-round honors captured by the worst dramatic and sensational revelations, and the endgame trophy captured by the organization that checkmates the candidate and thereby takes him or her out of the race.

Pack Journalism

Oddly enough, the intense competitive pressures we have just discussed cause reporters (and editors and producers) to move forward together in essentially the same story direction, rather than on different story tracks. It is called "pack journalism," a condition former U.S. Senator Eugene McCarthy (D., Minn.) once likened to blackbirds on a telephone wire: When one moves to another wire, they all move. Timothy Crouse, in his delightful book *The Boys on the Bus*, described pack journalism by comparing the press to "a pack of hounds sicked on a fox."[5] A third animal metaphor, fish schooling, may be even more telling. Fish in schools keep close tabs on each other and copy every school movement reflexively. The reason for the behavior is obvious: Any fish out of school loses the safety of numbers and is vulnerable prey.

For partly the same reason, the free market of journalism often leads to sameness instead of diversity. "Journalists want to do something their peers think is meaningful," notes Jim Gannon, formerly of the *Des Moines Register*. "Peer pressure matters in this big fraternity, and so you tend to turn to the sexy topic of the hour." *CBS Evening News* anchor Dan Rather puts it in practical terms for a newsman competing for an audience:

With journalists, as with almost everybody else, fear is the great motivator. Now, if you don't run the big scandal story of the day, Mabel is going to lean over the back of the fence and say to Ann, "What do you think about X's mistress?" and Ann's going to say "What are you talking about?"

"Where have you been, Ann, on planet Pluto?"

"Well, no, I just watched Dan Rather and he didn't say anything about it."

"Well, I watched Jimmy Jones and they did a lead piece and a follow-up piece on it."

That's the fear. That's what drives this. Once the herd moves, it's really hard to turn it and you find yourself just galloping along.

Most frequently, a major newspaper breaks the initial "big scandal story," and points the herd in a certain direction. But equally often today, a widely watched television broadcast — the evening news or a Sunday commentary show — will be the first indication of the conventional wisdom that will develop in reaction to the print story. David Brinkley's Sunday morning panel on ABC (*This Week with David Brinkley*) did the honors for Gary Hart after the *Miami Herald's* same-day publication of the Donna Rice affair, with Sam Donaldson, among others, suggesting the effective end of Hart's candidacy was nigh.

It is remarkable to observe just how quickly even the heavyweights fall into line with the pack when a frenzy begins. In retrospect, when one weighs the real importance of Gerald Ford's "free Poland" remark in his October 1976 debate with Jimmy Carter compared to the other vital subjects covered that night, the *Washington Post's* decision not to mention the "gaffe" until the thirty-third paragraph of its story was commendable and balanced. It was also clearly an independent one, since virtually every other major paper had placed the so-called slip of the tongue front and center. Yet within twenty-four hours the *Post* had capitulated and head-lined the comment as well.

Whether on the rise or not, the unfortunate effects of pack journalism are apparent to both news reporters and news consumers: conformity, homogeneity, and formulaic reporting. Innovation is discouraged, and the checks and balances supposedly provided by competition evaporate. Press energies are devoted to finding mere variations on a theme (new angles and wiggle disclosures), while a mob psychology catches hold that allows little mercy for the frenzy victim. CNN's Frank Sesno captures the pack mood perfectly:

I've been in that group psychology; I know what it's like. You think you're on to something, you've got somebody on the run. How dare they not come clean? How dare they not tell the full story? What are they trying to hide? Why are they hiding it? And you become a crusader for the truth. Goddammit, you're going to get the truth!

Watergate's Watermark on the Media

Sesno's crusader spirit can be traced directly to the lingering effects of the Watergate scandal, which had the most profound impact of any modern event on the manner and substance of the press's conduct. In many respects Watergate began the press's open season on politicians in a chain reaction that today allows for scrutiny of even the most private sanctums of public officials' lives. Moreover, coupled with Vietnam and the civil rights movement, Watergate shifted the orientation of journalism away from mere description — providing an accurate account of hap-penings — and toward prescription — helping to set the campaign's (and society's) agendas by focusing attention on the candidates' shortcomings as well as certain social problems.

A new breed and a new generation of reporters were attracted to journalism, and particularly its investigative arm. As a group they were idealistic, though aggressively mistrustful of all authority, and they shared a contempt for "politics as usual." Critics called them do-gooders and purists who wanted the world to stand at moral attention for them. Twenty years later the Vietnam and Watergate generation dominates journalism: They and their younger cohorts hold sway over most newsrooms, with two-thirds of all reporters now under the age of thirty-six and an ever-increasing share of editors and executives drawn from the Watergate-era class.

Of course, many of those who found journalism newly attractive in the wake of Watergate were not completely altruistic. The ambitious saw the happy fate of the *Washington Post's* young Watergate sleuths Bob Woodward and Carl Bernstein, who gained fame and fortune, not to mention big-screen portrayals by Robert Redford and Dustin Hoffman in the movie *All the President's Men.* As *U.S. News & World Report's* Steven Roberts sees it:

A lot of reporters run around this town dreaming of the day that Dustin Hoffman and Robert Redford are going to play them in the movies. That movie had more effect on the self-image of young journalists than anything else. Christ! Robert Redford playing a journalist? It lends an air of glamour and excitement that acts as a magnet drawing young reporters to investigative reporting.

The young were attracted not just to journalism but to a particular *kind* of journalism. The role models were not respected, established reporters but two unknowns who refused to play by the rules their seniors had accepted. "Youngsters learned that deductive techniques, all guesswork, and lots of unattributed information [were] the royal road to fame, even if it wasn't being terribly responsible," says Robert Novak. After all, adds columnist Mark Shields, "Robert Redford didn't play Walter Lippmann and Dustin Hoffman didn't play Joseph Kraft." (Kraft, like Lippmann, had a long and distinguished career in journalism.)

In the post-Watergate press there is also a volatile mix of guilt and fear at work. The guilt stems from regret that experienced Washington reporters failed to detect the telltale signs of the Watergate scandal early on; that even after the story broke, most journalists underplayed the unfolding disaster until forced to take it more seriously by two wet-behind-the-ears *Post* cubs; that over the years journalism's leading lights had gotten too close to the politicians they were supposed to check and thus for too long failed to tell the public about JFK's and LBJ's dangerous excesses, the government's lies about Vietnam, and the corruption in the Nixon administration and in Congress. The press's ongoing fear is deep seated and complements the guilt. Every journalist is apprehensive about missing the next "big one," of being left on the platform when the next scandal train leaves Union Station. The everlasting press search for another Watergate has produced one oversize "-gate" after another. Ironically, the Watergate analogy can actually help the targeted politician, as Ronald Reagan happily discovered during "Irangate." Despite his mismanagement and ignorance aplenty, in the end Reagan was judged "innocent by reason of analogy" because the investigations turned up no smoking-gun equivalent of the Watergate tapes directly implicating the president.[6]

Reagan's case was exceptional, and it was not for want of the press's trying that he escaped permanent damage. Ever since Watergate, most investigative journalists' goal has been not just sensational revelation but the downfall of their target, a trophy head for their wall that is the (im)moral equivalent of Richard Nixon. "We look for and hope for a really bad character to pursue because it can do wonders for our careers," observes ABC's Brit Hume. The sizable financial and personnel investments many major news organizations have made in investigative units almost guarantee that greater attention will be given to scandals and that probably more of them—pseudo and real—will be uncovered. The healthy adversarial relationship that naturally exists between the press and politicians has been sharpened to a razor's edge in the process. Many in the press are not merely skeptical of the pols, they are contemptuous of and corrosively cynical about them, and some reverse the usual presumption of innocence into "guilty unless proven otherwise." Partly this is an understandable reaction to their own earlier naïveté and betrayal. Robert Novak recalls, "When the Agnew story broke, the mood was, 'Come on, you've got to be kidding.' There was a disbelief among journalists that there was anything to it. But when you had a vice president accepting bags of money in the Executive Office Building, and Watergate—something out of a cheap Washington novel—on top of it, then anything seems possible." Yet the resulting cynicism, especially among their young colleagues, worries thoughtful veterans. "At times we're too adversarial," says *Los Angeles Times* Washington bureau chief Jack Nelson. "You shouldn't just assume politicians are lying." NBC News commentator John Chancellor somewhat wistfully recounts the days when he could "win an argument by citing U.S. government statistics" because they were considered the unquestionable "final word." Then came Vietnam, Watergate, and "hero worship for Woodward and Bernstein. Skepticism turned to cynicism, and in the White House press corps old-fashioned comity dissolved into a pack of attack dogs," notes Chancellor, regretfully. The Watergate-fed dogs are now used to red meat, and the pack is deeply addicted to the "-gate" scenario.

The Character Issue Takes Hold

A clear consequence of Watergate and other recent historical events was the increasing emphasis placed by the press on the character of candidates. As journalists reviewed the three tragic but exceptionally capable figures who had held the presidency since 1960, they saw that the failures of Kennedy, Johnson, and Nixon were not those of intellect but of ethos.

Chappaquiddick, Spiro Agnew, and the Eagleton affair reinforced that view. The party affiliations and ideology of these disappointing leaders varied, but in common they possessed defects of personality, constitution, and disposition. In the world of journalism (or academe), as few as two data points can constitute a trend; these six together constituted an irrefutable mother load of proof. "We in the press learned from experience that character flaws could have very large costs," says David Broder, "and we couldn't afford to ignore them if we were going to meet our responsibility."

The issue of character has always been present in American politics — not for his policy positions was George Washington made our first president — but rarely if ever has character made such a mark for so many consecutive elections as it did from 1976 onward. The 1976 Carter campaign was characterized by much moral posturing; Edward Kennedy's 1980 candidacy was in part destroyed by lingering character questions; Walter Mondale finally overcame Gary Hart's 1984 challenge in the Democratic preliminaries by using character as a battering ram; and 1988 witnessed an explosion of character concerns so forceful that several candidates were eliminated and others badly scarred by it. The character issue now dominates many state and local elections and a sprinkling of Supreme Court nominations, cabinet appointments, and Speakership selections for good measure.

This focus on character is undergirded by certain assumptions — some valid and others dubious. First, the press correctly perceives that it has mainly replaced the political parties as the "screening committee" that winnows the field of candidates and filters out the weaker or more unlucky contenders. Second, many journalists, again correctly, recognize their mistakes under the old Rooseveltian rule and see the need to tell people about candidate foibles that affect public performance. *Time* magazine's Ted Gup frames this point by contrasting the press's crimes of commission with those of omission:

If a guy has got a psychological problem, if he can't keep his zipper up, if he can't keep away from a bottle or whatever, we are not serving the public by concealing that fact from them. The press gets a lot of heat for the crime of commission, what it writes about. But we're equally guilty of crimes of omission, because if we have an obligation to write about something and we don't, that's just as egregious as if we write about something that we're not supposed to.

The press's third realistic presupposition is that it is giving the public what it wants and expects, more or less. The social factors that have led Americans to prefer more information about the private lives of public officials will be discussed in the next chapter. For now, though, television itself is a sufficient answer, having served as handmaiden and perhaps mother to the age of personality politics. Television has not only personalized campaigns but has also conditioned its audience to thinking about the private "lives of the rich and famous." The rules of television prominence now apply to all celebrities equally, whether they reside in Hollywood or Washington.

Less convincing, however, are a number of other assumptions made by the press about elections and the character issue. Some journalists insist that they have an obligation to reveal everything of significance discovered about a candidate's private habits; to do otherwise, they say, is antidemocratic and elitist. Such arguments ignore the press's unavoidable professional obligation to exercise reasonable judgment about what is fit to print and air as well as what is most important for a busy and inattentive public to absorb. Other reporters claim that character matters so much because policy issues matter so little. The issues change frequently, they say, and the pollsters and consultants determine the candidate's policy stands anyway. Brooks Jackson, now of CNN, voices typical sentiments:

The candidate stands for whatever his pollster tells him the public wants to hear at the moment. The question is not what his party stands for because party is irrelevant. We have candidates who have the ability to market themselves as anything they want. They're chameleons. And so the central issue in a campaign must be the character of the person running for office.

Bob Schieffer of CBS News adds, "We wind up with candidates who say about the same thing . . . but because it's a contest, people try to find a difference. The difference is character." Granted, journalists covering media-manipulating candidates who mouth tape-recorded, sound-bite answers to all questions can be forgiven a measure of cynicism. Nonetheless, even in contests between relative moderates, such as the 1976 presidential matchup, substantial policy differences exist — and the distinctions become a chasm in ideological polarized years such as 1972, 1980, 1984, and 1988. The illusion of issueless races cannot justify an overemphasis on character.

Perhaps most troubling is the nearly universally accepted belief that private conduct is a road map to public action. Unquestionably, private behavior can have public consequences, as the review of recent history suggested. However, it is a far-from-settled matter whether private vice inevitably leads to corrupt, immoral leadership or whether private virtue produces public good. An argument can be made that many lives run on two separate tracks (one public, one private) that ought to be judged independently. Too often, the press defines character just as Gary Hart once complained: "in a totally negative sense as everything a candidate lacks or every mistake a candidate has made."[7] A focus on character becomes not an attempt to construct the mosaic of attributes and features that make up an individual but a strained effort to find a sometimes real, sometimes manufactured "pattern" of errors or shortcomings that will automatically disqualify a candidate. It is a rare life that does not contain enough embarrassing incidents to give critics the opportunity to shred it. Similarly, there is not a human being who has not repeatedly exercised "bad judgment" — the standard flaw used to raise the character issue.

On the other hand, some public figures have made it impossible, and unwise, for the press to ignore the evidence of character defects. Before and after Chappaquiddick, Senator Edward Kennedy has rarely been accused of exercising much discretion in his personal affairs. *Washington Monthly* editor Charles Peters believes the press was compelled to examine this presidential aspirant's vices: "When you mix the womanizing with the excessive drinking and speeding, you get a combination of dangerous recklessness, a self-destructive pattern that very definitely needed to be reported." Despite his many protestations to the contrary, Senator Gary Hart can reasonably be classed with Ted Kennedy or brother John. Hart's bravado in asking the press to follow him around while he ran unacceptable risks with his reputation and future was reminiscent of President Kennedy's derring-do. Ken Bode, formerly of NBC News and one of the most experienced political correspondents in the nation, capsules the JFK–Hart comparison this way:

People who supported Hart said to me, "Well, what about John Kennedy?" And my answer . . . was that John Kennedy was also too reckless to have been president. . . . In fact, those people who say Kennedy proves one point, I think, got it backwards. Kennedy proves the point that adultery is something that must be looked into if it happens in the case of a presidential candidate.

The Hart character frenzy was nevertheless worrying to many journalists. Lines had been crossed, and methods used, that gave pause. Steven Roberts of *U.S. News & World Report* "object[s] in many ways" to the Hart story:

I just don't like the idea of reporters sitting in the bushes watching someone's bedroom, which is basically what the *Miami Herald* reporters did. But in hindsight I think it was very important that the material came out. I didn't like the means, but I liked the end, because the end clearly told us something critically important about Hart's ability to be president. It told us something profoundly important about his sense of judgment, something directly relevant to his capacity to be president. So in the end, the process worked, but I was always very uncomfortable with the way it worked.

Roberts's doubts were widely shared, but so was his conclusion. Bad means had yielded a good end; that is, Hart's demise as a serious presidential contender. In the process, however, those bad means may have been sanctified and, without doubt, the character issue had become even more firmly rooted in journalistic practice. The press would continue to play "character cop," its thin blue line society's first cordon of defense against vice-ridden candidates.

More Women in the Press Corps

Instrumental in the emergence of the character issue were women journalists, who have broken the "good ol' boy" mentality—and morality—prevalent in the press corps for decades. Right on target in her analysis is Cokie Roberts of National Public Radio and ABC News:

> Until a lot of women came into the press corps, the unwritten rule was that the guys worked together during the day and caroused together at night, and nobody reported on anybody. And on the bus, they pretended there were no marriages. We women all started arriving on the bus and we sort of pruded it up. There we were, friends of their wives, not that any of us were gonna run home and tell tales—but they couldn't be sure of it.

The numbers alone tell a good part of the story. In 1971 the newsroom workforce was just 22 percent female; by 1989, women had a contingent comprising 35 percent of the total. Moreover, about half of all newly hired print and television reporters today are women, and current journalism school enrollments are 60 percent female.[8] Women journalists do not yet have anything approaching equal visibility, especially on network television, where progress has lagged well behind that of newspapers. But great strides have been made since 1972, when CBS's Bob Schieffer recalls only two women traveling regularly with the McGovern campaign. "Today half the seats in most campaign planes are usually filled by women," claims Schieffer. (Others agreed with the thrust of Schieffer's comment but placed the proportion at 30 to 40 percent.)

As the boys on the bus—or plane—have gone coed, and as the press fraternity has made room for a sorority, the journalistic consensus about character has been profoundly influenced by feminism. In 1979, when *Washington Monthly*'s Charles Peters published a watershed article on Ted Kennedy's personal problems, he was much criticized for broaching the subject. The author of the piece, Suzannah Lessard, had difficulty getting on-the-record comments from committed feminists who were nonetheless deeply disturbed by Kennedy's behavior and found it abhorrent and disre-

spectful to women. The reluctant interviewees feared being seen as un-
trendy and unworldly. As Lessard later noted, those concerns had dissolved
in time for Gary Hart to reap the whirlwind in 1987.[9] This new-wave
thinking has "raised collective consciousness in the press corps," according
to Schieffer. The most significant effect has been to reinforce the character
issue and prepare the way for more feeding frenzies based on private vices.

Loosening of the Libel Law

In the old days, a reporter would think twice about filing a story
critical of a politician's character, and his editors probably would have
killed it had he been foolish enough to do so. The reason is clear: fear
of a libel suit.[10] Veteran journalist Jerry terHorst recalls the first question
his supervisors asked about even an ambiguous, suggestive phrase about
a congressman: "If we're sued, can you prove beyond a doubt what you
just wrote?" The chilling effect of libel laws tilted the press-politician
relationship firmly in the direction of the pols, reinforcing the Rooseveltian rule that governed coverage of elected officials.

Such inhibitions were ostensibly lifted in 1964, when the Supreme
Court ruled in *New York Times Co.* v. *Sullivan* that simply publishing a
defamatory falsehood was not enough to incur a libel judgment. Hence-
forth a public official would have to prove "actual malice," a requirement
extended three years later to all public figures, such as Hollywood stars
and prominent athletes. The Supreme Court declared that the First
Amendment requires elected officials and candidates to prove that the
publisher either believed the challenged statement was false or at least
entertained serious doubts about its truth and acted recklessly in publishing
it in the face of those doubts. The "actual malice" rule has made it very
difficult for a politician to prevail in a libel case. The most comprehensive
empirical study on the subject suggests that the *Sullivan* standard has
reduced public plaintiffs' success rate in libel cases by as much as 60
percent, with only about one in ten "public person" libel plaintiffs winning
against the press.[11]

Nonetheless, the threat of libel litigation has not dissipated, and some
deterrent effect on the press is still visible. At least two reasons account
for this persistent libel chill. First, the *Sullivan* protections do little to
reduce the expense of defending defamation claims. The monetary costs
have grown enormously, as have the required commitments of reporters'
and editors' time and psychic energy. Small news organizations without
the financial resources of a national network or the *New York Times* are

sometimes reluctant to publish material that might invite a lawsuit because the litigation costs could threaten their existence.

The second reason for the continuing libel threat is what defamation expert Rodney Smolla calls "the general thinning of the American skin,"[12] a cultural phenomenon of heightened sensitivity to the harm that words can do to an individual's emotional tranquillity. As a result, politicians are often more inclined to sue their press adversaries, even when success is unlikely. For example, despite the stringent *Sullivan* standards, elected officials and candidates brought 20 percent of all the defamation suits between 1974 and 1984.[13]

But high costs and the American propensity to sue cut both ways. The overall number of libel suits filed in recent years has dropped because plaintiffs also incur hefty legal bills, and — perhaps more important — they have despaired of winning. Some news outlets have added another disincentive by filing countersuits charging their antagonists with bringing frivolous or nuisance actions against them.

In practice, then, the loosening of libel law has provided journalists with a safer harbor from liability in their reporting on elected officials and candidates. Whether it has truly diminished the chill of press self-censorship, especially for less financially endowed media outlets, is a more difficult question. However, at least for the wealthy newspapers and networks, the libel laws are no longer as severe a restraint on "character" or private-life reporting about public officials, and this once-formidable barrier to certain types of feeding frenzies has been lowered considerably.

The Search to Validate the Subtext

With the threat of a libel judgment greatly diminished, reporters are relatively free to make known their frank evaluations of a candidate's basic character. Frequently, a near consensus (accurate or not) forms around a politician's personality and faults, and each pol is typecast with shorthand labeling of various sorts. This set of preconceived images and stereotypes becomes the candidate's subtext — that is, the between-the-lines character sketch that guides and sets the tone for press coverage. Journalists are always on the lookout for circumstances that fit the common perceptions and preconceptions about a candidate, especially his or her shortcomings. A major incident that validates the subtext (and therefore the press's own judgment) has a good chance of being magnified and becoming a feeding frenzy. The subtext is the "fertile ground in which a story is planted," observes *Nightline*'s Ted Koppel, "and when it rains, the story grows explosively like Jack's beanstalk." In other words, a campaign development that corroborates the news media's conventional wisdom about a candidate resonates and intensifies because it rings true to the scribes and broadcasters. When a politician seems to confirm his or her own subtext, a collective gleeful shout from the press of "I knew it, I told you so" becomes a reinforcing part of many feeding frenzies. Table 3.1 reviews the subtexts that have helped to define selected presidential frenzies. Pack journalism and the development of the character issue are much in evidence throughout the table's listing. Some of the subtexts are accurate, if incomplete, readings of the candidates; others are off base; all are simplistic and usually unidimensional judgments on complex people.

It is important to understand just how pervasive the subtext interpretations frequently are. In several dozen discussions of Joseph Biden with this volume's interviewees, for example, not one journalist departed from the conventional wisdom. "We all thought he was a blowhard, didn't have much to say, wasn't very deep," said ABC's Brit Hume. E. J. Dionne, formerly of the *New York Times* (which played a key role in Biden's demise), characterized the widespread impression of Biden as that of "mostly talk." Columnist Jack Germond's epitaph of a reminiscence sums up the sentiment: "All he was known as was a guy who gave a good speech. As it turned out, they were good speeches other people had already given." The prefrenzy coverage reflected precisely these evaluations. Noting "Biden's verbal excesses" and "the perception that he is a gabby lightweight," *Time* quoted a prescient Iowa activist months before Biden's troubles began, saying, "He just might talk himself out of the nomination."[14] Even earlier, *Business Week* had headlined a feature article, "Is Joe Biden More than 'Just a Speech'?"[15] *The Economist* declared at the outset that Biden's overriding task was to show that he was "not just a pretty face and articulate voice."[16]

This uniform perspective on Biden has undeniable elements of truth in it. Yet a fair evaluation of Biden's long legislative career shows it to be more substantive and accomplished than his typecasting would suggest. What mattered in the frenzy that engulfed Biden, however, was not a balanced view of his record but the nearly universally embraced substance of his subtext.

Biden is not the only candidate to have been victimized by an unleavened subtext. Later, during his presidency, Jimmy Carter also demonstrated that even a grossly insignificant incident could become a debilitating frenzy, given the right press subtext and spin. In the summer of 1979 when Brooks Jackson, then an AP reporter, first sent out the story of the swamp rabbit's "attack" on President Carter's Plains rowboat, he missed its significance. It was only when editors across the country began to

TABLE 3.1 PRESS SUBTEXT OF SELECTED PRESIDENTIAL FEEDING FRENZIES

FRENZY	SUBTEXT PREDATING FRENZY
Spiro Agnew's "fat Jap" (1968)	Agnew was viewed by many newsmen as insensitive and out of his depth.
Edward Kennedy's Chappaquiddick (1969)	Journalists knew of Kennedy's womanizing, drunkenness, tendency to speed, and general recklessness.
Edmund Muskie's New Hampshire "cry" (1972)	Muskie was seen as moody, temperamental, and given to emotional outbursts.
Jimmy Carter's "lust in his heart" *Playboy* interview (1976)	Some newspeople detected in Carter a false piety and sanctimony; others feared the religious zealotry of Carter's Southern Baptist religion; still others sensed a "weirdness" about Carter that worried them.
Gerald Ford's "free Poland" gaffe (1976)	Ford was seen as clumsy, ill-equipped mentally for the presidency and not up to the job, an amiable dunce given to malapropisms.
Jimmy Carter's "killer rabbit" (1979)	Carter's presidency had soured, and the press perceived him as managerially incompetent and politically impotent.
Gary Hart's name, age, signature changes (1984)	Journalists believed Hart to be aloof, arrogant, rootless, strange, and a loner who refused to play by the rules.
Jesse Jackson's "Hymietown" remark (1984)	Jackson's (and many blacks') tensions with the Jewish community were well known; Jackson's embrace of the Palestine Liberation Organization and previous anti-Jewish statements were also remembered.
Geraldine Ferraro's family finances (1984)	Ferraro's Italian heritage may have sparked tacit suspicions; this was combined with a previous lack of scrutiny and an initial press so positive that some in the news media were concerned about bias and imbalance.

TABLE 3.1   CONTINUED

FRENZY	SUBTEXT PREDATING FRENZY
Gary Hart and Donna Rice (1987)	Hart's past factual and rumored womanizing, as well as the recklessness perceived in his character, served as backdrop.
Joseph Biden's plagiarism (1987)	The adjectives reporters privately (and sometimes publicly) used to describe Biden were *consultant programmed, glib,* and *shallow.*
Michael Dukakis's mental health (1988)	The press had typecast Dukakis as a cold technocrat, who had difficulty showing emotion, and this rumor seemed to confirm the stereotype in part.
Dan Quayle's past (1988)	Many in the news media knew little of Quayle, but first impressions suggested a "pretty boy" lightweight who was out of his league, a rich kid who had led a life of cushioned privilege.

Note: Subtext descriptions, and many of the specific adjectives used here, are drawn from newspaper and broadcast stories printed or aired *before* the onset of the corresponding frenzies. Journalists' recollections during the interviews conducted for this volume also served as source material.

beseech the AP to permit early publication of the item that Jackson realized how the story fitted into the journalistic subtext about Carter. The "killer rabbit" became a press parable of Carter's political impotence, a perfect metaphor for a president at the mercy of plagues big and small. That even a "banzai bunny," as Jackson called it, would be free to trouble this weakened leader exposed Carter to an avalanche of ridicule at a make-or-break point in his presidency. Jackson himself called "irresponsible" some of the exaggerated play given his footnote of a story, but the subtext — and the intensity of the personal dislike many in the working press felt for Carter — made the result almost inevitable.

Gary Hart's evolving and expanding subtext over two presidential campaigns neatly encapsules many of the principles suggested here about subtexts. In 1984 Hart emerged so quickly from the Democratic pack that most reporters had not focused their energies on him, but many veterans remembered Hart in his role as George McGovern's 1972 campaign manager, and others had had contact with Hart on Capitol Hill during his years in the Senate. Bob Shogan of the *Los Angeles Times*, one of the most senior and respected reporters in the political corps, spoke for many if not a large majority of his peers in stating the common view of Hart as "one strange and quirky person." Fred Barnes of *The New Republic* gives a blunt evaluation: "Hart is a weird man, a very distant figure and the strangest guy I ever talked to." Adds the *Washington Post's* George Lardner, who first discovered Hart's misrepresentation of his age, "There was always something strange and inexplicable about him, like he was trying to carve out a new identity and transform himself into somebody else." Individually, Hart's shortening of his name (from Hartpence) earlier in life, his changes in signature, his claim to be a year younger than he actually was, and his seemingly studied imitation of JFK's body language were not all that bothersome. After all, millions of Americans have altered their names, tens of millions lie about their age, and every third politician tries to emulate John Kennedy. But as a package, and in combination with Hart's aloof manner, lack of close friends in the Senate, drifting marriage (at times), and estrangement from his strict upbringing and the fundamentalist religion of his early life, they constituted a convincing pattern to the press. "They seemed to symbolize to some reporters something that was inherently nongenuine in Gary Hart, and they were trying to figure out what it was. He seemed to be unable to come to terms with who he was and who he had been, and that seemed to bother a lot of reporters," says Hart's 1984 press secretary, Kathy Bushkin. Not just the changes but Hart's enigmatic lack of convincing explanation for some of them was puzzling to the press.

The other main feature of Hart's subtext right from the start of his first presidential effort was his image as a womanizer. Hart's own actions had fueled it, of course. In the 1972 McGovern campaign some reporters covering the campaign closely had been surprised to learn Hart was a married man, and he was quoted in the *Washington Post* then as saying, "Let's just say I believe in reform marriage." Both Hart and his wife, Lee, had also dated openly during two separations in the late 1970s and early 1980s. Further, reporters who had known Hart well were all too familiar with his extracurricular activities. NBC's Ken Bode, who had both a friendship and a professional relationship with Hart dating back to 1969, claims he personally knows of "eleven women" Hart has dated at various

times. Howard Fineman of *Newsweek* was in close touch during 1970 to
1972 with a college friend who was a ranking McGovern aide, and his
chum described in some detail Hart's "kind of pathological sleeping
around." A distressed woman correspondent for a prominent newspaper
chain confided to a few of her colleagues that she had been propositioned
by Hart in the spring of 1984 while interviewing him in his U.S. Senate
office. Despite these assorted rumors and hints in published articles, the
womanizing subtext never became a frenzy in 1984. No current incident
that could have been used to highlight this aspect of Hart's character ever
became public, and the campaign simply refused to talk about the subject.
Recalls Bushkin: "When people asked me a general, vague question like,
'Gee, we hear there are rumors,' I'd say, 'Fine, if you can come back with
something specific, then maybe there's something to talk about. If you
don't have a specific allegation, don't raise it.' And that's about as far as
it ever got in eighty-four."

All that smoke had convinced many in the media that Hart had started
forest fires and never been caught. They were determined not to let him
continue to break the post-Rooseveltian rules. The press was primed for
1988, particularly since Hart was the clear Democratic front-runner. This
time around "Hart could get away with less than anyone else because he
was perceived as getting away with more," Robert Novak surmises. "I
love danger, " Hart had once told journalists after shooting the rapids in
1984,[17] and everyone was on the watch now to see how risky Hart would
be, whether he would try to evade the ordinary rules that applied to
everyone else. At the *Washington Post*, according to political reporter
Edward Walsh, "a conscious decision was made early on that we would
basically declare a statute of limitations on whatever Hart may have done
in the past, but if the behavior continued in the eighty-eight campaign
cycle, if more rumors and allegations surfaced, then we would pursue
them." *Newsweek*'s Fineman, in a piece published just before Hart's 1987
declaration of candidacy, quoted John McEvoy, a key Hart aide in 1984,
warning that Hart would "always [be] in jeopardy of having the sex issue
raised if he can't keep his pants on."[18] The day after Hart's April 13
announcement, the main story filed was about the womanizing issue.
Time's Larry Barrett asked Hart about the "rumors" allegedly being circulated by other campaigns concerning his private life, and Hart briefly
suggested rumormongering would accomplish no good for any campaign
guilty of it. This inconsequential exchange containing no hard news sent
"virtually every single reporter on the campaign plane" diving for his
computer keyboard, according to Hart's then press secretary Kevin
Sweeney. By now the womanizing subtext was overpowering. Less than

a month later, Donna Rice and the *Miami Herald* provided the subtext its full-blown outlet. Gary Hart's character quilt now had its centerpiece.

Timing and Special Circumstances

Timing matters in both sex and politics. It also matters in press coverage. Feeding frenzies are more likely to develop in slow news periods, such as the doldrums of summer. The absence of much hard news in those weeks allows relatively insignificant events such as President Carter's "killer rabbit" to be blown well out of proportion. Candidates should simply beware the Ides of August, says Steve Roberts: "If you are going to fuck up, don't fuck up in the middle of August when there is nothing else to write about."

Other time pressures affect the likelihood and coverage of frenzies. Because of the sheer concentration of media focusing on politics in election seasons, transgressions that might be unseen or ignored at other times are closely examined then. So many potential stories flow past the desks of editors in peak seasons that the element of fortune becomes part of the mix. As Roberts notes,

How much attention a story gets, where it gets played, what kind of attention it gets, is always a comparative judgment. The *New York Times* is going to have eight stories on its front page every day. Some days fifteen stories are going to be worth the front page. Some days three are going to be worth the front page. But there is always going to be eight and there is always going to be twenty-two minutes on the nightly news, whether they have ten minutes or forty-five minutes of good stuff. Luck and accident determine what the competition is for public attention on any given day.

A candidate's good or bad luck in timing is thus reflected in the press coverage. Republican vice presidential candidate Spiro Agnew had the misfortune to utter his "fat Jap" comment in 1968 just before a three-day campaign tour of the Hawaiian Islands, whose population includes many people of Japanese descent. As a consequence, the remark took on added significance for the press.

The fact that front-runners get rougher treatment and closer scrutiny than back-of-the-pack contenders is but one of the many special press circumstances that govern feeding frenzies. Other factors include the following examples.

- Nonpolarized races bereft of big events (war, major recession, and the like) tend to breed frenzies. The 1976 and 1988 presidential elections fall into this category. So do party nomination races in many years, when large fields of lookalike, soundalike Democrats or Republicans compete to be their party's standard bearer.

• Candidates who may reap a windfall of favorable news coverage one day will probably have to pay the press piper the next. Geraldine Ferraro well understands this "zero-sum" principle of journalism. Having benefited from enormously positive, even euphoric media attention as the first woman nominated by a major party for national office, Ferraro came in for especially intense examination shortly thereafter by a press trying to restore balance to its coverage.

• The context of an incident or offense — including its age and extenuating circumstances — greatly affects a frenzy's development. For example, a "statute of limitations" is in effect at some media outlets for examination of private, illicit relationships. As earlier mentioned, Gary Hart benefited (however briefly) from such an amnesty at the *Post* in 1987. Marijuana use provides another illustration of the importance of context. The youthful indiscretions of 1988 Democratic presidential candidates Albert Gore and Bruce Babbitt had little political impact on their campaigns, but when Douglas Ginsburg was nominated for the Supreme Court, his drug use was given heightened relevance because of the vigorous antidrug policies of his sponsor, President Reagan.

• Certain frenzies gain greater relevance because they complement current fad or fashion in press coverage. Dan Quayle's membership in the National Guard became "one of those stories that reverberate because they tell other stories. . . . The United States had just gone through a period of rediscovering Vietnam again," notes E. J. Dionne. Moreover, Vietnam service and drug use are two story categories of ear-pricking interest for the baby-boom journalists how dominating American newsrooms.

• While the press sometimes triggers a frenzy by initiating its own investigation (as with the *Miami Herald* stakeout), it is frequently reactive in nature. Congressional action or partisan politics can jumpstart a reluctant press.

The most recurrent and important of all the special circumstances helping to explain frenzies is the exceptional nature of the presidency and vice presidency, and the distinctive forum in which nominees for those offices are chosen. Because of a president's life-or-death power, because he and his family become national role models, and because of the retrospective judgments rendered on past presidents' character flaws, most journalists are firmly convinced that there should be no limits to the scrutiny undergone by nominees for the office. "For the presidency there is virtually no reservoir of privacy left," says Jim Gannon of the *Detroit*

News. ABC's Hal Bruno draws an admittedly crude comparison to his days on the crime beat:

When I started out as a police reporter, we used to say, with every crime, except murder, certain things don't have to be revealed, but when it's murder, everything comes out; there is nothing left in the closet. And it's true in politics. When you run for president, unlike lesser offices, there can be nothing left in the closet; everything has to come out.

Eric Engberg of CBS News offers a "Manchurian Candidate" defense of the proctoscopic examination endured by today's leading presidential contenders. Referring to the 1962 movie of that name starring Frank Sinatra and Laurence Harvey, in which a soldier brainwashed by Red China assists the rise of a political candidate who is a tool of Communist foreign powers, Engberg asserts:

Anybody who would think that he could lead the free world ought to have every single thing about his past life [exposed] and every moment of it accountable. . . . It's very important that the man who gets elected president doesn't stand up some day and say "Oh, by the way, I happen to be a Soviet agent. During that year my official biography says I was a Rhodes Scholar at Oxford, I was actually a KGB trainee in Moscow."

These same rationales and standards are applied as rigidly today to vice presidential nominees, who were all but ignored just a few decades ago. The post–World War II era's experience with vice presidents easily explains why: Of the ten men serving in the post from Harry Truman to George Bush, fully half have become president (three by direct succession upon the president's death or resignation), and two more have been unsuccessful presidential nominees. The press feels more secure with some veep nominees than others, of course. Well-known national leaders who are picked for the position often get a mere once-over-lightly since it is presumed, perhaps incorrectly, that they have already been closely scrutinized. This axiom applies particularly to previous losing presidential candidates who wind up in the second slot, such as Walter Mondale in 1976, George Bush in 1980, and Lloyd Bentsen in 1988. Nominees who are virtual unknowns, though, are guaranteed microscopic inspection, as Geraldine Ferraro and Dan Quayle learned to their chagrin.

Ferraro's time of trial came postconvention, once the glow of her "historic first" had dimmed. Quayle had no such chit to use. Not only was he almost completely anonymous — one matronly GOP national convention delegate mistook the middle-aged, dark-haired comedian Mark Russell for the youthful, blond Quayle a full day after Quayle was chosen — Quayle was a *tabula rasa* (a blank slate) for most of the press corps. Jack

Nelson of the *Los Angeles Times* recalls, "Here was a guy who was suddenly thrust on the stage by Bush, as a surprise to everybody, including most of Bush's closest associates, for God's sake. . . . We'd had no chance to check him out because there were no credible trial balloons." In the memorable words of GOP media consultant Roger Ailes, Bush "dropp[ed] a hot dog in a tank of 15,000 bluefish [journalists]. . . . That hot dog goes quick, you know what I mean?"[19]

The national political convention itself is a tailor-made accessory to a feeding frenzy crime. Filled to the gills by the print and electronic press and tens of thousands of political activists, with no escape or surcease even in the hotels and restaurants, the convention becomes an amplified echo chamber where every whisper of a rumor can quickly grow into a deafening roar. The late Republican National Committee Chairman Lee Atwater was an acknowledged master of the convention scene, and he analyzed the press's role in it by stressing the convention's built-in ingredients of disaster:

A convention is the most unique thing in American politics because a convention is a world of its own and has a life of its own. And recent conventions have all been coronations. So what you're faced with is a self-contained world where every political reporter in the United States does *not* have a story. A convention more than anything else is an automatic breeding ground for a frenzy. You've got them all down there. They got to go with *something* everyday. Add to that the regular intense competitiveness among reporters multiplied by ten.

The synthesis of crowds, competition, and news famine is a stampede when a delicious morsel is produced. Robert Novak explains the mad mood when Quayle was served up as the chef's surprise:

Suddenly, you've got one of the great stories of all time. Here's a guy who is supposedly a multi-millionaire, draft dodger, sex fiend, Paula Parkinson's boyfriend, stupid. . . . Are they going to dump him? Is it over? . . . People call in with some tidbit that he dunked his donut somewhere sometime. . . . There's nothing else to write about—the platform has been put to bed, there are no floor fights. So everybody's a little guilty. I plead a little guilty: I think I hyped that story.

Press Frustration

Not surprisingly, politicians react rather badly to the treatment they receive from the modern press. Convinced that the media have but one conspiratorial goal—to hurt or destroy them—the pols respond by restricting journalists' access, except under highly controlled conditions. Kept at arm's length and out of the candidate's way, the press feels enclosed behind trick mirrors: They can see and hear the candidate but he or she does not see and hear them. Journalists' natural, human frustrations grow throughout the grueling months on the road, augmented by many other elements, including a campaign's secrecy, deceptions, selective leaks to rival newspeople, and the well-developed egos of candidates and their staffs. Despite being denied access, they are expected to provide visibility for the candidate, to retail his bromides. Broadcast journalists especially seem trapped by their need for good video and punchy sound bites and with regret find themselves falling into the snares set by the campaign consultants — airing verbatim the manufactured message and photo clip of the day. The press's enforced isolation and the programmed nature of its assignment produce boredom as well as disgruntlement, yet the professionalism of the better journalists will not permit them to let their personal discontent show in the reports they file.

These conditions inevitably cause reporters to strike back at the first opportunity. Whether it is giving emphasis to a candidate gaffe or airing an unconfirmed rumor or publicizing a revelation about personal life, the press uses a frenzy to fight the stage managers, generate some excitement, and seize control of the campaign agenda. Press emotions have been so bottled and compressed that even the smallest deviation from the campaign's prepared script is trumpeted as a major development. A slip of the tongue or a scandal is especially welcome so that reporters can freely release their pent-up emotion on a nonideological subject, with less fear that they can credibly be charged with bias.

Bias

Does press frustration, among other factors, ever result in uneven treatment of candidates, a tilt to one side or the other? In other words, are the news media biased? One of the enduring questions of journalism, its answer is simple and unavoidable: Of course they are. Journalists are fallible human beings who inevitably have values, preferences, and attitudes galore — some conscious and others subconscious, all reflected at one time or another in the subjects or slants selected for coverage. To paraphrase Iran-Contra defendant Oliver North's attorney Brendan Sullivan, reporters are not potted plants. The far-more-vital questions are: In what ways is the press biased? When and how do the biases show?

"There is a liberal tilt among the press that we refuse to recognize, and it is pointless not to acknowledge it because it is obvious," asserts *U.S. News & World Report*'s Michael Barone. In fact, a surprising number of our interviewees from the ideological right, left, and middle did acknowledge the bias. Liberal *Washington Monthly* editor Charles Peters concedes, "The conservatives have a point about liberal tilt"; the *Washington Post*'s relatively nonpartisan public editor, Richard Harwood, observes, "Most journalists are pigeonholed fairly as liberal Democrats"; conservative columnist James J. Kilpatrick perceives "a natural tilt in personal inclination toward the liberal side of the spectrum." Aside from the far right and far left, no one believes the bias to be overwhelming. As Kilpatrick put it, "Walter Cronkite and I used to agree on eighteen of the twenty items that should be on the 'CBS Evening News' on an average night, but our clashing vantage points could spark quite an argument over the other two!"

Cumulatively, of course, those two stories per night—assuming they always veered to the left—could make quite a difference. And, truth be told, they would indeed most likely have a liberal bias. First of all, the relatively small group of professional journalists (not much over one hundred thousand, compared to over four million teachers in the United States) are drawn heavily from the ranks of highly educated social and political liberals, as a number of studies, some conducted by the media themselves, have shown. Journalists are substantially Democratic in party affiliation and voting habits, progressive and antiestablishment in political orientation, and well to the left of the general public on most economic, foreign policy, and especially social issues (such as abortion, affirmative action, gay rights, and gun control). Second, many dozens of the most influential reporters and executives entered (or reentered) journalism after stints of partisan involvement in campaigns or government, and a substantial majority worked for Democrats. Third, this liberal press bias does indeed show up frequently on screen and in print. A study of reporting on the abortion issue, for example, revealed a clear slant to the pro-choice side on network television news, matching in many ways the reporters' own abortion rights views. The *Washington Post* gave extensive coverage to a 1989 pro-choice rally in Washington that drew 125,000 (a dozen stories, leading the front page), while nearly ignoring a pro-life rally that attracted 200,000 (two stories in the Metro section). *Post* reporters have also repeatedly been observed cheering speeches at pro-choice rallies. In addition, the press lists to the left on the agenda of topics they choose to cover. In the latter half of the 1980s, for instance, television gave enormous attention to the homelessness issue; in the process, some experts in the field believe the broadcasters both exaggerated the problem and grossly overstated the role of unemployment in creating the homeless.

Not only does liberal tilt help to predict the stories chosen for coverage, it can determine which subjects are avoided by the press. "Where you look for a story depends on your view of the world," explains Michael

Barone, "and you tend to find the stories you look for and *not* find the ones you *don't* look for." The alleged sexual preference of a public official is one such story. The case of Congressman Barney Frank might suggest otherwise, but many reporters insist that homosexuality, in and of itself, does not interest them even if it scandalizes their readers and viewers. "I don't care if someone's gay," declares CNN's Frank Sesno. "To me it's not a story and I wouldn't participate in covering it." Sesno also admits his decision is based on his own values; he recognizes that a substantial part of his audience believes homosexuality to be a major issue and might well object to being represented by a gay person. *Washington Post* managing editor Len Downie does not even concede that the public holds different values than he: "I believe we live at a time in which homosexual relationships between consenting adults, as far as society generally is concerned, are not thought to be illegal or immoral. I don't see that as something we need to inform people about."

The public, incidentally, senses that most members of the press have somewhat different beliefs than the citizenry at large. The Times–Mirror Center for the People and the Press, which has commissioned an enlightening series of Gallup surveys on public attitudes toward journalism, found in 1989 that 76 percent of a random sample of the U.S. adult population saw "a great deal" or "a fair amount" of political bias in news coverage.[20] And 68 percent believed that news organizations tended to favor one side rather than dealing fairly with all sides on political and social issues. (Just four years earlier the proportion citing one-sidedness had been only 53 percent.) By decisive margins, respondents who chose to classify press bias saw it as liberal leaning rather than conservative or moderate.

Conservative politicians do not need a Gallup survey to convince them the press is biased against their ilk. For decades, right-of-center Republican leaders have railed against the "liberal media." When former President Dwight Eisenhower attacked the "sensation-seeking" press at the 1964 GOP convention that nominated Barry Goldwater for president, delegates raged against the media assemblage, cursing and shaking their fists at them. No one has ever launched a more vigorous assault against the American media than did Vice President Spiro T. Agnew in November 1969, when he derided the "small band of network commentators and self-appointed analysts . . . who not only enjoy a right of instant rebuttal to every presidential address but more importantly wield a free hand in selecting, presenting, and interpreting the great issues in our nation."[21] And conservative journalists such as Republican activist Patrick J. Buchanan have built careers assailing their liberal brethren: Wrote Buchanan in a 1988 column, "America is bitter because the front pages of the prestige press and the major network 'news' shows are saturated with liberal bigotry, the practitioners of which are either too blind to see it or too dishonest to concede it."[22]

Most rankling to conservatives, though, was this pair of findings: The most liberal candidate for president in 1988, Jesse Jackson, garnered the best press, and the most conservative of the four national party nominees, Dan Quayle, secured the worst. Quayle's treatment has become a right-wing cause célèbre, with attention given to alleged press excesses large and small. The intensely critical focus on Quayle's avoidance of Vietnam service and the publication of rumors about his past enraged conservatives, as did unflattering characterizations of Quayle such as the insistence on calling the candidate by his full formal name (the elitist-sounding "J. Danforth Quayle") by some television broadcasters in the days following his nomination. No such moniker was forced on James Earl Carter—who was just "Jimmy" to the press, noted conservatives. And why, they asked, was Quayle derided as unqualified for the vice presidency after twelve years in the House and Senate when Geraldine Ferraro, with just three terms in the House and fewer legislative accomplishments to her name than Quayle, was hailed by the media (at least at first) in 1984? Incidentally, conservatives get some support within the press for their assertions about Quayle's coverage. ABC's Brit Hume, for instance, recalls hearing some newspeople make "vitriolic comments" about Quayle that made him "ashamed to be a reporter":

I was stunned by the extraordinary level of personal animus to this guy from major reporters. They knew enough about him to know they didn't like him. He was a conservative Republican, a young, attractive, apparently rich kid from Indiana who seemed to have coasted into the position in which he found himself. And that was good enough for a lot of reporters who decided they hated the guy.

The right wing is not alone in its disgruntlement with the news media. For very different reasons, the left wing joins in the condemnation. Liberals, while acknowledging the press's tough line on Quayle in August 1988, have taken the media to task for not keeping the pressure on him throughout the fall. The failure of the media to analyze and criticize the sometimes exaggerated claims made in Bush's anti-Dukakis advertisements is also cited, and many on the left are still furious that the media did not fully air the "Bush mistress" story. To the left, the perceived press kindness toward Bush was merely a continuation of its genuflection to Ronald Reagan during his presidency. "Because of government manipulation and voluntary self-censorship the major American news organizations too often abdicated their responsibility . . . during the Reagan years," wrote left-wing media critic Mark Hertsgaard.[23] Like others of his persuasion over the years, Hertsgaard points to the conservative status-quo interests of the corporate elites who run most media organizations to explain why a Reagan or a Bush would be pampered by the press. And there are many conservatives well placed in the television and print commentary areas to do the pampering, whether prompted by the media moguls or not.

From left to right, all of these criticisms have some validity in different times and circumstances, in one media forum or another. But this cornucopia of critiques ignores some nonideological factors probably more essential to an understanding of press bias. Owing to competition and the reward structure of journalism, the deepest bias most political journalists have is the desire to get to the bottom of a good campaign story (which is usually negative news about a candidate). In search of this holy grail of journalism was conservative Dan Quayle laid low — as were a host of candidates near and dear to reporters' assumed partisan preferences (Eagleton, Ferraro, Biden, and Hart). Pack journalism more than bias leads all media outlets to the same developing "good story" and encourages them to adopt the same slant. One of the newspapers that broke important information about Quayle's National Guard service was none other than the Quayle family–owned paper, the *Indianapolis News*. Commenting on the totality of his frenzy, Quayle himself remarked, "It just became so overwhelming [that] for anyone to step out and write something different about Dan Quayle, they would just [have] sort of said, 'Are you nuts?'"[24]

A related nonideological bias is the effort to create a horserace where none exists. Newspeople whose lives revolve around the current political scene naturally want to add spice and drama, minimize their boredom, and increase their audience. Runaway elections such as 1984 almost inevitably find the press welcoming a new face (Hart) or trying to poke holes in the campaign of the heavy favorite (Reagan).

Other human, not just partisan, biases are at work. Whether the press likes or dislikes a candidate personally is often vital. Former Governor Bruce Babbitt and U.S. Representative Morris K. Udall, both wisecracking, straight-talking Arizona Democrats, were press favorites in their presidential bids (in 1988 and 1976, respectively), and both enjoyed favorable coverage. Richard Nixon, Jimmy Carter, and Gary Hart were all roundly disliked by many reporters who covered them; from Watergate to Donnagate the press used exposed Achilles' heels to spear politicians it rated as overall heels. In Carter's case his press secretary, Jody Powell, concluded that "by August 1979, if the President had been set upon by a pack of wild dogs, a good portion of the press would have sided with the dogs and declared that he had provoked the attack."[25]

Media Bias, Front and Off-Center

A surprising number of prominent journalists and commentators, not all from the conservative wing of their profession, insist that in the 1992 general election the press leaned heavily in Bill Clinton's direction. Republicans are overwhelmingly of this opinion, having long ago consigned journalists to the rung of hell reserved for covert Democrats. The Perotistas would concur: George Bush and Ross Perot may not agree on much, but dislike for those Bush called the "nutty talking heads" and Perot termed "jerks" and "teenage boys" is one unifying element. (The first half of Bush's favorite slogan, "Annoy the Media — Reelect Bush" could easily have been adopted by Perot.)

Naturally enough, much of the media establishment disagrees with Bush, Perot, *and* some bold journalists. Yet NBC's political director, Bill Wheatley, declared, "I don't believe there was an active bias at work,"[26] while his network colleague, anchor Tom Brokaw, offered his own sound bite to dampen the controversy: "Bias, like beauty, is most often in the eye of the beholder."[27] Thus, fairness prevailed, say most of the news business's high priests, and the press did not defeat Bush: Bush beat Bush.

The more one studies the remarkable case of 1992, the greater the likelihood of judging both sides of this debate partly in the right. For 1992, the conclusions about press tilt are essentially these: "Of course" the news media are biased, but "press tilt has a marginal-to-moderate effect, no more and no less. . . . "

First, the bias itself. From Labor Day to Election Day, the Center for Media and Public Affairs found that 71 percent of the substantive comments made about George Bush on ABC, NBC, and CBS by reporters and other "nonpartisan" sources were negative. Bill Clinton's evaluations among the same group were 52 percent *positive*. These totals excluded horserace remarks about who was likely to win the election — portrayals that favored Clinton by an even greater margin.

Another study, by PR Data Systems and Mead Data Central, suggests that print-news organizations exhibited a similar bias. A painstaking content analysis of AP, UPI, and eleven major U.S. daily newspapers over the general election period showed that nearly three-quarters (72 percent) of all negative characterizations made in presidential debate stories and accompanying headlines were about Bush. Clinton garnered just 15 percent of these unfavorable mentions, and Perot only 13 percent. By contrast, Clinton was the beneficiary of almost half (48 percent) of the glowing characterizations and headlines, while Perot garnered 30 percent of the positive mentions and Bush a paltry 22 percent. Most observers rated Perot the best performer in the first debate, Clinton in the second, and Bush in the third, so even a healthy front-runner's bonus could scarcely entitle Clinton to such a lion's share of kudos if fairness prevailed. The tilt to Clinton in the news pages was matched on the editorial pages, too, as Clinton became the first Democrat since Lyndon Johnson in 1964 to win more newspaper editorial endorsements than the Republican nominee.

Seemingly, everywhere one looked in the summer and autumn of 1992, Bush and Quayle were being bashed and Clinton and Gore were being hailed in the media. The *Washington Post* certainly fit the pattern, and when its ombudsman, Joann Byrd, scrutinized the newspaper's contents (including headlines and photographs) covering the campaign's last two and a half months, she reached the conclusion that her paper had a "very lopsided" tilt in Clinton's direction.[28] For instance, the *Post*'s Style section featured a glowing account of a Clinton-Gore bus trip, headlined "New Heartthrobs of the Heartland." And, in one of the most embarrassing juxtapositions of the campaign, the *Post* hyped its mid-September public opinion poll showing a 21 percentage-point lead for Clinton with a front page, top-left headline, "Clinton's Lead Appears Solid, May Be Growing." Just a week later, when its next poll revealed a much narrower 9-point lead for Clinton, the *Post* buried the story inside on page A6 with the amusingly protective headline, "Clinton Slide in Survey Shows Perils of Polling." The news media tilt was supplemented by late-night comics, and even some prime-time entertainment shows, such as *Murphy Brown*, which piled on the Republicans and promoted the Democrats (see Table 3.2).

There were notable exceptions, of course. Broadcast personality Rush Limbaugh, with a weekly radio audience of over 12 million and growing rapidly, aimed daily broadsides at the Clinton bandwagon. The *Washington Times* was slanted against Clinton from its masthead to its classified ads, with headlines and news stories so enthusiastically pro-Bush that at times it appeared to be a throwback to the nineteenth century's cheerleading party press. And many of the news approaches to Hillary Rodham Clinton suffered from a subtle — or (sometimes) blatant — sexism. But even added together, these anti-Clinton transgressions were no match for the collective pro-Clinton fare of the leading networks and newspapers.

There is general agreement that the economy torpedoed Bush and

TABLE 3.2   LATE-NIGHT POLITICAL HUMOR IN THE 1992 CAMPAIGN

CANDIDATE	TOTAL NUMBER OF DAVID LETTERMAN, JAY LENO, AND ARSENIO HALL JOKES	EXAMPLES
Bill Clinton	423	"Top Ten Surprises in the United Nation's Sex Study: No. 10—Of the 100 million acts of love daily, most occur in Bill Clinton's campaign van." (David Letterman, June 25, 1992) "Bill Clinton said yesterday, 'It's not appropriate to go after someone's wife in the media.' He said, 'Going after someone's wife is better done discreetly, like at a cocktail party.'" (Jay Leno, August 25, 1992) On Clinton saying he's capable of commanding the U.S. military because he's headed the Arkansas National Guard: "Isn't that like saying you can fly the space shuttle because you've seen every episode of *Star Trek*?" (Jay Leno, August 31, 1992)
Dan Quayle	357	On Quayle being like Hamburger Helper: "You know he's in the Cabinet. You just hope you never have to use him." (Jay Leno, June 19, 1992) "Top Ten Ways Quayle Prepared for the Vice Presidential Debate: No. 7—Read book of inspirational stories about dumb guys who went up against smart guys—and won. No. 2—Reread his 'how a bill becomes a law' comic book." (David Letterman, October 13, 1992)

TABLE 3.2   CONTINUED

CANDIDATE	TOTAL NUMBER OF DAVID LETTERMAN, JAY LENO, AND ARSENIO HALL JOKES	EXAMPLES
Ross Perot	334	"I haven't seen a guy so mixed up about being in a race since Michael Jackson." (Arsenio Hall, September 25, 1992) "If he is not elected president he should go out to the airport. He'd make a great Hare Krishna." (Jay Leno, October 8, 1992) "Top Ten Reasons Clinton Is Losing His Lead: No. 2—More and more people like the idea of a tiny, insane millionaire running things." (David Letterman, October 29, 1992)

SOURCES: Numbers of jokes on *The Tonight Show with Jay Leno*, *Late Night with David Letterman*, and *The Arsenio Hall Show* were compiled by the Center for Media and Public Affairs. All of calendar year 1992 was surveyed. The joke examples were selected from campaign issues of *Hotline* from January 1, 1992, to November 3, 1992.

elected Clinton. But was it the economy itself, or the media depictions of it, that turned voters against Bush? No one can say with any certainty, but the networks' descriptions of economic conditions sounded more like the Great Depression than the moderate recession and prolonged period of sluggish growth that characterized 1990–92. Fully 96 percent of the economic evaluations on the evening newscasts during much of the general election were negative, as were 83 percent of the predictions about the economy's future performance.[29] The latter undoubtedly helped to drive down consumer confidence still further, and make Bush's predictions of recovery seem fanciful and "out of touch" to voters.

These media characterizations of the economy were no minor matter. The state of the economy was unquestionably the central issue of the campaign, and the chief source of President Bush's woes. A positive press spin suggested that economic recovery could have helped Bush regenerate lost momentum, and would have undercut Clinton's major campaign thrust. But not only did Bush not receive an assist; the news media repeatedly ignored or downplayed nearly every encouraging sign of an ongoing recovery that was slowly picking up steam. Near the end of the campaign, when the U.S. gross domestic product was announced to have grown by a strong 2.7 percent in the third quarter, most major media outlets pooh-poohed the news, some even implying that the government's books had been cooked to make Bush look good at a critical moment. After the election, when the government released the final revised GDP growth rate for the third quarter, the statistic turned out to be 3.4 percent — an even better showing than Bush had been able to trumpet.

Was this just an isolated incident, one wherein skeptical reportorial juices were flowing freely as Election Day approached? Not according to a number of experienced financial reporters who attended the Commerce and Labor Departments' briefings throughout the campaign. Some colleagues, they noted, openly cheered bad economic statistics and booed good ones, hoping for the best spin from Clinton's perspective. These personal reactions would be revealing but harmless enough, as long as the resulting stories were not affected by the bias. Yet many news reports of economic statistics seemed to share the same slant. When the civilian unemployment rate rose, the headlines logically reflected that bad news. But when it fell in the summer and autumn, that fact was sometimes deemphasized (or even buried) in print stories, with more obscure, unfavorable jobless statistics — such as private, nonfarm payroll employment — highlighted in the headlines. For example, in early September, when overall unemployment edged down a tenth of a point, to 7.6 percent, the front pages of both the *Washington Post* and the *New York Times* headlined instead the loss of 67,000 private nonfarm jobs. Said one financial reporter for a major news service, "Financial markets paid attention to the [private nonfarm] number, but even professional economists weren't uniformly focussed on that drop, and I have never [before] seen a paper lead with it in a general news report."

The media's Democratic tilt is not new to many voters. A postelection survey by the Times–Mirror Center for the People and the Press found that 35 percent of the voters believed the press had been unfair to George Bush, while just 19 percent termed the press unfair to Bill Clinton. Even many reporters acknowledged as much. An October 1992 study by the Times–Mirror Center revealed that 55 percent of the journalists surveyed believed Bush's candidacy was damaged by press coverage, while only 11 percent thought Clinton was similarly harmed.

True, the press targeted Clinton early on, thanks to Gennifer Flowers, the draft charges, and marijuana noninhaling — but this was the time when key reporters had tagged Clinton "easy meat" for the Republicans in the fall, and many newspersons were privately hoping a "stronger" Democrat would enter the fray. Once Clinton was the nominee and the alternative to four more years of Bush, the tone of his coverage changed markedly. Adding to Clinton's advantage was the shame and regret many reporters felt about their handling of the Flowers affair, not to mention embarrassment about their mispredictions of Clinton's "inevitable" demise.

What motivated the tilt? The obvious but incomplete explanation is party preference and ideology. A Freedom Forum survey of journalists revealed that newspersons are predominantly and increasingly Democratic: 44 percent of reporters in 1992 called themselves Democrats, up from 38 percent in 1982, while only 16 percent identified with the Republican party, down from 19 percent ten years earlier.[30] Whether Democratic, Republican, or independent, most reporters are ideologically liberal, especially on social issues. Thus, the Democratic National Convention platform was almost universally labeled "moderate" despite containing an absolutist pro-choice position on abortion and, for the first time ever, controversial pledges to end the ban on gays in the military, and seek civil rights legislation for homosexuals. (President Clinton and the news media were to discover, shortly after the new president's inauguration, just how explosive the proposal on gays in the military was.) By contrast, the Republican National Convention platform was repeatedly characterized as right-wing and extreme, even though it was little changed from the ones with which Ronald Reagan and George Bush won landslide Electoral College victories in 1980, 1984, and 1988.

The abortion issue in particular generated an extra shove in the Democratic direction in 1992, since another GOP presidential victory could have eventually provided the fifth Supreme Court vote to overturn *Roe v. Wade*, the decision guaranteeing abortion rights. Many reporters claim that their personal views on abortion and other issues do not influence coverage, but this assertion rings more true for some than for others. Journalists are not automatons, and at the very least their personal preferences influence the kinds of subjects they choose to cover, and the approach they take to that coverage. A few newspersons are quite blunt about the influence their views have on coverage. Margaret Carlson, *Time's* deputy bureau chief in Washington who once worked in the Carter administration, explained: "You couldn't have fought the battles you have fought to get where you are and not find what the Republicans say about women offensive — it's not possible, you cannot be that objective."[31] Of course, most Republicans find Carlson's statement not only offensive but proof positive of press bias. Another example often cited by the GOP is the statement by ABC News's Carole Simpson that she "believed Anita Hill" in her 1991 charges of sexual harassment against Supreme Court Justice-to-be Clarence Thomas. This declaration came less than a week before Simpson was to moderate the second presidential debate in Richmond, Virginia, on October 16.

Other factors besides ideology were also at work in 1992. The press is traditionally tougher on an incumbent administration, whatever its party affiliation, especially in hard times. The White House occupant's flaws are always well known, and the press's battles with him have usually left tender bruises that are easily inflamed or require the revenge of the pen. By contrast, the challenger is relatively unsullied, his transgressions less known or threatening. George Bush was an irresistibly inviting target because he had blown a massive lead and become unpopular with most viewers and readers — a development that actually predated the nasty turn in his press coverage. Bush took on the unmistakable look of a potential loser, and the possible fall of a once-invincible leader became a compelling story that shaped the context in which all other reporting was done. The scent of losing also emboldened enemies from the president's own party and ideology to carp and lash out, without fear of retribution, which made it all the more difficult for Bush to communicate a persuasive message. After all, the news media often only echo and amplify the biting criticism they readily find in the pundit class or on the campaign trail, and the source can as easily be on the right (Bush critics Patrick Buchanan, William Safire, and George Will, for instance) as on the left. In fact, the most dismissive, vicious remarks about Bush came from conservative, not liberal, commentators; the president's right flank was breathtakingly exposed, and relatively few ardent defenders of the Bush faith could be found to counteract the torrent of abuse heaped upon him.

Surprisingly, given Bush's apparent congeniality, many senior reporters also disliked him personally — and this group extended well beyond Dan Rather. Various explanations were offered privately, including Bush's inaccessibility, perceived favoritism, and even reverse class snobbery (the old "preppie factor" that long dogged the upper-crust Bush). Some journalists also harbored resentment about the way in which Bush won the presidency in 1988, especially his team's shrewd manipulation of the media and the use of Willie Horton, the pledge-of-allegiance issue, and the like; 1992 became the payback, the just deserts, for 1988. But whatever the cause, the press usually gives more favorable treatment to politicians they personally like (Bill Clinton, Ronald Reagan) than ones they do not like (Gary Hart, George Bush), regardless of ideology.

In addition, the newsrooms across America are now dominated by the baby-boomers, and in the main they identified with the Democrats' young and hip boomer ticket. The 46-year-old Clinton's Fleetwood Mac, saxophone, and experiences in the 1960s counterculture era had more resonance and relevance to youthful journalists than the 68-year-old Bush's country music, horseshoes, and World War II.

Perhaps most fundamentally, journalists' careers and personal satisfaction depend in good part on the importance of the news they cover. The defeat of an incumbent president, the end of the Reagan/Bush era, and the election of a Kennedyesque successor with the accompanying massive changes in policy and personnel all were simply better news, with the promise of years of drama and upheaval to come. More than a few newspersons who did the reporting on candidate Clinton knew they would likely win the assignment to cover President Clinton, sharing the White House limelight and — with visions of Ben Bradlee advising JFK dancing in their dreams — maybe even the Oval Office. Most of us just *hope* for change that will benefit our professions or businesses; journalists are in a position to nourish their kind of change to fruition.

So, on the whole, the press was certainly a Clinton ally in 1992. But George Bush probably could still have won the election had he held fast to his "no new taxes" pledge, capitalized early on his Persian Gulf victory, focused purposefully on domestic ills, and spent the campaign convincing Americans of the worth of his recovery plan, instead of mainly attacking Clinton's character and record. Bush and his managers ignored a fundamental lesson of American presidential elections: Voters cast ballots retrospectively, and any contest for the White House inevitably becomes a referendum on the performance of the incumbent administration, not the challenger. So the fault, dear George, lay less in your press clippings than in yourself and your truly awful campaign — one of the most inept in modern history.

In sum, then, press bias of all kinds — partisan, agenda-setting, and nonideological — can and does influence the development of feeding frenzies and the day-to-day coverage of politicians as well. But bias is not the absolutist be-all and end-all critics on both the right and left often insist it is. Press tilt has a marginal-to-moderate effect, no more and no less; it is but one facet of the mosaic that forms a frenzy.

CHAPTER FOUR

A Thousand Points of Gossip

*How the Politicians, the Public, and
the Pundits Feed the Frenzy*

SEVERAL POWERFUL frenzy forces are removed from the press's direct and full control. The sources adopted by journalists have a profound effect on the course and substance of any public controversy, yet they use the press as much as they are used by it. The politicians often bring the frenzy on themselves through stupidity, duplicity, and hypocrisy. Their mistakes, independent of the news media, provide the match that lights the frenzy's fire. Frenzies build on each other as well: The taboos broken and doors opened in one frenzy sometimes lead naturally to a new set of precedents and portals. Public opinion also influences the conduct of a frenzy. What the public wants, tolerates, is interested in, and judges to be right or wrong has clear impact on the press's pursuit of any offense. A fifth force, popular humor, is less powerful than the others but still of moment, especially when it is introduced and promoted by late-night television.

Sources — the Tips of the Trade

Tips and leaks from sources are the chief currency of investigative journalism, and most frenzies could not be sustained without them. All skilled journalists cultivate sources, and most recognize the dangers inherent in the undertaking, such as "sweetheart" arrangements whereby a frequent tipster (perhaps a political consultant) is immune from critical coverage or guaranteed an enviable quota of kudos in print. Nonetheless, it would be impossible for journalism to function well without these press "providers." They are the bits of string that, when pulled, frequently enable reporters to unravel the fabric of hidden scandal.

Sources for political stories come in three main varieties: intrapartisan (a Democrat or Republican providing a tip about a same-party rival); partisan (a Democrat feeding negative information about a Republican, or the reverse); and nonpartisan (generally a journalist's friend or a politician's associate with a nonpolitical motivation of some sort). Tips are "planted" by regular sources, especially the ubiquitous political consultants, but not uncommonly the unknown, even permanently anonymous source can be the bearer of a jackpot story.

Intrapartisan Sources

Occasionally a former party opponent tries to even an old score by slipping a damaging dossier to a reporter. For instance, diplomat William True Davis, who lost the 1968 Democratic U.S. Senate nomination in Missouri to Thomas Eagleton, was the one who told Jack Anderson about Eagleton's supposed (and nonexistent) drunk driving arrests. Dan Quayle also suffered at the hands of Republican rivals, some disappointed that they had not gained the vice presidential nomination. "Most of the negative information about Quayle that I got came from Republicans who were infuriated for one reason or another," discloses Robert Novak. More usually, though, a campaign staffer or consultant will have a less personal but equally mischievous motive: to win a current contest by injuring a rival. "They try to get us to do their dirty work for them," explains the *Washington Post's* Eleanor Randolph. The operatives rightly figure that charges will have greater credibility coming from a neutral press than from a competing campaign, so they often seek to break the findings of their "opposition research" via journalists instead of paid television advertisements.

Partisan Sources

The precise motivations of sources are not always apparent, but the easiest to analyze are those of clearly identified partisans. Their goal in the great game of politics has remained unchanged through the ages: to get the other party's rascals out and to get their party's rascals in.

Not a single major presidential campaign rumor in recent years has been spread without the assistance of partisan operatives. Most of the time the party apparatchiks' motivations are so transparent and the tips so flimsy that reporters offer a polite thank-you and place the material in File 13. Late in the autumn of 1988 one Democratic political consultant called around to Washington gossip columnists, while his party's presidential ticket was sinking into the sunset, offering "the name, address, and phone number of a woman who's servicing Dan Quayle," with no proof cited, according to Bill Thomas, formerly of *Roll Call*. (Thomas and apparently all the other recipients of this desperate scurrilous rumor discarded it.) Journalists suggest that many partisans overdo it in another way: killing reporters with kindness by overwhelming them with damaging information about the opposition.

The more astute party activists recognize that they can best achieve their objectives when they provide newspeople with specific, provable information. By serving as research assistants gratis, they can earn goodwill and facilitate the further development of breaking frenzies. For example, a relatively low-level Reagan White House aide extended Joseph Biden's plagiarism miseries by informing the *New York Times* of Biden's unattributed use of certain Robert Kennedy phrases. (Oddly, for a Republican, he was a fan of Bobby Kennedy's and knew his speeches by heart, thus enabling him to recognize Biden's borrowing.) More-senior Reagan White House and campaign staffers were involved in 1984 efforts to spread and emphasize the emerging character questions (age, name change, and so on) about Gary Hart. Concerned about Hart's youthful appeal and about their polls showing Hart to be Reagan's strongest potential Democratic opponent for the fall, the top Reagan people each called several journalists in the wake of Hart's New Hampshire victory to point out the problematic pattern in Hart's past — which at that juncture had not been made explicit in news media coverage. "These things were already on the public record," says Ken Bode, then of NBC, "but they had not been packaged together. The White House was one of the driving forces behind the age/signature business, and press interest was stirred up as a result."

Nonpartisan Sources

While dependent on their regular sources, reporters often find that the tips rounded up by their usual suspects are shopworn and well known, since most experienced partisans peddle their wares on a regular basis from media outlet to media outlet. The truly stunning revelations are frequently served up by nonpolitical sources who may be only indirectly or not at all connected to public life. Family, friends, and jilted lovers of public officials seem especially ripe for sourcing. In fact, the lesson learned by some pols is an ancient one: With family and friends like these, who needs partisan enemies?

One source of unflattering information about Jesse Jackson over the years has been Jackson's former allies in the civil rights movement of the 1960s. The *Atlanta Constitution,* for example, has been the beneficiary of stories supplied by some Atlanta residents connected to the late Dr. Martin Luther King, Jr. These individuals resented Jackson's claim to King's mantle, according to Bill Kovach, formerly of the *Constitution.* The associates who prove to be most damaging are not professional coworkers but spouses and "significant others." Similarly, former lovers who choose to kiss and tell can be poisonous.

Other nonpartisan sources with less direct personal interest can also provide a reporter with paydirt. Foremost among them are Secret Service agents who are aware of a presidential candidate's every movement. All the agents' observations are supposed to be confidential, but reporters frequently develop social friendships with them — they are together on the road a great deal — and over a drink or a game of tennis, gossip will inevitably be exchanged. About a dozen newsmen interviewed for this study cited Secret Service personnel as having been useful in developing stories (especially about Gary Hart and Jesse Jackson). This is true on the state level as well, where a governor's troopers or highway patrol guards will be privy to information that can be passed along to reporters. And not just law enforcement officers but those on the other side of the jailhouse door occasionally serve as sources.

Reporters are fierce competitors but also comrades in arms, and under certain conditions they will share good intelligence with a colleague. In addition, reporters feed off each other's published work. There is a food chain in journalism, and the larger publications (the big fish) not infrequently develop stories first discovered by less-visible publications, such as the hundreds of Washington policy and trade newsletters (the plankton) and elite-circulation papers like *Roll Call* and *Legal Times* (the small fish). As Washington journalist-writer Bill Thomas correctly saw it, "The young unknowns working for the less important publications often dig deeper and ask questions a big-time reporter might be embarrassed to ask." Those tough questions can lead to discoveries that become fodder for the frenzies that only larger papers can initiate and sustain.

For all the intentional cultivation of well-placed individuals, the accidental revelations from unwitting sources can prove just as golden. Gary Hart suffered from these happenstances in both 1984 and 1988. The careful background reporting of the *Washington Post's* George Lardner, Jr., had taken him to Hart's birthplace, Ottawa, Kansas, in 1983 for an interview with his uncle, George Hartpence. During the course of the conversation, "Uncle George said, 'You know, I've always thought Gary was a year older than he says he is,'" remembers Lardner. Sure enough, his wife had recorded Hart's birth in the family "baby book," and the uncle clearly remembered visiting Hart's parents that same year when "there was a baby in the crib." After Lardner repeatedly confronted Hart with his relative's recollection, the candidate "just shrugged and weaseled around," eventually admitting, "It's whatever the records say." (Incidentally, Lardner and others are convinced that Hart's deception began sometime during the 1960s, when the in-vogue slogan was Don't Trust Anyone over Thirty — or in this case, twenty-nine.) In the next presidential cycle, Hart's womanizing was the focus of partly coincidental exposure. The *Washington Post* first learned of Hart's longtime relationship with a local woman two days after the *Miami Herald* published the Hart-Rice exposé, when *Post* reporter Thomas B. Edsall received a copy of a Washington, D.C., private detective's report that included photographs of Hart entering the woman's house at night and leaving the next morning. The detective had been hired to follow Hart by a former U.S. senator (a Democrat and ex-Hart supporter) who was a jealous husband convinced that Hart was having an affair with his wife. The stakeout uncovered no evidence of that purported liaison but apparently by chance documented the other relationship. "Uncomfortable with that kind of story" and also convinced that Hart was "dead meat already, so piling on was unnecessary," Edsall decided not to pursue the matter personally, but out of a sense of obligation to his newspaper, he passed it along to executive editor Benjamin C. Bradlee, who decided to carry it further and assigned it to other reporters. After their painstaking verification of details contained in the detective's report (such as Hart's schedule and itinerary on the day and night in question), as well as the gathering of other suggestive evidence, a Bradlee intimate contacted Hart's mistress, who confirmed her relationship with Hart in exchange for a guarantee that the *Post* would not publish her name in connection with the presidential candidate.

By no means, however, are sources always critical to the breaking of a good story. The *Wall Street Journal's* Brooks Jackson, on a hunch, had collected Geraldine Ferraro's financial disclosure forms just before she was selected by Mondale in the summer of 1984. He simply followed the paper trail, and Ferraro's problems "just jumped out at me instantly," recalls Jackson, who did some groundbreaking spadework on the frenzy.

Other stories are delayed or never see the light of day because sources will not come forward. The *Washington Post's* Tom Sherwood, like other newspeople covering Mayor Barry, had had "very strong suspicions" about the mayor's drug use for years, and in fact had been given off-the-record but insufficiently documented confirmations by Barry's friends and associates. Sherwood did everything he could "to persuade the people who said they had used drugs with the mayor to come forward. I even went to several and told them, 'You're responsible because you know the mayor is drowning in public. I'm going to come back to you when the mayor dies of an overdose and ask why you protected the mayor instead of helping him.'" Sadly, even after Barry's drug arrest, the silence of many of these sources was deafening. It is a case like this that causes most journalists to agree with the *Post's* Ann Devroy: "I want anybody on God's earth to call me up and tell me anything they want to about anybody in politics. Let us check it out."

The Politicians Themselves

Marion Barry's case is extraordinary but not unique in at least one vital respect: Virtually all frenzy victims are responsible to varying degrees for the unhappy fate that befalls them; the blood they shed that drives the press to frenzy seeps mainly from self-inflicted wounds. Yes, press excesses intensify the frenzy; bad luck can magnify the unfairness; and the punishment may not fit the crime. But the politicians' own substantive offenses (hypocrisy, lying, gaffes, greed, lawbreaking, or sexual misadventures) as well as procedural errors (lack of full disclosure, refusal to admit error quickly, or inadequate preparation for scrutiny) loom large, as Table 4.1 suggests. In many cases, the candidate's mistake confirmed the preconceived press "subtext" about him or her—a subtext the candidate was well aware existed and ought to have been on guard not to reinforce.

Procedural errors can be every bit as politically damaging as the substantive ones. Dan Quayle's selection as a vice presidential nominee is a case study of blunder and mishap. (Again, see Table 4.1.) The actual wisdom of Bush's choice aside, the much-vaunted Bush campaign team did a remarkably poor job of preparing the way for Quayle's acceptance by press and public alike. Even David Beckwith, then a *Time* correspondent and later Quayle's vice presidential press secretary, admitted: "Quayle was not prepared and the Bush campaign was not prepared [when Quayle was announced]. . . . It could have been handled better." Brooks Jackson of the *Wall Street Journal* adds: "The Quayle frenzy resulted because we and they didn't have all the facts. . . . If the whole story had been presented at the beginning, no feeding frenzy would probably have resulted." Even some senior aides had been left in the dark about Bush's choice and were

TABLE 4.1   How Politicians Bring Frenzies on Themselves: A Few Case Studies

Frenzy Category	Selected Frenzy	Substantive Error(s)	Procedural Error(s)
Financial	Nixon's "secret fund" (1952)	Nixon chose to finance his political activities in an unconventional fashion that would invite extra scrutiny. Eisenhower had chosen the corruption issue to use against the incumbent Democrats without carefully checking the background of his vice presidential nominee.	Nixon had not previously publicized the existence of the fund. The fund turned out to be 14 percent larger than first disclosed. Eisenhower and his staff vacillated about Nixon's fate, sending out mixed signals and extending the length of the controversy. Despite some advance warning that the story was about to break, Nixon did not take it seriously enough at first to prepare adequately.
Gaffe	Carter's "lust in the heart" *Playboy* interview (1976)	*Playboy* magazine was an inappropriate place for a major presidential candidate interview, especially in a year when personal values were being stressed. The odd phrases and offensive language used by Carter in the interview were not accidental, but clearly intentional, designed to counteract his image of holier-than-thou religiosity.	Carter and his staff failed to recognize the explosiveness of his remarks and did not organize an appropriate damage-control operation in anticipation of their release.
Character	Eagleton's mental health (1972)	When asked directly whether he had any "skeletons in the closet," Eagleton said no, deciding not to divulge his mental hospitalizations to McGovern and his staff.	McGovern staff (led by Gary Hart) gave the most cursory examination to Eagleton's record and past; the senator had been well down on the list of possibilities.

Eagleton (cont'd)	McGovern's actions proved both indecisive and devious after the crisis developed. First McGovern said he was "1,000 percent" behind Eagleton, then he undermined him behind the scenes to ease him off the ticket. This helped to destroy his clean "new politics" image.	McGovern wasted most of his time in the vice presidential search on a fruitless quest to woo Edward Kennedy onto the ticket. The staff missed many signals at the convention, including warnings from prominent Democrats phoned directly to McGovern's headquarters, about Eagleton's problems.
Character		Republican party leaders, the press, and citizens were not prepared for the announcement through private consultations, tips, and trial balloons.
Dan Quayle (1988)	Bush picked a virtual unknown as his running mate, and someone not regarded as a person of great accomplishment who was prepared to be president.	Bush made a momentous decision in virtual isolation, without properly gauging reactions in advance.
	The hypocrisy factor was present: Quayle was a hawk but chose not to go to Vietnam.	The surprised Bush staff was disorganized and unable to get ahead of the press curve at the convention. Some were not particularly supportive of Quayle in off-the-record conversations with newspeople.
	Quayle was ill-prepared for the national spotlight, and not well briefed for his first few public appearances after Bush announced his selection; he fanned the National Guard controversy by mishandling inquiries about his motives for serving in and admission to the Guard.	The early convention announcement of Quayle gave the frenzy more time to build in the convention's news-starved echo chambers.

SOURCES: Interviews conducted for this volume.

in no mood to sell the party line. "We weren't getting any passionate defenses of Quayle from some of Bush's close associates," recalls NBC's John Chancellor. "To the contrary, we were getting winks and nods that Quayle was a strange choice and Bush hadn't thought it through." Compounding the difficulties was Quayle's own unsteady performance now that the klieg lights were on him. Though he defended his overall presentation, Lee Atwater acknowledged that "a couple of times [during convention] week Quayle appeared like a doe with headlights shining in his face, and the media saw and smelled weakness." Atwater and others also rue the decision to announce Quayle's selection on Tuesday, instead of the traditional Thursday of the convention. As one top Bush adviser explained:

If we'd done it Thursday Quayle would have been out of there before a frenzy would have had time to build in the special convention atmosphere. But by going with it Tuesday, we took away the only story [the vice presidential pick] the press tribe had, and so they had to gin up another story. And the ridiculous thing is we did it all because we didn't want to mess with [Senator Robert] Dole's ego and wanted to end his misery [since he was not selected], and in retrospect, Dole's gonna be mad about something everyday anyhow.

Other substantive misdeeds are seen as evidence of poor judgment and impure character. Gary Hart is the prototype, of course, though his case also blends in a generous measure of obdurate obtuseness. Hart had been warned repeatedly by staff, friends, and even sympathetic reporters that he would have to be on his best behavior and might well find himself under surveillance. The candidate repeatedly assured newspeople as well as aides that he was observing all the conventional rules. Just seven days before Hart's weekend with Donna Rice, Jack Germond had dinner with him, and the columnist was assured that "there's nothing to the womanizing charges" and that he was being careful to "observe community standards." Later that week Hart reiterated essentially the same message on videotape for NBC's Ken Bode. The crowning imbecility was Hart's declaration to *New York Times* reporter E. J. Dionne, "Follow me around. I don't care. I'm serious, if anybody wants to put a tail on me, go ahead. They'd be very bored."[1] Dionne himself was stunned by the statement, published in his *New York Times Magazine* profile of Hart the same morning the *Miami Herald* printed the Donna Rice exposé:

As soon as I heard the "follow me" quote ten percent of me thought maybe he really has changed and ninety percent of me thought, "Why did you say this?" Because I immediately started imagining all the ways either the media or his opponents would use that quote as an excuse for something.

Interestingly, while the *Miami Herald* had already made the decision to conduct the Hart stakeout, *Herald* reporters Tom Fiedler and Jim Savage had an advance copy of Dionne's story in hand when they flew to Washington for the surveillance and eventual confrontation with Hart. Dionne's story reinforced their rationale for the stakeout, though Hart had made similar "I have nothing to hide" comments earlier to Fiedler.

Most reporters found the Hart case an "easy call," as one put it, because he had been so blatant and had asked for intense scrutiny. A number of reporters such as *U.S. News's* Steve Roberts drew a distinction between Hart's behavior with Donna Rice and George Bush's alleged and unsubstantiated dalliances:

Whatever was true about Bush's sex life, he clearly was not reckless about his private life. If in fact he has had a mistress or a series of mistresses over the years, he has been extremely discreet about it. Now this sounds odd in a way, but a lot of people saw that as a defining difference. It wasn't how many times he cheated on his wife, it was how he handled it.

Some of his own staff members came to believe that Hart had adopted not just JFK's gestures but his reckless persona — in an age no longer tolerant of such shenanigans. Calling Hart's demise "unfortunate but inevitable," his 1984 press secretary, Kathy Bushkin, surmised, "He tempted fate and got caught." While denying immorality, Hart himself conceded "a mistake by putting myself in circumstances that could be misconstrued."

The frenzy offenses — whether major or minor — committed by politicians are amplified by any appearance of hypocrisy or attempt at lying and cover-up. The hypocrisy angle has particularly influenced the coverage of the private lives of public officials. To the extent that candidates portray themselves as family oriented and use their spouses and children as video backdrop, they ask for scrutiny of their life's private sector, says CNN's Frank Sesno: "We hear so much from our candidates about family values. If they're going to preach this stuff then they better be practicing it, and the more pious the candidate becomes, the more he or she opens up personal life to inspection." Hal Bruno of ABC agrees, and adds: "If the candidate stands there with his wife and family all exchanging loving glances, he's conveying the image of the solid family man. If it turns out that this is fraud, [press exposure] is perfectly legitimate."

There are many other varieties of hypocrisy, and since it is the oil that greases politics, a rare campaign is without any trace. In the situational ethics of hypocrisy, any action that contradicts a candidate's central image or motif is ripe for targeting. Joseph Biden's claim of high idealism and inspirational oratory was tarnished by his past and present plagiarism; Michael Dukakis's "attack video" violated the "open honesty" theme in his projection of presidential character. Oddly enough, the absence of hypocrisy at a critical moment can also prove damaging to a politician. Dan Quayle's most candid remark of the 1988 campaign, in response to a question about his Vietnam-era National Guard service shortly after he was chosen for the GOP ticket, was also one of his most injurious: "I did not know in 1969 that I would be in this room today." (Translation: He would have served in the military had he foreseen a big-league political career.)

Lying is even more deadly than hypocrisy to the modern campaigner. George Washington established the yardstick as a boy with his cherry tree, though standards slipped somewhat during the heyday of the Rooseveltian rule. Lyndon Johnson, for example, used to brag in speeches that his great-great-grandfather had died at the Battle of the Alamo, when actually he had died at home in bed; no one in the contemporary press apparently ever checked or corrected the record.[2] Truth telling became a sacrament again after Watergate, and a number of frenzies have been started or accelerated by lies, fibs, and half-truths. Sometimes the lie itself becomes the pretext for revealing a hidden private vice. More often, a politician's refusal to admit the truth worsens the original offense, as suggested by aspects of the frenzies involving Ted Kennedy, Tom Eagleton, Gary Hart, Jesse Jackson, Michael Dukakis, and Dan Quayle. Documented lying in past instances usually toughens the scrutiny, whether the deceit was willful (Hart on his name, age, and so on, in 1984) or relatively innocent (Dukakis misleading the press about the purpose of his wife's 1982 hospitalization for drug dependency.[3]) The cover-up — a politically perfected form of mendacity — always compounds the original error whenever the disguise is discovered, and Watergate is of course the modern original. Even the appearance of a cover-up is enough to send a shiver down the spine of most campaign managers. Finally, subterfuge and dirty tricks, once-common techniques out of style since Watergate, are forms of deception guaranteed to shake a campaign's foundations.

Frenzies Build on One Another

Frenzies get their rocket thrust not only from the fuel provided by candidates but also from the booster generated by other frenzies past and present. In short, frenzies build on one another. They do so by incorporation; that is, topics from each frenzy are incorporated into the repertoire of legitimate journalistic inquiry. In this fashion every frenzy sets new precedents that can be cited to justify another.

Sometimes the attempt is made to spawn more frenzies in the wake of a major one. An Associated Press reporter in Louisiana surveyed each candidate for governor after Gary Hart's fall, asking point-blank, "Have you ever committed adultery?" More important, candidates were given notice that the press would be scrutinizing this area of their lives in the future. And not just national politicians were affected; inevitably, frenzies have a trickle-down effect, and state and local campaigns adopt most of the same rules as federal ones.

The press's search for a trend line is obvious in all the "character frenzies" of recent years. A sensational revelation in one political camp leads reporters to search for similar discoveries and patterns elsewhere. Two Democratic presidential candidates, U.S. Senator Albert Gore of Tennessee and former Arizona Governor Bruce Babbitt, acknowledged youthful marijuana indulgence, as did a number of other Democratic liberals (such as U.S. Senators Claiborne Pell of Rhode Island and Lawton Chiles of Florida) and Republican conservatives (such as U.S. Representative Newt Gingrich of Georgia and Connie Mack of Florida). Perhaps because their drug use was basically restricted to casual experimentation, none suffered any noticeable political damage. Massachusetts politicians decided that on this issue there was safety in numbers. In 1990 about a dozen officeholders—including U.S. Senator John Kerry, U.S. Congressman Joseph Kennedy, and several statewide officials—rushed to confess mistakes of the past. The mass mea culpa was sparked by the state attorney general's admission of drug use, and it seemed to be a useful strategy. The developing frenzy was short-circuited and quickly converted into a revival meeting flooded by repentant sinners; all were guilty so no one stood out, and everyone's soul was cleansed in the process. Another lesson is apparent from the drug-use frenzies that have been building around the country: Only ye without sin had better cast that stone.

Social Conditions and Public Opinion

In a healthy democracy, public opinion affects all major developments in government and politics, frenzies included. And changes in public opinion—as well as evolving social conditions and popular culture—have helped to create circumstances favoring the development of virtually all the recent frenzies. In many ways the "new journalism" has merely reflected the modern desires of readers and viewers who financially sustain it.

Since the 1950s America has undergone a social glasnost that is sweeping and astounding. In 1962 David Brinkley, then of NBC News, was not permitted to use the words *venereal disease* on television; today, modest viewers are grateful when the formal term and not the slang is employed over the airwaves. Moreover, the range of subjects considered fit for public discussion is virtually unlimited in the 1990s, as just a glance at television or popular magazines will reveal. At the same time, attitudes on everything from acceptable language to divorce to homosexuality have liberalized, and the news media have both led and followed this cultural revolution.

Large-circulation personality magazines and "trash TV" have conditioned their audiences to thinking about the private lives of public figures. This "Oprah Winfrey–*People* magazine" mentality meshes nicely with the personalizing effect of television itself so that a kind of celebrity politics is created: Public careers become soap operas, coverage of elective stars becomes indistinguishable from the focus on the Hollywood or sports variety, and the appetite for tidbits about officials' private lives grows as a natural consequence. Inquiring minds want to know, so "there is virtually nothing we would not print in the newspaper now, if we had the goods," asserts *Washington Post* ombudsman Richard Harwood.

One event (Watergate) and two contradictory social movements (feminism and fundamentalist Christianity) have had special impacts on the public opinion that feeds frenzies. The post–Watergate generation of Americans is more cynical about politicians, less tolerant of corruption, and ever receptive to the explosion of public myths. Watergate's legacy was the passage of much tougher conflict-of-interest and ethics laws across the country, which have simultaneously raised the standards of good behavior and set new hair-trigger traps for public officials. As *ABC World News Tonight* anchor Peter Jennings puts it: "We in the media are playing against the backdrop of a fairly righteous, I almost said self-righteous, public at the moment, which calls men and women to higher standards than we might have held them to ten or fifteen years ago." Also after Watergate, politicians were encouraged by character-sensitive journalists and mood-sensing consultants to share more of the personal details of their lives with a suspicious electorate. Feminism reinforced the trend toward this examination of private character. "The women's movement made what we used to call the 'male prerogative' unfashionable," acknowledges *The New Republic*'s Fred Barnes. "Before feminism we envied and admired Jack Kennedy for dipping his wick all over town, but no longer." There is a parallel here to the civil rights movement's effect on journalism, as native Southerner Bill Kovach, who began his newspaper career in 1959, explains:

The notion that a powerful political figure, normally white male, would have an affair with a woman was long considered part of life. It wasn't until the women's movement came along and women became more active in helping define what behavior was acceptable that the definition of news changed, and how men treated women became newsworthy. It was the same way in the Old South where the most well meaning people in the world didn't consider the notion of segregation and discrimination a news story — not until the civil rights movement forced Southerners to confront the notion that, "wait a minute, by God, that's a story!"

Oddly enough, the rise of Christian fundamentalism has complemented feminism's enhancement of the character issue despite the ideological polarity of the two movements. In the 1980s, out of a rediscovered belief that government has a moral dimension, Christian evangelical preachers led their flocks to new heights of political activism. In the Christian view, public officials, as role models for the young, should be exemplary individuals in all sectors of life, private conduct most definitely included. Even as individual evangelicals, such as Jim Bakker and Jimmy Swaggart, fell from grace because of their own personal peccadilloes, the fundamentalist perspective had some appeal to an America more attuned to conservatism in the 1980s and less enamored of the sexual revolution after the onset of the AIDS epidemic. In addition to promiscuity, alcohol abuse became much less acceptable over the last decade — and therefore, more reportable for a press reflecting changing mores.

Just as overarching social trends determine the universe of legitimate frenzy subjects, so too does public opinion about any specific frenzy affect that frenzy's course. Granted, the effect is often diffuse and ambiguous. First of all, most of the public simply is not much interested in political events. Gallup surveys for the Times–Mirror Center for the People and the Press conducted from 1986 to 1989 showed that 80 percent of Americans paid close attention to the *Challenger* space shuttle disaster and 69 percent followed carefully the story of a young Texas girl's rescue from a backyard well, but only 37 percent closely followed the Quayle frenzy and 28 percent the Hart-Rice exposé.[4] Second, most polls about matters not near and dear to the public's heart can be misleading, since the minority that cares passionately about a candidate's offense — and as a consequence is permanently alienated from him or her — may be obscured by the majority's apathy. Third, one suspects the public does not always give completely honest answers to pollsters' questions about frenzies. As we shall see, many people claim to be wholly uninterested in the racy side of political scandals and critical of the press for reporting it. But "that's part of the hypocrisy of the great American public," says columnist Jack Kilpatrick. "They damn the media for being prurient, but by God, they've got their noses in the paper hanging on every word we write." This hypocritical voyeurism, combined with intense concern by a minority of individuals, guarantees a substantial readership and viewership for the media's coverage of frenzies. As for the general public indifference, most reporters seem to adopt the viewpoint of the *Wall Street Journal's* Al Hunt:

People tell me all the time "Oh, the public's bored with that." The public's bored with everything. The public's not nearly into politics the way we think it is. We love to believe that everyone's on the edge of their seat, waiting to learn the latest junk, but they're not.

At the same time there is evidence that public opinion, or at least the opinion of those paying attention, does make some difference in the frenzy's outcome. The *Washington Post's* Paul Taylor sees the interested public as "very shrewd" in its judgments: "Despite the fact that nuance and subtlety gets lost in coverage, people monitor these things with incredibly fine antennae and they decide whether we've gone too far or whether we've hit the nail on the head, and almost always that determines whether the target survives or doesn't survive." The public certainly has to be tolerant of, or predisposed to hear, the charges made against a candidate, or the electorate will ignore them — a decision frequently sensed by the press, which will consequently deemphasize the frenzy or desist entirely.

Subject to the cautions expressed earlier, there is a rough pecking order of public concern about candidate vices. On the whole, voters seem more interested in establishing whether they would buy a used car from a politician than whether he or she could be beatified by the pope. When forced to choose the sin raising "the most serious questions about the ethics of the candidates," Americans select "taking money in return for political favors" (54 percent) and lying (33 percent) by a mile over excessive drinking (7 percent) and extramarital sex (4 percent).[5] A 1987 CBS News/ *New York Times* poll (see Table 4.2) did not require respondents to make choices but rather asked whether it was "important for the press to tell the American people that a presidential candidate" committed certain errors and whether those mistakes would "be enough to make you vote against him, even if you agree with him on most of the issues." Once again, extramarital exploits came dead last on the public's list of election crimes.

TABLE 4.2   THE PUBLIC RATES CANDIDATE VICES

ACCUSATIONS ABOUT PRESIDENTIAL CANDIDATE	YES, PRESS SHOULD REPORT IT (%)	RESPONDENT WOULD VOTE AGAINST CANDIDATE (%)
Uses Cocaine	89	91
Was Guilty of Cheating on Income Tax	81	65
Lied about War Record	72	46
Had Been Hospitalized for Psychiatric Treatment	70	55
Was Guilty of Drunk Driving	66	39
Was Unfaithful to His Wife	40	36

SOURCE: CBS News/*New York Times* poll, May 5–6, 1987.

Interestingly, cocaine use is at the very top of the scale, an exception to the public's emphasis on a candidate's trustworthiness rather than personal habits, and this is undoubtedly a reflection of the seriousness of the drug problem in contemporary America. Voters make a clear distinction between cocaine and marijuana, however. Only 29 percent believe someone who has ever smoked marijuana "should be disqualified from being president" and that proportion drops to 19 percent when respondents are assured the candidate "only smoked it in college."[6] This small minority compares with the 88 percent and 95 percent who would disqualify a presidential candidate for "drinking too much" or "improperly using government information to make money for himself," respectively.

Already acknowledged is the public's hypocrisy of maintaining avid interest in private-life scandals while pretending indifference and condemning the media for covering them. Nevertheless, there appears to be some genuine concern about the growing invasion of privacy occurring during some frenzies. During the 1988 election season 68 percent in a CBS News/*New York Times* poll agreed that "too much attention is being paid to the private lives of people seeking high public office," and by 51 to 38 percent, Americans believed that "television and newspapers [were] probing too deeply into the private lives of candidates rather than getting at what the public ought to know."[7]

The emphasis in this section has been on the public opinion's effect on press coverage, but of course the reverse effect is at least as powerful: The news media's choice of subjects and slant directly influences public opinion. Often, when media organizations conduct polls, they are merely holding up a mirror to their own coverage. The impact of the press's intense focus during a frenzy is clearly seen by opinion trends registered after the Ford "free Poland" debate gaffe in October 1976, when President Ford's pollster conducted continuous surveying from the debate's end through the following day. The public's "instant analysis" was quite different from that of the press. Immediately following the debate the sample picked Ford as "having done the better job" in the debate match-up by 44 to 33 percent. The news media judged Ford the loser, however, almost entirely on the strength — or weakness — of the "free Poland" remark. All three networks focused on the costly mistake in their postdebate commentary. NBC's John Chancellor remembers running from the debate hall to his network's headquarters as the candidates concluded: "I told the producer to queue up the Poland gaffe, and he said, 'I've already done it.' There was no question in anyone's mind that that was the [sound bite]." Most of the major newspapers reinforced this message the following morning; so did the next evening's television coverage by concentrating on anti-Ford fallout among Eastern European ethnic groups and a press conference with the Ford campaign's key strategists at which the first eleven questions had been about Poland. The drumbeat of negative coverage took a heavy and steady toll on Ford's standing over the twenty-four-hour period. The president's original debate performance edge of 44 to 33 percent became a massive Jimmy Carter lead of 62 to 17 percent — an astounding net change of 56 percentage points. The horserace results ("If the election were held today . . . ") showed a complete reversal. On debate evening Ford led by 55 to 37 percent; the next evening Carter romped out front by 54 to 37 percent. The decline for Ford and the rise for Carter was fairly constant from time period to time period, as the impact of the news media's analysis presumably penetrated an ever-increasing proportion of the population. Over the final month of the campaign, Ford recovered some of the lost ground and almost overtook Carter, but there is little question that the events of October 6 and 7 were critical. The making of the president in 1976 occurred at many points, but the news frenzy over "free Poland" was surely one of them.

Humor

"Humor is the best medicine," goes the old aphorism, but for a politician in trouble, humor can be a deadly brew, a compound of sweet poison that finishes him or her off. For centuries editorial cartoonists have humbled the mighty, and occasionally helped to bring them down. But the most costly humor to a modern campaign is that sponsored by the princes of television comedy: Johnny Carson, Jay Leno, David Letterman, and Dana Carvey. Their one-liners and skits reinforce and extend the disasters that befall candidates, transforming the pols from subjects of sympathy to objects of ridicule, changing the way voters perceive the real events on the campaign trail. Political reporters such as ABC's Ann Compton have sensed the relationship between late-night comedy and real-life politics:

Much of the legend is set not on the evening news. . . . It's set by Carson, and Letterman, and "Saturday Night Live." In a campaign, the gossip and the fun bleeds into the coverage. It's not actually in the news, but it affects the way people receive the news.

The comics have significantly shaped the images of many recent officeholders and seekers. *Saturday Night Live's* Chevy Chase portrayed President Ford as an idiot and a stumblebum, preparing the way for the interpretation of the "free Poland" gaffe as more prima facie evidence of Ford's stupidity. President Carter's "killer rabbit" provided fodder for endless gags about his political ineptitude and impotence.

Gary Hart and Dan Quayle may be entitled to royalties for all the time they have filled as the subjects of monologues. Letterman's "Top Ten Pickup Lines" for each beleaguered politician became instant classics, as this sampler suggests:

HART	QUAYLE
"Can a Kennedyesque guy buy you a drink?"	"Can my father buy you a drink?"
"Want to go to a nearby polling place?"	"Didn't we flunk out of school together?"
"Have you ever seen a front-runner naked?"	

When Hart reentered the presidential contest in late 1987, he was nearly laughed back out of it. Said Letterman: "In, out, in, out — isn't that what got him in trouble in the first place? . . . The Hart campaign has had to operate on a shoestring; Gary has pretty much limited his activities to phone sex." Quayle also has proved to be a nearly irresistible butt of quips both as a nominee and as vice president. At times he has outranked all other national and world figures to become the top target of late-night television.

Letterman and company are not the only sources of popular ridicule that spear candidates. The freelance punch lines fanned by increasingly important "talk radio" take a toll, too. Perhaps the most damaging joke about Quayle's National Guard service was not ready for prime time: "What do you get when you cross a hawk with a chicken? A Quayle."

Occasionally the most politically devastating laugh line is supplied by the candidate instead of a paid comedian. Near the end of the 1984 presidential primaries, a punchy Gary Hart expressed relief to be in California and out of New Jersey, where he had held "samples from a toxic waste dump" while his wife cuddled a koala bear in the Golden State.[8] Californians appreciated the New Jersey joke, but Garden State voters did not. Newspapers headlined the quip, and Hart lost the New Jersey primary in a landslide.

The Dynamics of the Feeding Frenzy

Late-night humor is no laughing matter for many candidates, but it is merely the icing on a many-layered cake. These layers — the conditions and stages of a feeding frenzy — have been presented and analyzed (see Figure 4.1, pages 90–91). The prior conditions include those internal to the press's operation as well as the just-discussed external factors that shape journalists' worldviews at any given time. All these conditions taken together help to determine the intensity and extent of the frenzy's fire once the spark of the candidate's mistake or offense flashes.

That spark can be generated directly by the candidate (as Gerald Ford did with his Poland gaffe on nationwide television) or indirectly by the press (for example, the *Miami Herald*'s Hart stakeout) or a rival camp (the Dukakis staff's "attack video"). Usually the press jumps to cover the offense, though occasionally it needs a nudge, as in Debategate. When *Time*'s Laurence I. Barrett revealed the Reagan campaign's 1980 unauthorized acquisition of the Carter briefing papers in his 1983 book, *Gambling with History*, journalists seemed to yawn collectively at this latest example of "politics as usual." But as mentioned earlier, former Carter aides and a Democratic congressional investigation jump-started a scandal probe.

The news media's interest in a candidate's mistake is always piqued by the error's sexiness or universality as well as the politician's hypocrisy, partial disclosure, attempts at lying and cover-up, or "spins" (that is, attempts to downplay or deflect) by the staff and political consultants. The Carter White House committed a classic goof in refusing to release the innocuous photograph capturing the attack of the "killer rabbit," for instance. Instead, "they left it to the cartoonists to illustrate" and exaggerate the story, explains its author, Brooks Jackson.

Press reactions to any revelation include a ratcheting up of coverage, with more resources devoted to the issue and generous doses of pack journalism and rampant speculation. "The conventional wisdom becomes set in concrete so quickly," observes *National Journal*'s James Barnes. "You get a sense that everyone is on the phone on one big party line, and everybody's so sure what's going to happen." Columnist Robert Novak adds, "There's a hype, a hysteria in the air where all disbelief is suspended, and the press is always going to the next step: 'When's Quayle going to be dropped from the ticket?' 'Are they going to have a miniconvention to replace Dukakis [because of his alleged mental illness]?' "

The candidate under fire also usually reacts predictably, directing his or her anger at the press, sometimes as an excuse to avoid full disclosure or to buy time before defusing the controversy or withdrawing altogether. There is probably less time to buy for a little-known candidate, such as Joseph Biden, who was defined by the allegations of plagiarism before he had the opportunity to define himself for the larger public. Also critical at this juncture is whether television decides to make the story a major focus. If it does, the battle escalates dramatically since "television *is* the front page," as *CBS Evening News* executive producer Tom Bettag termed it. Of course, TV news coverage is not quite an independent variable in all this, as Bettag's on-air colleague Dan Rather explains: "If the *Washington Post*, the *New York Times*, or the *Los Angeles Times* runs a front-page story, particularly for more than one day, the heat's on to run it and we usually do. I don't enjoy saying that, but that's the way it works." This competitive pressure also contributes to the previously discussed lowest-common-denominator journalism and "wiggle" disclosures (also called "water-torture" journalism).

Irresistibly, rival candidates are drawn to the fray, whether to fan the fires with off-the-record leaks to the press or to maneuver and attract the candidate's supporters if it looks as though the frenzy victim will not survive. Undercover, campaigns have frequently been known to encourage hecklers and demonstrators to show up at a frenzy target's public events, both to raise the temperature of the controversy and to give the news media colorful video backdrop and a hook to extend the life of the story. Dan Quayle was such a target in 1988 ("This Quayle is a chicken" was a common placard), just as Richard Nixon had been in 1952. It was in response to a protest sign reading "No Mink Coats for Nixon—Just Cold Cash" that Nixon came up with the line he later used to good effect in the "Checkers"

FIGURE 4.1   MODELING THE MODERN FEEDING FRENZY

Prior Conditions (Internal to Press)

News media's replacement of political parties in screening/ winnowing of candidates	Press subtext (preconceived notions) about candidate	Press bias, including like/dislike of candidate	Press competition	Growing intensity of coverage
More women in press corps	Relaxed libel laws	Elements of timing (such as slow news periods)	Post-Watergate/ Vietnam cynicism	Post-Watergate emphasis on investigative reporting
Decline of news business standards and civility in coverage	Character-issue emphasis	Pack journalism	Celebrity journalism	Press frustrations (such as no access to candidate)

Prior Conditions (External to Press)

| Pattern of known or unknown candidate behavior | Sources (intraparty, opposition party, nonpartisan) | Public opinion (crystallized and uncrystallized) | Decline of political parties | Prevailing social conditions and trends |
| Special atmosphere of a national political convention | No previous scrutiny for candidate | Celebrity politics and the personalizing effect of television | Prevailing political conditions (such as degree of competition) |

Candidate "Offense"
(Disclosed by Press, Candidate, Rival, or Combination)

| Intensified by hypocrisy | Intensified by lying | Intensified by partial disclosure | Intensified by simplicity, sexiness, universality of offense |

Press Reactions

| Shock, outrage, rampant speculation | Pack journalism | Increase in number of press covering candidate and amount/intensity of coverage | Devotion of more resources (time, money, people) to issue |

Possible Candidate Reactions

| Anger/antipress stance | Refusal to discuss: cover-up: downplay | Full disclosure | Withdrawal | Retrenchment; new strategies, spin, or focus (political consultant activity) |

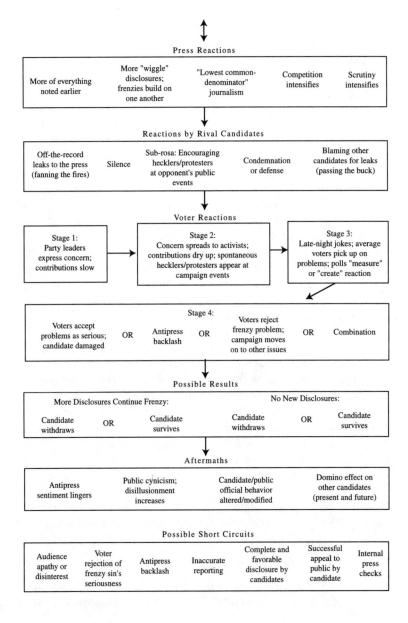

speech: "My wife Pat wears a good Republican cloth coat." (The "mink coat" reference was to a Truman administration scandal in which a secretary had accepted the gift of a nine-thousand-dollar mink coat.)

Many of the rival campaigns' challenges are actually on the record, with contenders attempting in full public view to capitalize on a wounded opponent's troubles. National party chairpersons frequently initiate attacks, too, as do interest groups offended by a gaffe or aligned with other campaigns. Thus, Polish Americans leapt into the fray to criticize Gerald Ford in 1976, *Playboy*-offended fundamentalist Christians savaged wayward son Jimmy Carter the same year, and Japanese Americans took on Spiro Agnew in 1968. Not every rival camp launches an assault on a tempting target, however. Some adhere to the old rule of politics that commands, "Never interfere with an enemy who is in the process of committing suicide." For instance, the 1972 Nixon campaign, so intent on surreptitious sabotage earlier that election year, stayed conspicuously away from all comment as the Eagleton crisis unfolded.

At long last the public beyond the campaign circle is drawn into the controversy. Earlier, party leaders, activists, and contributors went on alert, but with an intensifying frenzy, campaign donations may dry up, unprompted protesters begin trailing a candidate, and average voters start to pay attention. Public opinion polls measure citizens' reactions (or create them, depending on the wording and interpretation of questions), and the first late-night jokes creep into the monologues. At this juncture, the electorate — as (fallibly) measured by polls and pundits — may either judge the candidate's offense as serious, forcing him or her to withdraw or limp along in a damaged state, or deem it insufficiently weighty to merit severe punishment, in which case the candidate survives to fight another day. (The giveaway hint that it's all over is often when an official's staunchest allies defect.) New disclosures can revive the frenzy at any time, of course, though as the *Wall Street Journal*'s Al Hunt insists: "Whether it should or it shouldn't, the news business has to move on. You can't freeze-frame a campaign and hold it there until every [leftover] question gets answered." This appeared to be the prevailing sentiment in the press corps both in 1984 after Ferraro's late-August press conference on her family finances and in 1988 once Quayle had endured close press scrutiny for about two weeks.

The Frenzies of the 1992 Campaign

The year 1992 was the best of times and the worst of times for press coverage of politics. On the one hand, many news organizations made a determined effort to focus on issues in the presidential campaign, and thus inform their readers and viewers more fully than ever before. Yet, on the other, such well-intended plans still could not stop journalistic standards from sinking to new lows along the way.

How could this have happened, especially after the press had fervently promised not to repeat — much less augment — the mistakes of the 1988 campaign? The same factors that produced so many earlier feeding frenzies once again took control. Lowest-common-denominator journalism accelerated, the obsessive character issue was still front-and-center, and unproven rumors were even more carelessly splashed across many front pages than four years before. From time to time the campaign was hijacked by the tabloids, and the establishment press meekly followed the lead of their low-life brethren as the focus shifted from substance to sleaze.

Campaign '92 was replete with regrettable press practices and stumbles, many of them just more of the same from past years. In 1988 the press dutifully swallowed Republican media events whole (such as Bush's visit to a flag factory); the next cycle's uncritical reviews went to Democratic media events, such as the packaged Clinton-Gore bus trips. Despite a brief summer effort by CBS to expand the length of presidential candidates' sound bites, the average sound bite on the networks' evening news continued to shrink — to 8.4 seconds in 1992.[9]

Short sound bites were but a tiny part of the overall problem. The three oldest networks cut back their national party convention coverage substantially in 1992, devoting only a miserly two or three hours per night. CNN and C-SPAN's gavel-to-gavel efforts admirably filled the void for citizens fortunate enough to have cable TV, but nothing can excuse the networks' diminishing devotion to these vital quadrennial conclaves of American democracy. What airtime the networks offer is also increasingly filled with the chattering of their celebrity anchors and correspondents, rather than the actual words and deeds of the candidates, parties, and campaigns. From Labor Day to Election Day the TV reporters and anchors consumed 71 percent of the evening newscast time devoted to the 1992 campaign, while the presidential candidates were given a mere 12 percent of the time.[10] It is not just that the voters often benefit from seeing and hearing from the candidates directly; it is also that the network correspondents and pundits, predictable dispensers of inside-the-Beltway conventional wisdom, are so frequently off-base. During Bill Clinton's difficult spring of Gennifer Flowers, marijuana usage, and draft evasion, for example, virtually every major television newsperson and commentator wrote Clinton off, as the following sampling suggests:

Clinton . . . will either not be the nominee or not be the president.

— MARGARET WARNER, *Newsweek*

In November's general election Clinton will be clobbered by Bush.

— JOHN MCLAUGHLIN, *The McLaughlin Group*

I think he's got to get out of the race in the next two or three days; otherwise he's going to get badly damaged.

— ED ROLLINS, Republican (and, briefly, Perot) political consultant

I think he is dead . . . Clinton is unelectable.

— ROBERT NOVAK, CNN commentator[11]

With commentary of this ilk, one can easily understand why Bill Clinton and his fellow candidates sought refuge on the talk shows (*Larry King Live, Donahue,* etc.) and other nontraditional television forums (MTV, *Arsenio Hall,* and so on). This approach is obviously good for candidates who want to escape the usual news-media filter and speak to voters at length and without instant analysis. Ross Perot, who launched his protocandidacy on Larry King's CNN show, was the first to demonstrate talk TV's power, but Bill Clinton quickly set the record for quantity and variety of appearances on "alternative" television. Come the fall, George Bush joined in, albeit somewhat reluctantly, as he made the rounds of *Larry King* and the network morning shows. Overall, Clinton appeared on talk shows forty-seven times, Perot thirty-four times, and Bush only sixteen times.

Talk-show democracy added a surprise element to Campaign '92, and it proved its worth not just to candidates but also to voters, the political system, and even the press. Thanks to talk shows, votes probably glimpsed more facets of the presidential candidates than ever before, and they also were often able to make a direct connection with the contenders, due to the call-in component that was usually present. The political system was strengthened by this new diversity of approach, because the talk shows broadened the audience for politics, educating some citizens not regularly reached by news programming. The competition provided by nontraditional venues also proved healthy for the traditional news organizations. Voters' issue-oriented questions were a welcome change from the horse-race-obsessed fare of many reporters, for instance, and kept the press focused on people's real concerns. Also helpful was the reminder — a revelation to some of the news media's oversized egos — that many citizens believed they could happily do without much of the press. Of course, what voters frequently missed on the talk shows was the hard questioning and tough follow-ups that expose politicians' inconsistencies, the type of interrogation that only trained journalists can usually provide. So talk-show democracy has its limits, and it ought to be seen as either a complement or a supplement to mainstream news coverage. Nonetheless, the talk-show phenomenon, likely now a permanent part of the campaign landscape, is a useful revolt against the press insiders, and potentially a powerful tool to produce wider participation and interest in politics.

Throughout the year, some journalists derided candidate appearances on talk shows as undignified, characterizing the shows as more entertaining than informational. Whatever the truth of those criticisms, journalists ought to be at least as concerned with the Hollywoodized behavior of some of their colleagues. In 1992, as before, an apparently insatiable thirst for celebrity led many prominent television newspersons to blur the line between journalism and entertainment by appearing on such comedy/variety shows as those of Jay Leno, David Letterman, and Arsenio Hall. As usual, these infotainment artists (led by all-time-appearance record-holder Tom Brokaw of NBC) filled guest slot after guest slot without a peep of criticism from anyone in their star-struck profession.

Talk-show democracy also had its effects on the network evening newscasts. CBS, ABC, and NBC all employed panels of "average voters" for intermittent discussions throughout the fall with Dan Rather, Peter Jennings, and Tom Brokaw. Like all other unscientifically selected, nonrandom samples, these so-called focus groups were unbalanced in some way. For example, ABC's and CBS's participants seemed disproportionately hostile to Bush, while not a single undecided voter in NBC's small sampling eventually went to Clinton's column.

Other network innovations included regular "truth checks" on claims made in candidate advertising and speeches. In this area, the work of ABC's Jeff Greenfield, CBS's Eric Engberg, CNN's Brooks Jackson, and NBC's Lisa Myers, among others, was one of the highlights of 1992's television press coverage. However, there was at times an unfortunate tendency to present only one possible, narrow interpretation of a TV spot's assertions or a candidate's statements, when alternate explanations were equally credible, if less critical. The newspaper "ad watches" that rapidly and blessedly became a standard feature of campaign coverage around the country usually avoided this pitfall, allowing space for the criticized campaigns to respond. Television should do the same.

The network news divisions also made an effort to match the serious mood of 1992 voters by focusing on the key issues — especially the economy. All of the evening newscasts beefed up their issue-oriented segments, and the regular viewer probably did receive adequate tutelage in the major areas of campaign debate. Surprisingly, as a proportion of total election news, issue coverage declined from 40 percent in 1988 to 32 percent in 1992, while horserace coverage galloped ahead (35 percent in 1992, compared to 25 percent in 1988).[12] Yet the absolute numbers of issue segments in 1992 almost precisely matched those of 1988,[13] and many of the 1992 issue pieces were, by network TV standards, lengthy and in-depth. In addition, the issue pieces were competing with an unprecedent-ed orgy of horserace polls, including at least four sets of daily "tracking polls" in the final weeks of the campaign. Senior broadcast and print journalists are among the first to admit that polling—and reporting about it—got completely out of hand in the latter stages of 1992.[14] The survey results determined the headlines and drove the context of the coverage to an appalling degree, while the faults and inherent inadequacies of polls (high refusal rates, difficulties in screening out nonvoters, and so on) rarely received appropriate attention. Compounding these difficulties was the pronounced tendency of each news organization to hype its survey, to the minimization or exclusion of surveys with different results. And almost all the preelection polls missed the size of the Perot vote—a final caution that ought to give all journalists pause before the next poll-a-rama begins.

Because of time constraints, the three oldest networks are unable to match the news efforts of CNN and C-SPAN. CNN's *Inside Politics* and its six-part series *Democracy in America* were major contributions to voter education, and C-SPAN's complete coverage of almost all major campaign events (gloriously without commentary) allowed viewers to evaluate the candidates for themselves.

The aftermaths of feeding frenzies as well as possible short circuits in the frenzy process range from lingering antipress sentiment among the public and politicians to growing cynicism after another would-be emperor is unclothed to increased scrutiny of the remaining candidates. Antidotes to the frenzy's power might include a direct and successful appeal to the public by the candidate (à la the "Checkers" speech) or a public backlash against press tactics (perhaps stakeouts) that rebounds to the candidate's favor.

This model of the modern feeding frenzy is merely a sketch of the dynamics that might apply in a given controversy. By no means does the frenzy always unfold in precisely this way, nor does the model convey the complexity of interactions among the various institutions and individu-als constituting the political universe. Despite these obvious limitations, the model suggests a beginning of the next task at hand: a fuller description and analysis of the excesses that have characterized press coverage of some feeding frenzies.

CHAPTER FIVE

Rumor and Excess

Junkyard Dog Journalism on the Prowl

Almost every big story is invariably carried to excess; the news media tend to run everything into the ground.
— TOM BETTAG, executive producer, *CBS Evening News*

Maybe there's more of a relationship between news and pornography than we realize.
— HOWARD FINEMAN, chief political correspondent, *Newsweek*

A CRITIC IN SEARCH of press excess need not exert him- or herself. As most journalists freely admit, it is everywhere, and nowhere in such abundance as during a feeding frenzy. This chapter will explore the extent and the circumstances of many frenzy excesses, concentrating especially on the nefarious and increasingly common practice of publishing or airing rumors for which a convincing body of evidence does not exist.

Journalists offer many reasons and excuses for the excesses documented here. Some are convincing and acceptable. Deadline pressures take an inexorable toll on quality and accuracy. ("In the middle of a massive campaign explosion we have to decide what to report by 7:00 P.M.; we don't have two weeks to debate the nuances," argues David Hoffman of the *Washington Post*.) Since the press prints only what it is told and can find out, it unavoidably publishes partial truths and distortions of reality. And every human frailty possessed by journalists is magnified because of the attention given their work by the millions who read and hear them daily.

Yet a critic's central concern about the abuses and excesses to be described shortly is that so many in the media appear to shrug their shoulders and dismiss the "inevitable" problems with one of three hack-neyed formulations that might have been borrowed from *Bartlett's Familiar Quotations* or textbooks about the Fourth Estate:

> "This is the price we pay for a free press."
> "The public has the right to know."
> "Life, and especially politics, isn't fair."

As this chapter's stories unfold, the reader may well want to ask a set of companion questions: Must the price of a free press be so high in some instances? Does the public have the right to know gossip, rumor, and innuendo? Should the news media add in such generous measure to the inherent unfairness of politics?

The Parade of Excess

The Reverend Pat Robertson once came up with a strange but appro-priate (for him) theological explanation for the frenzies sweeping not only politics but religion: "Maybe God is cleaning house all around."[1] If political frenzies are divinely inspired, the press is serving as God's instrument with evangelical fervor. Many of the root problems generating journalistic abuses have already been identified: competitive pressures, pack journal-ism, biases of various sorts, the decline of news standards, and the corrosive post-Watergate cynicism, to mention a few. Moreover, many of the ex-cesses that result — lowest-common-denominator journalism, "wiggle" disclosures, the overemphasis on the character issue, and so on — have also been discussed. Traces of these regrettable aspects of coverage can be found in virtually all the recent frenzies, even ones where the public official was unquestionably in the wrong. In the case of Mayor Marion Barry, for instance, every trivial tidbit and morsel about his 1990 drug arrest became a new story fed to viewers and readers, including completely false rumors broadcast during the competitive war that erupted among local television stations at the time. The cameras and bright lights that were focused on Mayor Barry intruded on the privacy of innocent and publicity-shy patients in a drug treatment center, and even the movements of Barry's young son were recorded for the public to see.

Just the sight and sound of the frenzied press pack can be excessive. "Once we start, we're awful," observes CBS's Bruce Morton. "Pack jour-nalism is ugly: four dozen reporters yelling questions, two dozen cameras in pursuit of the prey. It's not very thoughtful and it's certainly not journalism at its best." ABC's Brit Hume notes that the excessive nature of the pack is contained even in the terminology pack reporters use:

The famous phrase we employ is, "the candidate was dogged today by controversy. . . . " Now usually he wasn't dogged by anybody except us. We go pester somebody about something all day, and then write a lead based on it.

As the frenzy takes hold, the press becomes mesmerized by the subject and obsessed with the target. "The press absolutely blocks out every other topic and can't talk about anything else," says Ellen Hume, formerly of the *Wall Street Journal*. Journalists get carried away, caught up in an overreaction of their own making. With a loss of perspective, they cease making judgments about how much is too much and instead lock into the story line for the duration of the unfolding soap opera.

The lack of balance in the coverage of most frenzies often encompasses trial by media, with an inherent presumption of guilt. "What concerns me as much as anything is the rush to judgment, with guilt assumed and extenuating circumstances rarely reported," admits *NBC Nightly News* anchor Tom Brokaw. The media also can lavish attention on a budding scandal out of all proportion to the offense.[4] Frequently the worst possible interpretation of a given set of circumstances becomes the press "spin," as Gerald Ford discovered after his Poland debate statement. While *Washington Monthly* editor Charles Peters "loved it because I'm a Democrat," he also calls the controversy "hideous and phony": "Any reasonable, well-informed person knew exactly what Ford meant, and the press certainly did. This was the most spectacular example of a story the press in their hearts knew was false, but willfully seized on anyway." Adds ABC News's Ann Compton:

I was at the presidential debate and in the travel pool the next day when we hounded Ford at every stop with, "What do you mean?" Now we all knew in our hearts exactly what he meant. We had been to Poland, we had seen the strength of the Catholic Church there. We knew that Poland felt this yearning for Western values and religious freedoms. What we got Ford on was a technicality, that the state of Poland was a Warsaw Pact nation. . . . The Poland frenzy lasted too long and was unforgiving.

Press mistreatment of candidates can take many other forms, including guilt by association and sensationalism. The strained efforts to link Geraldine Ferraro and her husband, John Zaccaro, to the Mafia in 1984 provided a sad example. In many instances using the most tenuous connections — such as a reputed mobster's renting of an apartment in a building Zaccaro inherited from his father in 1971 and immediately sold — some reporters seemed hell-bent on proving Ferraro's underworld ties. The *Wall Street Journal*'s Albert Hunt criticized one of his own newspaper's editorial writers, Jonathan Kwitney, as "particularly unfair. He went back for generations trying to see if anybody's name ended in a vowel." CNN's Frank Sesno believes "there were strong ethnic overtones in the commentary, basically saying 'they're Italian, so they must be connected with the Mafia.'" In some stories, too, unnamed "law enforcement officials" were conveniently on hand to express a considered, nonspecific opinion that the allegations were true.[2] Sensationalism was present in the Ferraro case and is a part of most frenzies, but it moves front and center in any incident involving sex. From *Geraldo* to the print tabloids, Barney Frank and his male prostitute were assured top billing. Yet much of the establishment press was happy to ride the publicity wave as well. "I doubt *Newsweek* put Frank on its cover because the magazine is profoundly interested in homosexuality," ABC's Peter Jennings wryly commented. The *Washington Times*, which first broke the scandal, showcased Frank in banner headlines for days. A disapproving rival, the *Washington Post*'s Len Downie, charged that the *Times* was "clearly crusading to drive Frank out of office; they wanted his scalp." And indeed, many of the front-page leads lend support to Downie's allegation: "Tide is rolling against Frank," "Democratic leaders desert Frank: 'Death drums are pounding,' lawmaker says," and so on. Congressman Frank's refusal to resign and his subsequent reelection in 1990 proves beyond doubt that politicians can sometimes survive the press's excesses — and their own.

More disturbing than sensationalism are the unethical practices, uncorrected errors, and invasion of innocent individuals' privacy that occur in some frenzies. Watergate's investigation established the modern standard for ends-justifies-means rule bending, with *Washington Post* sleuths Bob Woodward and Carl Bernstein underhandedly obtaining confidential telephone records and other information. An apparently more common unethical practice about which several of our nonpress interviewees complained is the "refused-call barb," an unflattering reference to a public figure included in a reporter's story to punish the official for not returning the reporter's phone call.

Rumors

People may expect too much of journalism. Not only do they expect it to be entertaining, they expect it to be true.
          — reporter and editor LEWIS LAPHAM[3]

Lapham is wrong. People have every right to expect the truth from the press, and most journalists fully accept their responsibility to report the news accurately. Despite deadline pressure, and even though the news is only the proverbial "rough first draft of history," newspeople by and large do a remarkably good job of delivering a reasonably reliable version of events. That is why the trend toward publishing and airing unverified rumors is so deeply disturbing, a throwback to the unbridled days of the early nineteenth century when journalists were little more than gossip-mongers.

Granted, the reader's appetite for titillation has always motivated the press, and "half the people in the newsroom are here because they like to gossip and get paid for it," as the *Washington Post*'s Milton Coleman puts it. Then, too, rumors are part of the fabric of the political community, woven into the day-to-day contact reporters have with political consultants, activists, and officials. But the trafficking in innuendo has accelerated dramatically in recent years. A newsman for one of America's most prestigious publications recalled that in 1988 rumors were coming in so fast and furious "we had to separate them into categories of 'above the belt' and 'below the belt.'" When the telephone would ring at the desk of National Public Radio's Nina Totenberg, her colleague Cokie Roberts would tease, "Sex or drugs, Nina?" The sewer of hearsay has become the new mainstream of American politics for a long, sick season. Partly, the age of pervasive negative campaigning has created the conditions conducive to the spread of sleaze. Political consultants apply the knife of gossip with surgical skill, "getting a dozen people aggressively asking, 'have you heard the one about . . .' until enough chatter develops so that the press starts to think it's true," as Democratic political operative Michael McCurry describes it. But mainly, tattle is taking center stage in politics because everyone knows the press will print it, even without proof, if not on the front page then in "style" sections or gossip columns where lower standards sometimes prevail. And under the lowest-common-denominator rule, only one media outlet need give the story legitimacy before all can publish or broadcast it guilt-free.

The on-the-record rumor mill is being fed by a growing belief among some journalists that even *unproved* facts, if widely accepted as true, can have a substantial effect on a campaign or public official, and are therefore reportable. "If you haven't been able to confirm the rumors, but the rumors won't die, that is a legitimate news story," insists one senior television journalist. Also supposedly appropriate for public consumption are allegations made by only indirectly connected but "credible" sources, whether evidence is on hand or not. Both guideposts represent a substantial and unwise lowering of the threshold for publishing and broadcasting information, which results in unwarranted damage being done to public figures and inaccurate reports reaching the public. It may sometimes seem to journalists that "everyone knows" the scuttlebutt, but that is only because a newsperson's universe of contacts is public affairs oriented. In truth, the circulation of any unpublished political rumor is usually restricted to a small circle of political elites — until the press makes it a general topic of conversation via newsprint and the airwaves. Consider the unfairness and injustice in these examples:

- When Michael Dukakis's campaign sent out the "attack video" that torpedoed Joseph Biden's candidacy, Richard Gephardt at first received the blame. Private speculation about the identity of the perpetrator was unavoidable, but when the conventional wisdom fingered Gephardt and this conclusion seeped into print — as it did almost everywhere — the Missouri congressman's campaign for the Democratic presidential nomination was dealt a body blow. Gephardt's 1988 press secretary, Don Foley, offered this assessment:

> It did us a lot of damage. Up until that time Dick Gephardt was viewed by most people as someone who would not engage in dirty campaigning, and he had a Boy Scout image. But this incident painted him as somebody who was a bit overanxious for the prize; in the eyes of a lot of people this took the shine off of the Gephardt aura.

Even when Dukakis's staff was revealed to be behind Biden's troubles, the tarnish seemed to stick to Gephardt's image.

- Not long after Biden's plagiarism became the focus of the nascent 1988 campaign, the Champaign, Illinois, *News-Gazette* published an article based purely on hearsay alleging that Jesse Jackson had left the University of Illinois in 1960 after plagiarizing an English term paper. The sole sources for the story were two college acquaintances of Jackson's who told the newspaper they had heard about the incident from others. The Associated Press sent out a dispatch based on the *News-Gazette* account that was used by many major newspapers throughout the country. As it turned out, the professor who supposedly discovered Jackson's perfidy could not recall it, and the president of the University of Illinois certified that Jackson's academic record contained no notation of any disciplinary action for plagiarism.

Such incidents are not isolated examples, but part of a pattern every bit as convincing as the "character" continuums that capture the attention of the contemporary news media. Again and again, the same questionable practices noted in the above examples have arisen in national politics, affecting the careers of Jack Kemp, Gary Hart, Michael Dukakis, Dan Quayle, Bill Clinton and Ross Perot. Each of these national cases will be examined in turn, in the rough chronological order of their development.

Jack Kemp

Some candidates have provided the press with satisfactory answers to questions about rumors on numerous occasions, only to be asked the same questions over and over again.[4] For two decades this has been the problem facing Jack Kemp, the former New York congressman and 1988 Republican presidential candidate who ran the Department of Housing and Urban Development for the Bush administration.

When Kemp was a star quarterback for the Buffalo Bills in the 1960s, he donated much of his free time to the campaigns of prominent Republicans. In 1967 Kemp was rewarded for his efforts with a three-month, off-season job as an assistant to one of California Governor Ronald Reagan's highest-ranking aides. Unfortunately for Kemp, this was precisely the time when a "homosexual clique" among Reagan's staff was exposed. An internal investigation mounted by Reagan's legal affairs adviser Edwin Meese and communications director Lyn Nofziger identified the members of the ring that included Kemp's boss, and those involved were asked to resign. The reason for the resignations was not reported at the time, but two months later, after Nofziger leaked word of the incident to six reporters, an October 31, 1967, syndicated column by Drew Pearson reported "that a homosexual ring [had] been operating in [Reagan's] office." Pearson also said that an "athlete" was involved.[5]

Pearson's column was the original published source of a false rumor that would grow and persist for decades: that Jack Kemp had been or was still a homosexual. Everywhere Kemp turned in the 1970s, the gossip seemed to follow him. It was the subject of private speculation in his congressional campaigns (Kemp was first elected to the U.S. House from a Buffalo district in 1970), it surfaced behind the scenes at the 1976 Republican National Convention, and it threatened his presidential ambitions as he geared up for a possible White House run in the late 1970s.

Some of Kemp's advisers decided on a bold move to spike the rumor: Absolutely confident the allegation was false, they would attempt to have the rumor fully investigated by a reputable journalist, with the results published independently of the campaign. One of Kemp's closest confidantes, writer Jude Wanniski, told all to the New York Times's White House correspondent Martin Tolchin, who was preparing an October 1978 article about Kemp for Esquire.[6] When Tolchin questioned Kemp about the matter, the congressman stated flatly, "There is absolutely not a shred of evidence. There is nothing, and there was nothing." Kemp explained that he had simply invested in property with his Reagan administration boss. Unknown to Kemp, his boss had used the property (a Lake

Tahoe ski lodge) for parties with other homosexual members and associates of the administration. Kemp said he had never seen the place, and that his investment was strictly a financial decision. Tolchin confirmed Kemp's account, published his findings, and concluded, "Everyone who has looked into the case has come to the same conclusion." It seemed like a vindication, but two months later columnists Rowland Evans and Robert Novak were moved to write a column about the "ugly and malicious calumny" being spread about Kemp by an unnamed, high-ranking Carter White House aide as well as John White, then chairman of the Democratic National Committee. Sure enough, the "garbage" and "gutter communications" riling Evans and Novak turned out to be, once again, the gossip about Kemp's sexual orientation. The columnists launched their own exhaustive inquiry, and summarized the results for their readers:

After considerable checking, we can now report that the rumor comes as close to being disprovable as any personal slander ever is. For example, contrary to one recurrent part of the rumor, there never was any police file on Kemp; he was not investigated.

One principal in the 1967 case whom we tracked down with some difficulty to his new job and life said he never had known or been told of any illicit association between Kemp and those who resigned under a cloud. Indeed, the sole source of the rumor that has haunted Kemp's career for eleven years is the fact that he traveled, on an official basis, several times with one of the Reagan aides who later resigned. That, and nothing more, is the "case" against Kemp.[7]

Yet, in a telling commentary on human nature, the charge continued to be remembered better than the emphatic exoneration. Despite these back-to-back 1978 debunkings, the squalid rumor continued its underground life. In the summer of 1985, as Kemp was gearing up for his 1988 presidential campaign, his aides again decided to confront the rumor in interviews with reporters for *Vanity Fair* and *Newsweek*. Kemp's press secretary, John Buckley, had learned of the *Vanity Fair* reporter's interest in the "gay" rumor; one of Kemp's friends from the National Football League had tipped Buckley after an inquiry from the reporter. So Buckley called the newswoman (Marie Brenner), informed her that he had "heard the drums along the Mohawk," knew what she was up to, and proposed the following ground rules:

You can ask him any question you want. If you find anything based on your investigation, print it. If you find that the guy is gay, print that he's gay. But if you can't find anything, do one of two things. Either don't go into it, or print the fact that you've looked into it and there is nothing there.

And that, says Buckley, became the Kemp camp's formula for rumor control, at least in the beginning of the campaign. At about the same time, Howard Fineman of *Newsweek* approached Buckley, interested in the same subject. It was not a coincidence. According to Buckley, Brenner had told colleagues of her belief that *Newsweek* had had the goods on Kemp for years but had not published them; this got back to *Newsweek*, which decided it had better investigate what it didn't have.

Fineman's article ran before Brenner's, but both reached the same predictable conclusion: The rumors were untrue. Fineman retraced the history of the gossip, and quoted Lyn Nofziger: "They are vicious rumors [and] there is no evidence at all that anything happened." Kemp himself opened up to Fineman, expressing his hope "that any fair-minded person who reads about a rumor — many of which float in and out of Washington all the time — will dismiss something that has nothing to back it up." Instead Kemp's explanations only fueled more speculation and investigation. CBS's *West 57th* show explored the rumor but eventually decided not to air the matter. "I could have done what everyone else was doing at the time [which] was gathering all the rumors up and passing them off as a story," executive producer Andrew Lack says. "[But] four rumors don't make a story. I found no evidence that supported those rumors or . . . that would lead you to believe that [the rumors] were true, and so I dropped the story."

NBC's *Today* show, on the other hand, took a less admirable approach and aired a story about Kemp on March 13, 1986, in which Kemp was asked point-blank whether he was gay or had ever been involved in a homosexual incident; he once again "categorically" and "absolutely" denied the rumors.[8] The segment's producers showed pictures of the *Newsweek* and *Vanity Fair* stories, not as Kemp's vindication or as proof that the rumors were false, but rather as a pretext justifying their decision to pop the question themselves. Kemp's answers to the *Today* questions were reported in an Associated Press story that was subsequently picked up by a number of daily newspapers.

Meanwhile, all the stories helped perpetuate the Kemp rumor, further damaging his campaign. Kemp's fundraisers encountered a number of major contributors who refused to give, citing their fear that "scandal" would engulf the candidate. After the *Today* fiasco, the Kemp staff changed their rumor-control method, essentially refusing to cooperate when reporters sought to explore the topic further. But the campaign's leaders understood that if Kemp's presidential bid began to succeed, it would all be revisited with greater intensity. Kemp's failure to catch on in 1988, perhaps in some measure due to the rumor that would not die, had one small benefit for the exasperated candidate, his family, and his staff: No additional confrontations with what *Washington Post* columnist Richard

Cohen termed "sexual McCarthyism" occurred. In the absence of damning evidence, without even an accuser, Jack Kemp had nonetheless been forced by various media organizations to deny repeatedly that he "is now or has ever been" a homosexual. As Cohen sadly observed, "Journalism has had prouder moments."

Gary Hart

There are often disturbing excesses in the most justifiable of feeding frenzies. Gary Hart is a case in point. The Colorado candidate invited his troubles and brought controversy to himself. But at times even Hart critics sympathized with his plight. In 1984 legitimate concerns about his age, name change, and so on became "obsessive," as his then press secretary Kathy Bushkin noted: "How many times did he need to answer those questions? There were other important topics that also needed to be addressed." The scrutiny of Hart's résumé became ridiculously overwrought after the initial disclosures, too, with Hart criticized, among other things, for deemphasizing in his official biography his work as national campaign director of George McGovern's 1972 presidential campaign. What ambitious politician would not have wanted to downplay a leadership position in a campaign that lost forty-nine states?

The Donna Rice exposé itself is the focus of much concern about the press's investigative methods and procedures. First of all, the justification cited by the *Miami Herald* that made its news story on Hart "legitimate" was the candidate's "pattern of behavior," according to political editor Tom Fiedler. And what established this pattern? "The allegations had already been in place; the rumors had been there." In other words, gossip — allegations and rumors — constituted presumptive evidence of Hart's behavior, requiring a press trap to prove the candidate's guilt for the public to see. In Hart's case the presumption was almost certainly correct, but the standard of probable cause was a dubious one — a disturbing precedent waiting to be applied to future candidates in less compelling circumstances.

The *Herald*'s stakeout also comes in for criticism, since it was less than airtight. The rear entrance to Hart's town house was not watched continuously, nor was the surveillance maintained at all for two hours in the middle of the night. The poorly edited story was rushed into print as well (missing some of the *Herald*'s own Sunday editions) and for the wrong reason: The reporters did not want to give Hart any extra time to concoct an alibi or give a covering story to another newspaper. Jim Savage, a member of the stakeout team, explained why the paper would not "sit" on the story for another day to allow for more checking and precision: "We knew Hart had an aggressive group of operatives, and we would have given them twenty-four more hours to counterattack." This strategy might have been more appropriate for a competing presidential campaign than a newspaper. Overall, journalists inside and outside the *Herald* have ambivalent feelings about the Hart stakeout. A large majority believe it accomplished a good end (the exposure of Hart's character and judgment flaws), and some agree with the *Washington Post's* Bob Woodward that the *Herald's* stakeout was "unseemly but necessary and important—and it's not against the law to sit in a car." Many others, however, made statements like National Public Radio's Nina Totenberg's:

Most of us did not get into this profession to become private eyes. While completely legitimate, I find staking out houses to be extremely distasteful. If given the chance, I doubt very much I would have done it. That's just not the way I want to spend my time.

By no means is the *Herald* alone as a target of criticism for excessive behavior during the Hart affair. The *Washington Post's* handling of the "other woman" story was also highly unpopular with many journalists. One of the *Post's* own most-respected reporters, Bill Peterson, had refused to participate in the newspaper's New Hampshire request to question Hart because he was "queasy" about the invasion of the candidate's privacy and also believed there were "unanswered questions and holes" in the detective's report that revealed Hart's liaison. Outside the newspaper, the *Post* was judged severely because of the widespread belief that the editors in effect "negotiated" Hart's withdrawal from the race in exchange for not publishing the details of the candidate's long-term relationship with a Washington woman. Hart's precipitous withdrawal may well have occurred on account of the *Post's* inquiries; when informed of the *Post's* information, an exasperated Hart threw in the towel and headed back to Colorado within hours. And the *Post* did indeed decide not to publish the full story of the relationship once Hart had left the race; at that point, according to the *Post's* Ann Devroy, the story became moot, irrelevant to a presidential contest that no longer included Gary Hart. But the decisions made by Hart and the newspaper were reached separately; inextricably bound together, they were at the same time isolated and independent. Furthermore, as related earlier, the *Post* apparently had already given Hart's D.C. mistress a promise of anonymity.

The second reason for the drubbing administered to the *Post* was the question asked Hart by one of its reporters, Paul Taylor, at a news conference a few days after the *Herald's* exposé. Taylor posed an excruciatingly personal and unprecedented series of queries to a presidential candidate, twice requesting a reply to this interrogatory: "Have you ever committed adultery?" It was "overstepping the bounds . . . a cheap shot, an unfair ambush question," said the *Los Angeles Times*'s media reporter, Tom Rosenstiel, reflecting the opinion of many news colleagues. "The *Post* wanted Hart to deny guilt on adultery, so they could print their [D.C. mistress] story to prove Hart lied." Taylor, of course, saw it differently. Responding to a torrent of criticism from the *New York Times*, he pointed out that Hart had insisted nothing "immoral" went on with Donna Rice. "What did Mr. Hart mean by his denial of immoral behavior? . . . What I did was ask Gary Hart the question he asked for."[9]

Legitimate or not, Taylor's prying was part and parcel of the "mass pursuit of naked sensationalism" — as Hart's campaign manager called it[10] — that enveloped the Hart frenzy. Respectable newspapers were competing with the tabloids, playing one-upmanship in titillation. No personal detail was too private for exploration. In the end Hart bitterly bowed out, but his unintentional legacy to politics was already clear. Rumors of illicit activity, if widespread enough, had become a sufficient news peg to entrap and publish.

Michael Dukakis

While the judgmental evaluation of Hart's frenzy is necessarily equivocal, no such ambiguity is possible about Michael Dukakis's 1988 "mental health" controversy, one of the most despicable episodes in recent American politics. The corrosive rumor that the Democratic presidential nominee had undergone psychiatric treatment for severe depression began to be spread in earnest at the July 1988 national party convention. The agents of the rumormongering were "LaRouchies," adherents of the extremist cult headed by Lyndon LaRouche, who claims, among other loony absurdities, that Queen Elizabeth II is part of the international drug cartel. The LaRouchies passed around leaflets headlined "Is Dukakis the new Senator Eagleton?" and after the convention they contacted numerous reporters and media organizations to follow up, stoking the competitive fires by telling each that rivals were already hot on the story's trail.

Shortly after the Democratic convention, the Bush campaign — with its candidate trailing substantially in most polls — began a covert operation to build on the foundation laid by the LaRouchies. As first reported by columnists Evans and Novak,[11] Bush manager Lee Atwater's lieutenants asked outside Republican operatives and political consultants to call their reporter contacts about the matter. These experienced strategists knew exactly the right approach so as not to leave fingerprints, explains Steve Roberts of *U.S. News & World Report*:

They asked us, "Gee, have you heard anything about Dukakis's treatment? Is it true?" They're spreading the rumor, but it sounds innocent enough: they're just suggesting you look into it, and maybe giving you a valuable tip as well.

At about the same time the *Detroit News* sent a questionnaire to Bush and Dukakis mildly reminiscent of the earlier *New York Times* grand inquisition, asking in part whether the candidates had ever been hospitalized or treated for depression or other mental illness. The Bush camp was delighted and began to alert key Republicans around the nation to the forthcoming Detroit story, which they hoped would include revelations about Dukakis's past. This fed the already developing frenzy and brought to a boil the speculation in political circles — all of it reaching the ears of reporters. Incredibly, the fever pitch of gossip even broached the subject of Dukakis's possible resignation from the ticket and the identities of his potential replacements.

The Bush strategists actually received little satisfaction from the *Detroit News*'s August 2 story, which contained no discussion of Dukakis's mental history because Dukakis had refused to provide his medical records. But in anticipation of the story, the behind-the-scenes gossip had become so intense that a reporter from the *Boston Herald* asked Dukakis about the subject at a July 29 press conference. Dukakis merely shrugged and brushed the question aside, yet the *Boston Globe* (but not the *Herald*) printed an account of the encounter in the two bottom paragraphs of a page 6 article on July 30. Included was a brief explanation of the rumor and a notation that no evidence supporting it had been uncovered. Dukakis's press secretary, Dayton Duncan, also issued a blanket denial that the candidate had ever been treated for any form of mental illness.

At this juncture the conservative *Washington Times* swung into action. On August 2 (the same day as the *Detroit News*'s nonstory), the *Times* published a front-page article entitled "Dukakis Psychiatric Rumor Denied." The story was officially pegged to Duncan's statement and the *Globe*'s report, but the paper also revealed that a Dukakis press aide had piqued its interest with a telephone call on July 28. As the *Times* editorially explained later, the aide wanted "to deny rumors that hadn't been placed in print — and which we had no intention of printing. . . . Such denials traditionally produce news reports, especially when they're unaccompanied by documentary proof." With this highly questionable rationale for publishing a rumor without evidence, the *Times*'s August 2 story suggestively drew a strained parallel between Dukakis's situation and Thomas

Eagleton's 1972 resignation from the Democratic ticket. This was child's play compared to the thoroughly deceptive, front-page banner headline the *Times* ran two days later: DUKAKIS KIN HINTS AT SESSIONS. The lead paragraph began, "The sister-in-law of Massachusetts Gov. Michael Dukakis said yesterday 'it is possible' the Democratic presidential candidate consulted 'on a friendly basis' with psychiatrist Donald Lipsitt." (Lipsitt was a Dukakis family acquaintance who lived in their neighborhood.) Four paragraphs later the extent of the sister-in-law's actual knowledge, and her real opinion, became clear: "It's possible, but I doubt it. . . . I don't know." This manipulation of the facts was so egregious that both of the bylined reporters quit the *Times* in protest. Incidentally, the psychiatrist in question, Dr. Lipsitt, was not even interviewed by the *Times*; when the *Baltimore Sun* contacted him, he emphatically denied treating Dukakis, discussing any personal problems with him, or referring him to any other doctor.

Many newspapers, including the *Sun* and the *Washington Post*, had at first refused to run any mention at all of the Dukakis rumor since it could not be substantiated. But on August 3, an incident occurred that made it impossible, in their view, not to cover the rumor. During a White House press conference, a correspondent for *Executive Intelligence Review*, a LaRouche organization magazine, asked Reagan if he thought Dukakis should make his medical records public. A jovial Reagan replied, "Look, I'm not going to pick on an invalid." Reagan half apologized a few hours later ("I was just trying to be funny and it didn't work"), but his weak attempt at humor propelled into the headlines a rumor that had been only simmering on the edge of public consciousness. Opinions differ as to whether the "gaffe" was intentional. The *Sun's* Jack Germond says no. "Reagan was always making mischievous cracks without thinking." Steve Roberts strongly disagrees: "I was sitting twenty feet from Reagan when he said it, and I'm convinced it was a shrewd and calculated way of planting that story. Reagan and his staff knew much of the press was trying to ignore the rumor, but when a president says something like that you can't ignore it."

Whether spontaneous or planned, there is little doubt that "Reagan and the Bush people weren't a bit sorry once it happened," as CNN's Frank Sesno asserts. The Bush camp immediately tried to capitalize on and prolong the controversy by releasing a report from the White House doctor describing the Republican nominee's health in glowing terms.[12] But this was a sideshow compared with the rumor itself. The mental health controversy yanked the Dukakis effort off track and forced the candidate and then his doctor to hold their own press conferences on the subject, attracting still more public attention to a completely phony allegation. False though it was, the charge nonetheless disturbed many Americans, raising serious doubts about a candidate who was still relatively unknown to many of them.

As is usually the case, though, the candidate unnecessarily complicated his own situation. Until events forced his hand, Dukakis adamantly and stubbornly refused to release his medical records or an adequate summary of them, despite advance warning that the mental health issue might be raised. Gossip had circulated for years in Massachusetts about Dukakis's "deep" depressions after the death of his brother Stelian in a 1973 automobile accident and again in 1978 when he was defeated for reelection as governor. Dukakis's wife, Kitty, had called his reaction to the 1978 loss "like a public death," although it would be a strange individual who would not be considerably affected by such a voter rejection or by the death of a close relative. More to the point in 1988, a senior civil servant with direct access to Reagan and Bush White House aides delivered a very specific warning right after the convention to Dukakis adviser Kirk O'Donnell. The Bush side intended to undermine the Democrat's reputation by stoking the mental health rumor, the source said with assurance. Yet, even apprised of this fact, Dukakis still held firm for nondisclosure. Some of Dukakis's top staffers are convinced that the nominee mainly wanted to protect Kitty, fearing that a policy of complete openness on health records would eventually lead to requests for fuller information about his wife's past medical treatment and counseling for drug dependency.

In retrospect, several newspeople said they regretted not giving more attention to the LaRouche role in spreading the rumor, given what Ellen Hume called the LaRouchies' well-deserved reputation as "dirty tricksters." President Reagan also received no more than a light rap on the wrist in most newspapers and broadcasts for his successful move to highlight the rumor. "The incident was an outrage right from the get-go, but all the more so because of the president's misuse of his national platform," commented CBS's Dan Rather. And the press was far too reluctant to expose and alienate a source or two in order to piece together the clever rumor-marketing effort conducted by Republican party operatives. Kirk O'Donnell asked a question that begs attention from the press: "If they're pushing false rumors, why should they be protected?" Overall, one of the most important lessons of the Dukakis mental health frenzy is an enduring one, with applicability to many of the rumors discussed in this chapter. "The media are really liable for criticism when we get stampeded by competitive instincts into publishing or airing stories that shouldn't be on the record," says Nina Totenburg. "We were stampeded on the Dukakis story, and we should never have let it happen."

Dan Quayle

The megafrenzy of post-Watergate campaigns, the perils of Dan Quayle, became perhaps the most riveting and certainly the most excessive feature of 1988's general election. For nearly three weeks, coverage of the presidential campaign became mainly coverage of Quayle. Most major newspapers assigned an extraordinary number of reporters to the story (up to two dozen), and the national networks devoted from two-thirds to more than four-fifths of their total evening-news campaign minutes to Quayle.[13] Combined with the sexy material being investigated, this bumper crop of journalists and stories produced, in the words of a top Bush-Quayle campaign official, "the most blatant example of political vivisection that I've ever seen on any individual at any time; it really surpassed a feeding frenzy and became almost a religious experience for many reporters." Balance in coverage, always in short supply during a frenzy, was almost absent. First one controversy and then another about Quayle's early life mesmerized the press, while examination of the most relevant parts of his record, such as his congressional career, got short shrift. "You saw lots of reporters camped out at the registrar's office at DePauw University [Quayle's alma mater] and at the National Guard headquarters in Indiana, but you didn't see many talking to people on the Hill about what sort of reputation he had," said David Beckwith, then of *Time* magazine and now Quayle's press secretary.

It is not surprising to find Quayle's staff criticizing the press. What may startle observers who view the media as thin-skinned and defensive is their widely shared retrospective agreement with the charge that the Quayle frenzy was chock-full of excesses. "I had second thoughts from the first day. Our pursuit of Quayle was relentless, and our demeanor was terrible," said Peter Jennings of *ABC World News Tonight*. Even the minor but revealing digs at Quayle are well remembered by concerned journalists. *U.S. News & World Report*'s Michael Barone recalled that CBS's estimate of Quayle's financial worth, broadcast at the GOP convention, was an astounding six hundred million dollars: "It was part of the press's irresponsible attempt to paint Quayle as a mindless rich kid, to put him into a slot that he didn't quite fit." (While Quayle will eventually inherit a large, family trust fund, his total assets in 1988 totaled approximately one million dollars.) Another previously mentioned aspect of the press's "slotting" of Quayle at the convention was an insistence by some broadcasters on calling him "J. Danforth Quayle III" rather than "Dan," by which he was usually known. This denial of a courtesy commonly extended to all politicians was decried by Roger Mudd: "The one thing you don't do is make fun of a person's name. With [the surname of] Mudd, I've been through it myself, and it's probably the cheapest shot you can take at anybody."

Of course, it was the big-ticket items about Quayle — his National Guard service, the alleged affair with Paula Parkinson, and his academic record — that attracted the most attention. As discussed earlier, the question of whether Quayle used special influence to gain admission to the National Guard and avoid the Vietnam War draft when he graduated from college in 1969 served as the original lightning rod for criticism of the young senator. At the convention, wild rumors flew, such as the false one that Quayle's family had paid fifty thousand dollars to gain him admission to the Guard. The controversy was beginning to come to a boil when Bush and Quayle traveled to Indiana on August 19 at the conclusion of the Republicans' national conclave. At Huntington, Indiana, a hometown crowd of twelve thousand had gathered to root for Quayle, and in a classic setup, Quayle answered questions from a swarm of reporters as Hoosiers alternately cheered the candidate and booed the journalists. This threatening atmosphere may explain what NBC's John Chancellor called some "astonishingly vicious questions" from the press, but the nationally televised encounter in Huntington lives on in popular memory as an example of frenzy journalism. Even before the jeering crowd appeared, many members of the press corps were spoiling for a fight, says Brit Hume:

Riding on the press bus into Huntington I heard remarks of a highly personal nature directed at Quayle. Once we got there, the press acted disgracefully. Some reporters were shouting and screaming at Quayle, arguing with him, saying things that were not questions at all, but comments.

The National Guard issue was unquestionably a legitimate one for the press to raise, although once the picture was clear — Quayle's family did pull strings, but not to an unconscionable degree — some journalists appeared to be unwilling to let it go.

Some of the rumors engulfing the press corps about Quayle stretched even farther back into his past. Quayle's academic record was particularly fertile ground for rumormongers. By his own admission, the vice presidential nominee had been a mediocre student — and the evidence produced during the campaign suggests that *mediocre* was a charitable description. When the administration of Quayle's undergraduate college, DePauw University, proposed giving the new senator an honorary degree in 1982, many on the faculty heatedly protested and hundreds of students signed

petitions objecting to the choice. In good part, the dissenters opposed
Quayle's politics, but his exceedingly lackluster academic performance
gave them powerful ammunition. (Quayle got his degree anyway.) At the
time, though, a rumor swept DePauw, and especially its faculty, that
Quayle had been caught plagiarizing during his senior year. This rumor,
which had a specific teacher and class attached, was widely accepted as
true and became part of the Quayle legend on campus.

Within a day of Quayle's selection as the vice presidential nominee,
the rumor had reached the New Orleans convention hall. Apparently there
were two primary sources. One was the core of Democratic operatives
who had worked on U.S. Senator Birch Bayh's unsuccessful reelection
campaign in 1980 (when Quayle defeated Bayh). Some staffers remembered the opposition research done on Quayle — research that included
references to possible college plagiarism. The other source was DePauw
University faculty, who shared their recollections when reporters called
them seeking "color" quotes for profile pieces on the country's newest
political star. Hours after the adjournment of the GOP convention, the
Wall Street Journal published a lengthy article on Quayle's problems that
included unsubstantiated "rumors" of "a cheating incident."[14] The source
cited was English professor Robert Sedlack, who said, "There was an
allegation that [Quayle] had plagiarized in a political science course." The
reference to the plagiarism rumor was near the bottom of the article, noted
the *Journal*'s Washington bureau chief, Al Hunt, who further justified its
inclusion by pointing to the "credible, reputable faculty member who
was willing to be quoted making the charge and who, in checking with
other people, did not appear to be a guy who was on the payroll of the
Indiana Democratic party." In fact, as noted in the *Journal* article, Professor
Sedlack was an outspoken Democrat and president of the Greencastle,
Indiana, city council, where DePauw is located.

The *Journal* mention helped to push the plagiarism rumor high up
on the list of must-do Quayle rumors, and soon the press hunt was on —
for every DePauw academic who had ever taught Quayle, for fellow
students to whom he might have confided his sin, even for a supposedly
mysterious, extant paper or bluebook in which Quayle's cheating was
indelibly recorded for posterity. (A variation on the bluebook rumor was
that it was up for sale to the highest media bidder.) Michael Lawrence,
a former political science professor in whose class some said the incident
had occurred, was tracked down to his new home in Albuquerque; he
was hounded by reporters, some of whom accused him of keeping it
under wraps. Several other present and former faculty members confessed

that they did little but answer the telephone and the door for days. And reporters were often rewarded with tantalizing suggestions that the rainbow's pot of gold might be at the end of the next telephone connection. But it was fool's gold, recalled NBCs Jim Polk:

We chased professors all over the country. And each one kept saying, "I think it's true and professor so-and-so knows all about it." Then we'd call so-and-so and he'd say, "no, not me, it's this other guy," and by the time we finished running around in circles it was clear that there wasn't anybody who knew a real fact.

As it happens there appears to be a possible, logical explanation for the plagiarism allegation against Quayle, and it was apparently first uncovered by the meticulous and painstaking efforts of two *Journal* reporters, Jill Abramson and James B. Stewart (the latter a graduate of DePauw, a happy circumstance that gave him a leg up on the competition). Abramson and Stewart managed to locate almost every DePauw student who had been a member of Quayle's fraternity, Delta Kappa Epsilon, during his undergraduate years. Approximately ten did indeed remember a plagiarism incident from 1969 (Quayle's graduating year), and the guilty student was in fact a golf-playing senior who was a political science major and member of DKE fraternity—but *not* Quayle. The similarities were striking and the mix-up understandable after the passage of nearly twenty years. What was remarkable, however, was that an undistinguished student such as Quayle would be so vividly remembered by faculty. Abramson and Stewart also uncovered the reason for this, and even two decades after the fact, their finding makes a political science professor blanch. Quayle, the future vice president of the United States, was one of only two 1969 seniors to fail the political science comprehensive examination, a requirement for graduation. (He passed it on a second try.) Abramson's conclusion was a reasonable one: "Jim Stewart and I believed that people had confused Quayle's failure on the comprehensive exam with his . . . fraternity brother's plagiarism, especially since both events . . . occurred at about the same time." Unfortunately for Quayle, and also the public, this reasonable but not airtight supposition did not reach print, though it might have provided a fair antidote to the earlier rumor-promoting article. Instead the firmly established fact of Quayle's comprehensive exam failure was prominently displayed in the *Journal*, undoubtedly if unintentionally reinforcing suspicions that Quayle must have cheated his way through college.[15]

Other academically oriented rumors congregated around Quayle's admission first to Indiana University's law school and then to the bar. Many wondered how a student with a poor undergraduate transcript could gain admission to a competitive law school. Then there was the rumor that Quayle had convinced or paid someone to take the bar exam for him.

An observer reviewing the academic stories about Quayle is struck mainly by two elements. First, despite the windstorm of rumor that repeatedly swept over the press corps, there was much fine, solid reporting with appropriate restraint shown about publication, with the exception of the original *Journal* article mentioning plagiarism as well as some pieces about Quayle's law-school admission. Of equal note, however, was the overweening emphasis placed on his undergraduate performance. As any longtime teacher knows, students frequently commit youthful errors and indiscretions that are not necessarily indicative of their potential or future development. Many students are also late bloomers, and maturity levels differ dramatically among college-age individuals. It is true, as the *Journal's* Al Hunt contends, "Here was a guy who stood out for his lack of achievement"; from all indications there is little or nothing on his transcript about which Quayle can be proud. And Quayle made his own situation worse by steadfastly refusing to release his records, substantially increasing the damaging speculation that he has something to hide. Yet, once again, a question of balance is raised: How much emphasis should have been placed on, and precious press resources devoted to, Quayle's life in his early twenties compared to his relatively ignored senatorial career in his thirties?

Another high-voltage rumor about Quayle concerned his alleged drug use in the early 1970s. This electrifying gossip galvanized the press from Washington to Los Angeles and became the hidden election-eve crisis of the 1988 presidential campaign. The rumor's real strength was its universally accepted premise: Any college student of Quayle's generation must have tried drugs. (Actually, many surveys at the time indicated that a substantial minority of college students had not experimented even with marijuana, much less harsher drugs.) This premise became the basis for the press's instantaneous fishing expedition at the Republican National Convention; ABC's Peter Jennings, in an anchor-booth interview with Quayle at midconvention,[16] asked the nominee-designate directly, "Did you smoke marijuana?" and Quayle's response was unhesitating: "I did not."

Shortly thereafter, a telephone call was placed that would attempt to cast doubt upon the vice presidential candidate's veracity. Brett Kimberlin, a federal prisoner serving a fifty-year sentence for drug smuggling and a 1978 series of bombings in Speedway, Indiana, contacted *Los Angeles Times* reporter Douglas Frantz, who had written a story about Kimberlin in 1982 while the prisoner was serving time in Chicago and Frantz was on the staff of the *Chicago Tribune*.[17] With a conviction for perjury also on his record, the so-called Speedway Bomber was never considered a particularly credible accuser, but he told a detailed and circumstantially plausible story. He had met law student Quayle at a 1971 Indiana University fraternity party, claimed Kimberlin, who at the time was sixteen years old and a self-described "high-school pot dealer." According to Kimberlin:

Danny found out I had some pot for sale and he told me he wanted to buy some. At first I thought he might be a narc [narcotics policeman] because he looked square. But a friend of mine said he was all right, so I gave him my phone number in Indianapolis. A couple of weeks later he called and used the name DQ on the phone . . . and for the next sixteen to eighteen months I sold him an ounce of pot about once a month.

By Kimberlin's account, he and Quayle struck up such a good relationship that when Quayle got married, Kimberlin presented him with the gift of an ounce of hashish and "Acapulco Gold" marijuana. The relationship began to go sour, though, when Kimberlin watched the rising political star denounce drug use and insist he had never tried, much less regularly enjoyed, marijuana. As Kimberlin explains it, he had the purest of motives in "reluctantly" blowing the whistle on Quayle: "Everybody knows the way he smoked pot," and the American people needed to know what a "hypocrite" Quayle was. "Everybody" may have known about Quayle's college affinity for pot, but Kimberlin had great difficulty pointing to any witnesses who could corroborate his story.

From drugs to women to plagiarism, rumors about Dan Quayle absorbed a disproportionate share of the press's time and resources in the 1988 general election campaign. Some of this focus was an inevitable and perhaps necessary by-product of Quayle's national anonymity, not to mention the acknowledgment even among staunch Republicans that Quayle was nowhere near the most-qualified person Bush could have chosen to be next in line for the presidency. But once nominated, Quayle was entitled to have his abilities, public accomplishments, and ideas evaluated fairly—and at least as fully as the rumor of the week.

Even later, in 1992, it was business as usual—same old, same old—in the press's treatment of Dan Quayle. Four years of incumbency in the vice presidency, general acknowledgment behind the scenes that Quayle had been an effective second-in-command, and substantive accomplishments during his term mattered not a whit. Much of the press continued to hold Quayle in contempt as a dim-witted, lightweight, rich, and pampered pretender to the throne. Many journalists extended the scorn they felt for Quayle to any colleagues who dared suggest that Quayle might not be as bad as his press clippings suggested. The *Washington Post's* David Broder and Bob Woodward wrote an extensive seven-part series on Quayle for their newspaper in January 1992 that credited the vice president with *some* political talent and administrative savvy. While Broder and Woodward's overall judgment of Quayle was actually quite mixed, it was entirely too positive for the media's conventional wisdom mainstream, and the two respected and experienced *Post* reporters were widely ridiculed in the journalistic community. Instead, many journalists chose to focus on other Quayle incidents. Two that would haunt him during Campaign '92 were the *Murphy Brown* speech and the "potatoe" incident. Quayle's unhappy season began on May 19, 1992, in a speech he delivered in San Francisco on "restoring basic values [and] strengthening the family." Toward the conclusion of a serious address with some thoughtful passages about the decline of families as a root cause of the recent Los Angeles riots, Quayle condemned "bearing babies irresponsibly" and added:

It doesn't help matters when prime-time TV has Murphy Brown—a character who supposedly epitomizes today's intelligent, highly paid, professional woman— mocking the importance of fathers, by bearing a child alone, and calling it just another "lifestyle choice."

In many respects there was nothing exceptional about this passage. Quayle and the Republicans had already been developing their "family values" issue, and virtually every major Democrat, including Bill Clinton, Jesse Jackson, and Mario Cuomo, had preached similar sermons against unwed motherhood. Nor was rhetorical reference to a television show, or criticism of television's standards and morals by politicians, very unusual. Yet Quayle's poke at Murphy Brown set off a firestorm that consumed for many weeks the vice president's usefulness on the campaign trail.

Partly, this was the result of Quayle's choice of an exceptionally popular CBS television show and character, a news anchorwoman played by Candice Bergen. As a subsequent poll showed, she was considerably better liked than the vice president, even as a potential president, and Quayle simply could not compete with her legions of fans who resented Quayle's passing harsh judgment on her. (They saw Quayle's message much as the New York *Daily News* did, in its headline QUAYLE TO MURPHY BROWN: YOU TRAMP!) Partly, too, Quayle's tar-and-feathering was because of a seemingly unresolved, illogical, and hypocritical aspect of his criticism and its root Republican philosophy. Once impregnated, Brown chose *not* to have an abortion — the GOP preference — but, instead of being celebrated for her pro-life stance, she was condemned. Most of all, Quayle was pummeled in this circumstance because he could not escape his press subtext, the dismal caricature of him that had been created and validated and reinforced over four years of virtually nonstop derision. The Quayle subtext instantly established an unshakable premise for the Murphy Brown episode: This cartoon stick-figure, this callow gaffe-prone youth, this nincompoop of a vice president, had attacked a nonexistent television sitcom character! David Letterman captured Quayle's quandary better than any columnist or commentator when he deadpanned, "Mr. Vice President, I don't know how to tell you this, but Murphy Brown is a fictional character." Other less humorous pundits used the opportunity to relive past Quayle controversies, including the usual parade of unsubstantiated rumors. This sound bite from Jesse Jackson was widely used, for example: "No exam-cheating, pot-smoking, draft-dodging, privileged youth vice president . . . can speak with moral authority about abandoned moral values and assuming personal responsibility."[18]

The Murphy Brown controversy intermittently stretched almost to October, thanks to a "family values" Republican National Convention as well as a revenge-minded Hollywood. Emmys were awarded to Candice Bergen and her series in a late August production filled with anti-Quayle invective. And in late September the *Murphy Brown* season opener was a virtual nonstop rebuke to Quayle. But by April 1993, when Quayle had left office and the issue he raised could be considered outside of his subtext, *The Atlantic* magazine ran a much-discussed cover story by a liberal academic, with the headline "DAN QUAYLE WAS RIGHT" followed by "The dissolution of two-parent families, though it may benefit the adults involved, is harmful to many children, and dramatically undermines our society."[19]

Quayle's image as a lightweight, already secure as a result of Murphy Brown and a dozen earlier frenzies, was irreversibly elevated to dogma on June 15, 1992, with the so-called [or so-spelled] "potatoe" incident. Quayle was visiting an elementary school in Trenton, N.J., when, as planned, he conducted a spelling bee for sixth-grade students. Working off an inaccurate flash card prepared by a teacher,[20] he corrected twelve-year-old William Figueroa when the child spelled "potato" on the blackboard — prompting the nervous boy to add an unnecessary "e" at the end of the word.

It proved to be a costly letter for Quayle. Reporters ran for their dictionaries, and CNN aired the clip over and over, all day long. "Quayle Opens Mouth, Inserts Toe," read a typical newspaper headline. MTV broadcast a spoof (Pink Floyd singing "We don't need no education"),

David Letterman invited Figueroa on his show, and Jay Leno joked that Quayle "should stop watching 'Murphy Brown' and start watching 'Sesame Street.'" The elementary-school principal was inundated with press calls from England to Colombia, and journalists camped outside the Figueroa home.[21]

As all fair observers will attest, the average day of almost any national candidate contains at least a gaffe or two — a mispronounced word, a garbled sentence, confusion about one's current location (the towns all blur together). Only rarely does the press focus on any single one, much less blow a minor slip-up into a monumental goof. But Quayle's subtext guaranteed inordinate attention. Young Figueroa himself saw the point, and was quoted as saying the misspelling "showed the rumors about the vice president are true — that he's an idiot." As for the news media, they were unwilling to let Quayle remove his dunce cap easily. When the vice president tried to laugh off the incident by noting that "Mark Twain once said, 'You should never trust a man who has only one way to spell a word,'" the Associated Press surveyed Twain experts and quickly put a report on its wire that "Twain may never have said that." Whether Twain did or did not, the piling-on was clearly excessive, the whole episode one of the silliest frenziettes ever. The "potatoe" incident, once pursued, became an embarrassment for Dan Quayle, but it ought to have embarrassed the press even more.

The unfairness in Quayle's coverage is all the more apparent when compared with that of his opponent. If Dan Quayle was the ultimate media goat, then Albert Gore was the classic media darling. Nary a discouraging word was said about Gore, a former journalist, in most media quarters; to the contrary, he was hailed upon his selection by Clinton, and given one of the softest rides for a national party nominee in recent times. The double standard that existed through the campaign continued even after election day. Shortly after becoming vice president–elect, Gore and his wife, Tipper, went hiking in some woods near Washington. They got lost and had to depend on the Secret Service for rescue. Modest to nonexistent accounts of the event were carried by most news organizations, despite Gore's reputation (subtext?) as a bright and resourceful environmentalist. As Thomas Palmer of the *Boston Globe* observed, "Who doubts that, had Dan and Marilyn Quayle lost their way, they would have been featured on Page 1?"[22]

Other Frenzies of Campaign '92

There was a frenzy or two in store for other candidates as well in 1992, and voters could be forgiven for thinking they had seen it all before.

The circumstances were familiar: mistresses, imagined or real; drug use; the Vietnam draft; deeply rooted subtexts; unsubstantiated rumors in print and on air. Here is a sampling of the frenzies of '92.

Bill Clinton

Damaged but unbowed, Bill Clinton has survived more feeding frenzies than anyone else in modern history. And despite a barrage of frenzies, he emerged from the media's trial-by-fire holding the keys to the White House. Few in Clinton's camp, and hardly anyone outside of it, imagined this happy ending in the snows of New Hampshire when Flowers bloomed early in 1992.

Ever since Clinton had begun to consider a 1992 White House bid seriously, profiles of the prospective candidate had often included vague and completely unsubstantiated references to Clinton's "womanizing" and "marital difficulties." Clinton himself was concerned enough about the early press coverage, as well as the specter of what lay ahead (given the Gary Hart precedent), that he brought his wife to a Washington press breakfast in September 1991. The couple attempted to head off further inquiries by admitting they had not had "a perfect marriage" free of difficulties, yet insisting that the details were no one's business, especially since the marriage had overcome those past problems. All the Clinton's close friends and associates privately confirmed to reporters that the pair had indeed worked through their difficulties and were happily married.

The Clintons' thoroughly reasonable claim to privacy was not to prevail, of course. When Clinton announced his presidential candidacy on October 3, 1991, most stories in the mainstream press contained the obligatory unsourced paragraph noting that Clinton was "dogged by rumors of marital infidelity," and the subsequent candidate profiles over the succeeding weeks retained this questionable dimension. Some broadcast journalists also helped to create the climate conducive to Clinton's adultery frenzy. On January 19, 1992, ABC's Cokie Roberts served as a moderator for a WMUR-TV (Manchester, N.H.) debate among the Democratic presidential hopefuls that was seen nationally on C-SPAN. Roberts turned to Clinton and launched this broadside of innuendo:

There is concern among members of your party that [with] these allegations of womanizing . . . the Republicans will find somebody, and that she will come forward late, and that you would lose the all important — to Democrats — women's vote. What do you say?

Despite all the well-intentioned seminars and the promises to conduct business differently than in 1988, the press had splashed enough rumor-combustible gasoline about Clinton in the early months of Campaign '92 so that only a spark was needed to start an enormous fire. Arkansas state employee and cabaret singer Gennifer Flowers decided to be the spark, for a hefty and still undetermined amount of money. On January 23, 1992, the *Star*, a gossipy, trashy supermarket tabloid, released a squalid cover story on Flowers's supposed "12-year affair with Bill Clinton." Subsidiary headlines included "Mistress Tells All," "Dems' front-runner lied to America, says his former lover," and "The secret love tapes that prove it." Over the next week this incident would not only nearly torpedo the Clinton campaign but prove anew the dominance of lowest-common-denominator journalism.

Gennifer Flowers was a name unfamiliar to the public but well known to many in the political press. For many months she and several other women had been romantically linked to Governor Clinton by his oppo-nents, and even by some neutral observers in Arkansas. Given the centrality of the post–Gary Hart character issue, most major broadcast and print-news organizations had sent reporters — some had dispatched teams of them — to Arkansas, to investigate. *At the time, not one news outlet uncovered enough evidence to warrant a single published or broadcast story.* The claims simply did not check out, were unprovable, or suffered from other fatal flaws. Therefore, one might presume that well-prepared news organiza-tions, having already thoroughly investigated these allegations, would dis-card them as without merit once they reached print in a sleazy, suspect publication.

Certainly, some news outlets attempted to do just that. On the first evening, only NBC among the networks even mentioned the subject, but some large local television stations, such as WNBC in New York City, covered it extensively. More important, ABC's *Nightline* devoted its program to the "media's handling of the Clinton allegations," a backdoor way of discussing the infidelity claim. The ABC, CBS, and CNN networks waded in with stories on the second day (Friday, January 24), as did most major newspapers, with the exception of the *New York Times*, which appropriately downplayed the frenzy from beginning to end. But the floodgates opened after Clinton made the decision to appear on *60 Min-utes* with his wife right after the Super Bowl on Sunday, January 26. Up to 50 million Americans watched the affectionate Clintons try to shake off the charges without discussing their marital history in detail. Whatever their success, the broadcast fully legitimized public discussion of the tab-loid story, and all networks led with the subject on their Monday broadcasts, aided by a *Star*-sponsored Monday afternoon press conference attended by over 200 journalists. At this session, edited tapes, surreptitiously recorded by Flowers, were played disclosing ambiguous telephone conversations between Clinton and Flowers—he called her "baby" once in closing, and a sexual allusion was made. Flowers also fielded questions ranging from Clinton's preferences in sex acts to his wearing or nonwearing of condoms. In one of the worst news decisions of the election year, CNN chose to carry this tawdry press conference live, a decision which in retrospect CNN political director Tom Hannon regretted.

There can be little doubt that in another election year the Flowers incident would have proved fatal to Clinton's candidacy. As it was, Clinton fell from near-certain winner of the New Hampshire primary to a poor second-place finish (well behind the victor, former U.S. Senator Paul Tsongas). Clinton survived and eventually triumphed because, first, the importance of the economy and the voters' determined focus on it overrode all other issues in 1992; second, Clinton was the beneficiary of a weak Democratic candidate field, and most party leaders recognized that probably he alone of the announced contenders would have a reasonable chance of victory in November; and third, the establishment news media were genuinely embarrassed about their latest detour into the gutter, and happy to move on to other matters at the earliest opportunity. *Newsweek*, the Arkansas *Democrat-Gazette*, and other publications quickly seized upon discrepancies in Flowers's story and résumé, while few major news organizations ever put much stress on the seemingly incriminating elements of the tapes.

The Flowers frenzy yet again made obvious the inability (or unwillingness) of the mainstream media to resist a juicy story from the seamier side of their business. Instead of news standards trickling down from best to worst, they were now bubbling up from worst to best—truly a Mad Hatter's affair. And, without either group of media overtly acknowledging the favor done the other, it was beginning to resemble a cooperative arrangement, as former *New York Times* reporter Christopher Lydon suggested:

The upscale media baited the trap with hints about womanizing; their downmarket cousins bagged the trophy; and the quality commentators returned, bright clothespins on their noses, to dissect the evidence and tell us what it meant. To audiences it did not look like real warfare in the media but rather like a face-saving division of labor.[23]

One salutary effect of the Clinton-Flowers story was to turn the public even more strongly against this type of reporting. A CNN/*Time* poll at the height of the Flowers incident found that 82 percent of the respondents believed the press paid too much attention to candidates' personal lives, and only 25 percent wanted to "be informed about the private lives of presidential candidates, including any extramarital affairs" — down dramatically from the 41 percent who wanted to be told such things in 1987.[24] Furthermore, the public gave a forceful thumbs-down on lowest-common-denominator journalism. "If a competing medium reveals charges about a candidate's personal life," only 4 percent thought "an editor should consider the charge to be news in itself and report it on that basis." Rather, 42 percent preferred that the editor "check out the stories and do a story only if it can be independently verified," while another 50 percent wanted the editor to "ignore the charges unless they seem clearly connected to the candidate's public duties."[25] While the press was less critical of itself, it was not particularly proud of its performance. In a June 1992 *Times–Mirror* survey of journalists, more than a third (36 percent) admitted that news organizations had handled the Clinton controversy "not too responsibly" or "not at all responsibly."

The press fiasco that was Gennifer Flowers may have helped insulate Clinton from additional intrusive coverage of his private life, despite many opportunities and provocations. As is standard practice, journalists were inundated with "helpful" calls from agents of Clinton's Democratic rivals, as well as the Republican party and longtime Clinton foes in Arkansas. The Clinton campaign undertook a "bimbo eruption watch" that was kept busy throughout the primaries and general election. Clinton aide Betsy Wright oversaw the effort, which included monitoring seven such allegations in the preconvention period and nineteen similar charges in the days following the Democratic National Convention. Some of the "bimbo fever" was traced to the large, six-figure sums of money being offered to women by tabloid publications. By and large, the Clinton effort at containment was successful, both because the accusing women had credibility problems and the post-Flowers press had little stomach for the chase. Even when one outlet published or aired a story, few if any others were willing to follow up. An April *Washington Times* top-of-the-front-page piece on Roger Clinton's use of his brother's Little Rock gubernatorial mansion for sexual liaisons went nowhere; even the *Times* noted that no evidence existed that Bill Clinton even knew about Roger's romantic activities. In its lead story on July 13, the *CBS Evening News* examined an apparently baseless claim by a conservative independent political committee that a young woman committed suicide after being made pregnant by Bill Clinton in the 1970s. (As the report noted, the woman's family denied the allegations, which correspondent Eric Engberg termed a "nasty hoax."[26]) Shortly after the Democratic convention, syndicated television talk-show host Sally Jessy Raphael irresponsibly featured the completely unsubstantiated claims of former Miss Arkansas Sally Miller Perdue, who said she had a brief affair with Clinton in the fall of 1983. No major news organization picked up the story, which was also being pushed by the far-left New Alliance party headed by presidential candidate Lenora Fulani.[27]

The real tests for the press came as the campaign moved into its tense final days in October. Often, in this pressure-cooker atmosphere, it becomes easier for questionable stories to reach print or air, and to ricochet across the media landscape before good judgment can intervene. In mid-October, *Penthouse* magazine chose to release its upcoming December issue interview with Gennifer Flowers, and in thirteen raunchy pages she leveled explosive charges (such as her claim to have aborted Clinton's child) and described in excruciating detail the couple's purported sex acts and pet names for various body parts. If ever the press might yield to the temptation to sell papers, this opportunity would be choice. Yet the matter was downplayed and sanitized almost everywhere (except in the *Washington Times*), perhaps prodded by *Penthouse* publisher Bob Guccione's statement that he had sought to verify Flowers's charges, "often without success."[28] The Republicans took up where *Penthouse* left off, as they desperately sought to turn the tide in the campaign's waning hours. During the final week, a number of major news organizations received telephone calls from GOP officials demanding that a story be written about Clinton's "current extramarital affair" with a reporter covering the Clinton campaign that the Secret Service "knew all about." On election eve (November 2), U.S. Representative Guy Vander Jagt (R., Mich.), the chairman of the National Republican Congressional Committee, publicly made this charge at an Omaha news conference. When only a local television affiliate aired the allegation, Vander Jagt sent a transcript of his comments to national news organizations. No one aired or published the story, and the Secret Service denied that any of their employees had knowledge of a Clinton affair.

Gennifer Flowers was Clinton's defining feeding frenzy, but hardly the only one to which he was subjected. The frenzy over Clinton's draft record was almost as disruptive for the candidate as the Flowers episode, and it lasted longer. Like Dan Quayle, Bill Clinton was forced to relive the painful Vietnam era through the ambiguities in his own past. Quayle had served in the National Guard while Clinton avoided service entirely, but both had clearly benefited from special connections and privileged treatment not available to most young men, and both suffered most from their own lack of candor and mishandling of the issue. Both the 1988 Bush/Quayle ticket and the 1992 Clinton organization were inexplicably unprepared for press inquiries on a legitimate subject — a national candidate's military record — and they let information about their pasts dribble out, in a confusing and contradictory way. Clinton had even less excuse than Quayle, who was unexpectedly chosen for the 1988 GOP ticket and had not faced prior intense press scrutiny on his Vietnam record. By contrast, Clinton had been extensively questioned on the matter during earlier campaigns in Arkansas, and he also had ample opportunities during the presidential primaries to lay out the particulars of his draft status. Instead, as the *Washington Post*'s Dan Balz concluded, Clinton wounded himself "largely because it took him months to reveal" the details, "and sometimes only after repeated questioning from news organizations."[29] The more evasive Clinton sounded and the hazier his usually sharp memory, the more the media's interest was piqued. At the height of the frenzy, for instance, the *Los Angeles Times* had eight staff members working on the story. "We've had a bigger bureau in Little Rock than we've had in New York," boasted the *Times*'s Jack Nelson,[30] and as a result the newspaper broke new ground repeatedly. Such a pattern of evasiveness would come to haunt him later.

As is often the case with similar controversies, the issue became not just draft evasion but also the candidate's trust and credibility: Was Clinton telling the truth? Every new "wiggle disclosure" was hyped because it suggested that the candidate had lied, or hidden something from public view; and every news organization tried to get a piece of the big story, and thus was likely to uncover an unrevealed fact. So Clinton could correctly insist, as he did about one such minor disclosure, "You've got a feeding frenzy on about something that even if it's true, it doesn't amount to a hill of beans,"[31] and yet it did matter, in another sense. The draft story became one more vehicle for the omnipresent character issue, another chance for the press to test a presidential contender, and another opportunity for the opposition to seed land mines.

Building on the doubts about Clinton created or reinforced by the draft debate, the Bush campaign tried to generate a potentially more destructive frenzy that went to the heart of Clinton's patriotism. Had Clinton been disloyal by participating in a 1969 anti–Vietnam War demonstration on foreign soil (in London) and by visiting the Soviet Union while that nation was supplying arms to America's Southeast Asia adversary? This frenzy probably started in September 1992 on the floor of the U.S. House of Representatives, where a group of Republican congressmen led by California's conservative fire-breather Robert K. Dornan had been asking the Moscow question and darkly suggesting an answer: that young Clinton was somehow a Communist dupe. But since the insinuations were based on mere speculation, most news organizations ignored the matter. The rumor continued to fly, however, in part because C-SPAN necessarily broadcast these House floor discussions as part of its comprehensive coverage of Congress. The *Washington Times* went far beyond C-SPAN's dutiful reporting, of course, touting the Democrat's 1969–70 Moscow trip in a banner headline ("Clinton Toured Moscow at War's Peak"),[32] and quoting a retired British intelligence officer as asserting that Clinton "fit the profile perfectly" of a candidate ripe for recruitment as a Soviet "agent of influence."

With the gas on the stove turned to high, President Bush decided to throw the lighted match himself. On October 7, 1992, in an appearance on CNN's *Larry King Live*, Bush gave a seemingly well-rehearsed answer when King asked him about the Moscow trip:

> Larry, I don't want to tell you what I really think 'cause I don't have the facts. I don't have the facts. But to go to Moscow, one year after Russia crushed Czechoslovakia, not remember who you saw — I think, I really think the answer is level with the American people. . . .[33]

Bush's remarks intensified a wave of electrifying rumors in press ranks. The Bush forces, it was said, knew Clinton had had KGB contacts; was part of a Soviet-sponsored and -financed antiwar network; had once prepared to renounce his American citizenship as part of his effort to evade the draft; and had possessed more than one passport under different names. Within a few days, though, it became clear that Bush had no facts at all to sustain his innuendo, despite an ill-fated, improper search of Clinton's and his mother's passport files by members of the Bush team,[34] and that not a single stitch of evidence existed to verify any of the rumors floating about. Press commentary and punditry turned harshly critical of Bush, and he paid a political price for his venture into McCarthyism.

This pseudo-issue never fully died, though many members of the press did their best to inter it. Variations on the theme continued to circulate right up to election day, and even Rhodes House at Oxford University was besieged by reporters "in pursuit of imaginary material to support various calumnies about Clinton's Oxford days."[35] In the final week of the campaign one Oxford-related rumor briefly took on a printed life and nearly became a last-minute controversy. On October 29, 1992, a widely circulated Boston bond wire reported a rumor that CNN and ABC News's *20/20* show would soon be airing photographs or videotape of Clinton burning the American flag at an antiwar rally in England.

ABC was flooded with calls from domestic and foreign news organizations, propelling a frazzled network news publicist, Arnot Walker, to secure a retraction (of sorts) by the bond wire about a day later.

Gennifer Flowers, the draft controversy, and Clinton's antiwar activities all were part of the character issue for the Democratic nominee. A great deal of the press's energy, not to mention newsprint and airtime, was wasted in pursuit of unrevealing aspects of these and other campaign matters. At the same time the news media once again failed to focus on some truly consequential facets of character. For example, in the case of Bill Clinton, a much ignored but significant and easily documentable character trait is his often uncontrolled temper — surely a legitimate worry for voters about any potential occupant of the Oval Office.

There were many open public examples of Clinton's blowing up during the campaign, but oddly the press never pointed to the obvious pattern of behavior. When Clinton was incorrectly told in late February that Jesse Jackson was supporting one of his rivals, Iowa U.S. Senator Tom Harkin, his angry outburst — "It's an outrage; it's a dirty, double-crossing, back-stabbing thing to do" — was picked up by an open satellite microphone and then aired by a Phoenix television station and, later, by some of the networks.[36] About a month later, Clinton exploded on stage in response to a heckling AIDS activist who was in attendance at a fundraiser; Clinton's videotaped retort was widely aired. In an April *Nightline* production that followed Clinton around during one day's campaigning for the New York primary, Clinton was shown sharply berating an aide because of some loud heckling at a Wall Street rally.[37] Reporters also personally watched other blowups at staff members, Secret Service agents, and fellow newspersons, and they were privy to his advisers' estimates that Clinton lost his temper at staff from five to ten times a day. Yet the first major publication to devote serious attention to the subject was the British newsmagazine *The Economist*, in an article published four days *after* the election. Concluded *The Economist*, in an observation that American journalists should have offered the American electorate for its consideration before they cast their ballots: "None of this proves that Mr. Clinton is an ogre. But it does show that . . . the 'real' Mr. Clinton is rather more complex than the folksy, schmoozy man that America thinks it has just elected as its next president." The U.S. media finally awoke from its slumber about Clinton's temperament after the president-elect cursed and dressed down his personal aide, David Friendly, on November 7 for permitting photographers near him on the golf course.[38] Interestingly, while the press widely reported this incident (and a later one shortly after Clinton was inaugurated[39]), almost no mention was made when Clinton had angrily rebuked the same Mr. Friendly *prior* to election day for allowing cameras to record his morning jog from the driveway of the Arkansas governor's mansion.[40]

Ross Perot

No other presidential candidate in American history has been treated to a wilder media roller-coaster ride than Independent candidate Ross Perot, and Perot's extraordinary evolving relationship with the news business helped to define a jarringly strange political year. An early love affair between Perot and journalism eventually turned into mutual contempt, as the press sought to unmask a super salesman while the sometime candidate found solace away from the press, on the talk-show circuit. Ironically, despite numerous press efforts and a series of mini-scandals, the only real frenzy that engulfed Perot (a bizarre charge that Republicans had plans to disrupt his daughter's wedding) was essentially self-generated.

Nothing was conventional about the "Perot for President" campaign — least of all its inception. Appearing on CNN's *Larry King Live* on February 20, 1992, Perot indicated his willingness to run for president if voters put him on all fifty state ballots. While Perot's personal money began to flow freely to fund the effort, there was also a great deal of genuine, enthusiastic grassroots support for the Texas billionaire-turned-politician. The "mom-and-pop" nature of the ballot drive in many locales was a made-to-order attraction for television, as was the Texan's homespun, simplistic, straight-talking style. Perot rapidly became *the* story, portrayed as a breath of fresh air — a welcome alternative to a failed Republican president and a slick, sleazy Democratic pol. Even more than Clinton, Perot invented the talk-show approach to politics, and as he went merrily from TV studio to TV studio his poll numbers kept climbing. The mainstream press could not get much access to Perot, in part because he did little stumping, had no traditional campaign schedule or entourage, and at first was immune from criticism by Bush and Clinton, both of whom were afraid to alienate his millions of followers. Oddly, given that Perot had shut them out, many normally skeptical big-name journalists signed on as boosters in the early months of Perot's protocandidacy, serving up powder puff, gee-whiz coverage, such as the March 29 Perot segment on *60 Minutes* in which an enthralled Morley Safer gushed, "And what Americans love most is a maverick, an untamed cowpoke willing to ride in and clean up the town, especially one who's willing to blow $100 million to get hired for a job he doesn't really want." Of course, journalism was welcoming a good story, and one supposedly untainted by the cynical machinations of partisan politics. But just as reporters take on an unseemly guise in pursuing a frenzy, so too are they unattractive and out of place in the role of cheerleader.

The press's natural instincts finally brought the extended honeymoon with Perot to an end. As Perot shot up in the opinion polls, the scrutiny of his candidacy increased. The defining moment of the new press-Perot relationship occurred on Sunday, May 3, when Tim Russert of NBC's *Meet the Press* pushed Perot hard for details of his deficit-reduction plan. When a flustered Perot couldn't deliver the goods, the candidate groused about "the interesting game we're playing today. It would've been nice if you'd told me you wanted to talk about this and I'd had all my facts with me. . . ." The Wizard of Texarkana had lost a bit of his magic, and the press began to pay attention to the man behind the curtain.

Fascination intermittently gave way to investigation, as tough pieces on Perot appeared in many publications and on broadcasts. The *Wall Street Journal* focused on Perot's alleged videotaping of employees, sometimes to obtain evidence of marital infidelity.[41] The *Washington Post* revealed Perot's attempts to smear a senior Pentagon official, Richard Armitage, with whom Perot disagreed on the Vienam MIA issue.[42] The *Post* also exposed Perot's work as a source for reporter Bob Woodward in 1988, when Perot sought to uncover damaging information about then Vice President Bush and his family.[43] This story proved controversial for the *Post* as well, mainly because of Woodward's decision to break a confidentiality agreement with Perot, formerly his off-the-record informant.[44] The *New York Times* focused on unflattering aspects of Perot's professional dealings,[45] and columnist William Safire hit Perot hard again and again about a host of alleged transgressions.[46] All three networks also broadcast skeptical pieces investigating Perot's activities and contradicting some of his assertions; many zeroed in on the rapidly emerging "Inspector Perot" image.

Singly, none of these charges reached the boiling point of a feeding frenzy; cumulatively, while they began to soften some of Perot's support, many voters were not yet paying close attention, so the effect was still limited. But there were more potentially explosive controversies on the way. *Newsweek* and ABC News were exploring whether Perot had had his daughter Nancy's Vanderbilt University boyfriend (who was a professor) investigated while she was at the college. ABC, which had seven reporters assigned to Perot, had also discovered but did not broadcast a story about a Perot employee named Bobby Joe King, who had been fired in March 1986 after disclosing he was HIV-positive.[47] Other Perot employees may also have been dismissed because of their, or their dependents', illnesses.

Ross Perot short-circuited these and other stories with his abrupt and somewhat mysterious withdrawal from the presidential race on July 16, 1992, the last day of the Democratic National Convention. The press quickly turned the spotlight on an energized Democratic campaign, and Perot receded to the background. Hints of the independent's potential reentry continued to trickle out from his core supporters, but reporters had shelved, stored, or discarded their Perot investigations to deal with more pressing election matters. By the time Perot actually reentered the race on October 1, there was only about a month to go, and little time, talent, or energy to spare for more background research on Perot. Much of the coverage was also on prearranged autopilot because of four debates, scheduled issue pieces and candidate profiles, and the usual avalanche of horserace speculation and opinion. In other words, intentionally or not, Perot chose to exit and reenter at precisely the optimal moments to minimize the amount and the effects of tough investigative reporting.

Moreover, the press was less interested in doing investigative research on Perot because most reporters viewed Perot II as a minor candidate. He was relegated to single-digit support in the polls, and his coverage was dismissive (as suggested by the October 12 cover of *Newsweek*, labeling Perot's reentry an "EGO TRIP"). As it turned out, this electoral reading of Perot was badly off the mark, but it nevertheless served to protect him from the scrutiny he might otherwise have faced had he been seen as a stronger force. There were in fact a few exceptions to the once-over-lightly coverage of Perot. For instance, CBS News revealed that Perot's petition committee paid $56,000 to private investigators to check out certain campaign volunteers,[48] and *U.S. News & World Report* and *The New Republic* published stories about Perot's keeping tabs on his daughter's Vanderbilt University professor-boyfriend.[49]

Perot might have escaped a full-blown frenzy, save for himself. As was so often the case with other frenzies, Perot brought the press club down on his own head, and proved to be his own worst enemy. The media instrument of Perot's self-mugging was CBS's *60 Minutes*. In a segment aired on Sunday, October 25, Perot made sensational charges: The Republicans had planned to disrupt his daughter Carolyn's church wedding in August 1992; conspired to circulate to the tabloids a phony, computer-generated photograph of Carolyn in a lesbian pose, in order to smear her; and intended to wiretap his office and break into his computerized stock-trading program, and ruin him financially. "This is Watergate II," declared Perot, who also announced that the potential attacks on his daughter were the real reason for his July withdrawal from the presidential race. Perot offered loads of specifics about the alleged dastardly deeds, but not a shred of proof to support any of them. Nor was this the first unsubstantiated plot Perot had "uncovered." In earlier times he had insisted he had been targeted by drug lords as well as five armed terrorists hired by the North Vietnamese to assassinate him.[50]

Even for conspiracy-addicted reporters who might have been inclined to believe the worst about a desperate Republican campaign, Perot's charges were over the top and simply incredible. Widely derided for his Perot-noia, the independent presidential candidate's allegations were believed by only a quarter of the voters (though half of his own support-ers).[51] Perot struck back hard at the press, telling reporters to "run your bizarre stories and your twisted, slanted stories," continuing an all-out war with the establishment media waged in the spring and intensified after Perot's reentry. (Minutes after rejoining the race, Perot said to the assembled newspersons, "I don't care what you do. Just have fun, get raises and bonuses, play gotcha. . . ."[52])

Perot also used press-bashing to counteract the predictable media chorus that suggested Americans were "throwing their vote away" by casting a ballot for an Independent candidate unlikely to win. Almost one in five voters apparently agreed with Perot, deciding they would be squandering their vote more recklessly by supporting Bush or Clinton. Meanwhile, Perot brought the oddest presidential campaign in American history to a close as it had begun, by talking to Larry King to thank him for "a hell of a ride." Perot's love-hate relationship with the media had been easily divisible: The talk shows were lovable, the working press detestable. And all future candidates took note of the media lessons Perot taught.

Such frenzies, regardless of origin, demonstrate the "coverage to ex-cess" that has become so much a part of the news media's political focus. Occasionally, however, the abuse is in the opposite direction: the press's failure to discover or reveal official venality, or to apply a uniform standard of scrutiny to all candidates. This less prevalent but still noteworthy occur-rence is the other side of the frenzy story.

CHAPTER SIX

Frenzies that Weren't

The Other Side of the Story

"THERE ARE THINGS we don't publish, lots of them, all the time," insists Len Downie, managing editor of the *Washington Post*. "There's far more restraint in this business than we're given credit for," asserts NBC News's Jim Polk. Despite all the excesses discussed previously, considerable evidence exists to confirm Downie's and Polk's contentions. Many of the stories that reach print or broadcast are like icebergs: Only an eighth of the material gathered is ever made visible to readers and viewers, discretion keeping the other seven-eighths from view. Several of the cases already discussed demonstrate as much. Moreover, most of the rumors heard by members of the press are never published or aired at all, and not simply for lack of proof. Serious journalists are truly concerned about the appropriateness of publication in many instances, and together with their editors they try to exercise considered judgement. "At least once every other week we have really wrenching discussions about whether or not something should be published," reports *Time*'s Ted Gup. "I have files having to do with private indiscretions that would make wonderful chatter, but I'm not going to publish them." Of course, the problem is that not all journalists are as responsible as Gup, and in this age of lowest-common-denominator journalism, the rules of coverage are sometimes set by those on the ethical periphery. Moreover, the decisions about what is and is not revealed are often disturbingly arbitrary, with the informal rules being unfairly applied to different candidates in similar circumstances. In a couple of cases, as we shall see, one could even argue that *too* much discretion was employed by the press, and the public was denied legitimate information critical to evaluating a candidacy.

Frenzies Delayed and Denied

Earlier we discussed the reasons for the lack of frenzies through the Kennedy and Johnson administrations. Once standards began to change, and the Rooseveltian rule was no longer universally honored, some potential frenzies were delayed or never happened at all simply by chance, circumstance, and missed opportunities. Ben Franklin of the *New York Times* spent months in Maryland during the 1968 presidential campaign "digging around, looking for the evidence of corruption on Governor Spiro Agnew's part. . . .We had strong intimations that Spiro had taken kickbacks [a form of illegal payoff by government contractors], which by then were a way of life in Maryland." Franklin at times came tantalizingly close to the story that would eventually cause Agnew to resign the vice presidency in disgrace, but alas he could not substantiate his suspicion by the end of the campaign. (Given the closeness of the final 1968 vote, it is entirely possible that corruption revelations about Agnew in midcampaign would have been enough to elect Democrat Hubert Humphrey president.) The Watergate scandal, of which Agnew's resignation was a somewhat unrelated subset, was another frenzy delayed by early missed signals. CBS News's George Herman scooped everyone on the original GOP-sponsored burglary of the Democratic party's Watergate headquarters when a friend who worked part-time for the Democratic National Committee dropped by Herman's house for a neighborly visit in the summer of 1972:

He came to borrow the rose sprayer and said to my wife, "What has George heard about the break-in at the DNC?" So she called me, and the friend gave me the details he had heard on the job. Then I called the police department, making them believe I knew all about the story, and they told me everything. And I put it on the air immediately, an hour and a half before a wire service came out with it. . . .I knew that it was some kind of an espionage operation because the burglars had microfilm and cameras with them. But I really wasn't all that interested because I was working on some economic story that I thought was very important at the time.

Herman was certainly not alone in missing the significance of the break-in. Less than 3 percent of all the print stories and 17 percent of the broadcast pieces during the 1972 general election campaign even mentioned Watergate.[1] And the Watergate reporting team of the *New York*

Times ignored an explosive tip from one of their newspaper's own photographers, who had been told by a Secret Service friend that President Nixon had an extensive Oval Office taping system. The journalists dismissed the suggestion as too outrageous to be true — until Nixon aide Alexander Butterfield revealed just such a taping system to the Senate Watergate Committee fully eight months later.

Some frenzies seem almost predestined to happen, so determined are a few politicians to advertise their odd proclivities. Tales of Jimmy Carter's homilies on sensitive subjects were legion in the 1976 campaign press corps even before his infamous "lust in the heart" *Playboy* interview. What has not been widely known is that Carter had given virtually the same talk with even juicier details in an on-the-record session to historian Doris Kearns Goodwin three months prior to *Playboy's* "scoop." While visiting Carter in Plains, Georgia, in July 1976, Goodwin asked Carter about a comment he had made to his campaign staff to avoid extramarital affairs. Carter responded by describing with graphic intimacy "about how every night when he prays to Jesus Christ he feels so guilty because he has to describe to Christ the dimensions of the women that he lusted after, and he felt that Christ didn't really want to hear this from him, but he has to go through it."[2] When Goodwin returned home and wrote a commissioned article for *Ladies Home Journal*, she decided to leave out what Carter had called his "battle of lust" because it was "too bizarre." In addition, at least one premier publication, the *New York Times*, refused the opportunity to print an exclusive advance article on the upcoming *Playboy* revelations. Jim Wooten, then covering the Carter campaign for the *Times*, relayed the *Playboy* offer to his editorial superiors, whose response was, according to Wooten: "We are not amused; thanks but no thanks." The editors believed the topic too racy, the source too seedy, and the opportunity to manufacture a phony issue too great — all commendable sentiments in part that, by 1990s "anything goes" standards, appear hopelessly anachronistic. Incidentally, the *Times* only printed a "lust in the heart" story after other publications had done so and the furor was manifest. Furthermore, the *Times* cited Carter's use of the word *screw* only as "a vulgarism," and when Carter employed the obscenity "fuck" in a *New York Times Magazine* interview with Norman Mailer released the same week,[3] the *Times* substituted four dashes for the four-letter word.

Again and again, we have returned to Gary Hart's 1988 frenzy as a watershed in reporting about the private lives of politicians. While bad luck combined with recklessness (and perhaps predestination, as with Carter's *Playboy* interview) resulted in Hart's demise in 1987, it should be remembered that fortuitous timing prevented Hart's sexual exploits from receiving greater scrutiny in 1984. Good timing also may have stopped another potential Hart minifrenzy in its tracks. In 1984 James Perry of the *Wall Street Journal* wrote a long profile of Hart, published at the apogee of the candidate's meteoric rise.[4] In the story was the revelation that Hart and a friend had stolen a high school chemistry test in advance of the examination, scoring near-perfect grades despite being very weak in the subject. The school principal almost refused to graduate the two seniors on account of the incident. Had Hart remained in the 1988 presidential contest, this might well have become a frenzy, or at least a flap, building on the Biden plagiarism controversy.

The Straight-Line Exception for Gays

Many journalists seem skittish about revealing homosexual entanglements, short of the truly outrageous cases such as that of Barney Frank. Partly this may be because the public opprobrium attached to homosexuality is far greater, and therefore the potential damage done by a story is more severe and long lasting.

A particularly striking example of press discretion about homosexuality came in early June of 1990, when two gay activists held a Capitol Hill press conference to announce the names of three U.S. senators and five U.S. House members they claimed were gay. It was an example of "outing," a despicable new movement by gay extremists that calls for "unclosseting" politicians who are homosexuals both to punish those who do not support the gay activists' agenda and (somewhat contradictorily) to produce more "role models" for the gay community. This practice is shunned even by many prominent avowed homosexuals as a violation of the privacy rights most gays hold dear. After the press conference, not a single one of the dozen correspondents covering it reported the names, nor was there apparently the slightest interest in seeking proof of the allegations. (No evidence was provided by the event's organizers.) Since 1988 "outing" advocates have organized at least a half dozen demonstrations at the homes or offices of prominent officeholders (mainly congressmen but also a midwestern governor), using signs, chants, and speeches to label the targets as hidden homosexuals. In only two instances has the mainstream press identified the substance of the "outing" allegations. One circumstance was partly unavoidable: In 1990 a gay activist announced on a live television news show panel his belief that a leading candidate for governor in his northeastern state was homosexual. No proof was forthcoming, but nonetheless some other media outlets reported the scurrilous claim in full.[5] A second example of press complicity happened at about the same time on the other side of the continent. During a western U.S. senator's 1990 reelection race, two of the incumbent Republican's most centrally located billboards were defaced with boldly visible statements such as "Closeted Gay. Living a Lie — Voting to Oppress." Several major West Coast newspapers, some Knight-Ridder newspapers (including the *Miami Herald* and the *Philadelphia Inquirer*), at least one local television station in the senator's home state, and National Public Radio named the senator in their accounts of the vandalism, thus acceding to the agenda of the vandals. This senator was one of those accused of "anti-gay" votes and thus hypocrisy, but in most cases the press appears to judge homosexual hypocrisy as more understandable than the heterosexual variety due to society's prejudices. As a consequence, journalists may see a less compelling need to publish or broadcast the inherent duplicity of gay public officials.

Discretion or Timidity? The Case of Jesse Jackson

Journalistic discretion, whatever the cause, may seem a welcome respite from the regular fare of scandal and tease. Yet too much discretion leads easily to abuses evident in John Kennedy's heyday. Such instances of excessive timidity are rare today, but they still can be found.

Known and widely discussed has been the press's hesitancy to treat Jesse Jackson on the same terms as other presidential candidates. Not only did Jackson receive the most favorable coverage of any 1988 White House aspirant,[6] but with the exception of the alleged plagiarism incident previously described, controversies that plagued his rivals' campaigns never had much of an impact on his, even when there was an obvious parallel. Jackson's wife, Jacqueline, was more than two months pregnant at the time of their 1962 marriage, but little was said about it. A number of reporters had heard Jackson use the slurs "Hymie" and "Hymietown" over the years, but none until the *Washington Post's* Milton Coleman thought this manifest example of prejudice sufficiently serious to report.[7] And Jackson's privacy was almost consistently respected despite strong circumstantial evidence linking him to women other than his wife. As early as 1975 Chicago journalist Barbara Reynolds, in her book on Jackson, reported on Jackson's "close personal relationship" with singer Roberta Flack, who crooned a passionate love song entitled "Jesse" on national television in 1974.[8] Other entertainers, including Nancy Wilson and Aretha Franklin, have also been tied to Jackson.[9] Still another celebrity, actress Margot Kidder ("Lois Lane" of *Superman* movie fame), nearly provided the hook for 1988 press scrutiny of Jackson's private life. Before the California primary, in the late spring of 1988, Kidder campaigned extensively with Jackson. As one reporter covering the campaign put it, "Jackie Jackson was conspicuously absent, and Kidder would almost take on the physical role of the campaign wife; she was there by his side campaigning with him everywhere." Late on the evening before the primary, Kidder came out of Jackson's hotel room apparently somewhat lightheaded, and said on tape to CNN and ABC camera crews waiting for an expected Jackson-Dukakis conclave: "I'm Margot Kidder and I'm whacked." In the elevator after this encounter, Kidder remarked to a Jackson aide within earshot of a CNN crew that she hoped someone cleaned up Jackson's bedroom "since it's a mess." The interest of the press was piqued by these events, and ABC's Brit Hume requested Marianne Keely, an off-the-air reporter for his network, to ask Jackson off-camera about Kidder's remarks. Jackson and later Kidder made it abundantly clear to Keely and others that the inquiry was not appreciated, and that all the circumstances, however suggestive, were in fact quite innocent. Jackson told Keely that his wife Jackie had been present that evening in his hotel room, and "the mess" to which Kidder referred was leftover food. A short time later ABC News received a letter from Kidder's lawyer threatening legal action and demanding that its personnel cease and desist from spreading rumors. The ABC reply insisted that its employees were innocent of rumormongering and noted that the network could not prevent other people from gossiping, but since it had no proof of a Jackson-Kidder relationship it would air no story. The only reference to the matter appeared in an AP dispatch filed by Rita Beamish on June 20, 1988, in which Kidder "angrily scoff[ed]" at "the inevitable campaign plane rumors that arise from her working relationship with Jackson." This single exception aside, the decision not to publish or air the unproved rumors was laudable, especially since the explanations offered by Jackson and Kidder were credible and plausible. On the other hand, the hesitation to pursue the more general topic of Jackson's alleged womanizing suggested a double standard in light of the press's aggressive pursuit of the character issue for other candidates. "I was convinced that a lot of people were afraid to touch that story for any number of reasons, first and foremost, a fear of being charged with being racist," commented CNN's respected anchor Bernard Shaw, who is black. Many interviewees also noted the paradox in Jackson's relationship with the press: Jackson insisted that he be treated as seriously as any other candidate — and when he was so treated, and was given the scrutiny that comes with the territory, Jackson often became incensed.

One newspaper that did devote substantial resources to investigating Jackson's private life was the *Atlanta Constitution*. But even the *Constitution* downplayed the matter, admitted the paper's respected former editor Bill Kovach (now curator of the Nieman Foundation) and staff writer Priscilla Painton.[10] Painton's extensive and aggressive research turned up substantial information about Jackson's links to several women, but the reporter and her editor chose to maintain a very high standard of proof not always present in the press's recent coverage of political figures. Painton makes an argument that Gary Hart would surely have welcomed in his time of trial:

Adultery is very hard to prove. Even if you have the woman involved claiming she's had a relationship, even if you have a time and a place, even if you have friends of the woman telling you this, even if you have the husband of the woman involved telling you this, it still boils down to their word against his. It's not like anything else in journalism where you can come up with documented proof.

Kovach pointed to his decision not to publish some of Painton's most suggestive material: "Priscilla got a lot of information about Jackson checking into motel rooms with a woman not his wife, and when the maid cleans up the room it's pretty obvious somebody was romping around in bed. I would not let those stories get into the paper because after all, he could have had a nightmare and she could have been sleeping on the floor. Jesse Jackson or anybody else could go into a lot of rooms with a lot of women and it does not necessarily prove anything." Jackson was undoubtedly delighted by Kovach's high standards, though the candidate took nothing for granted. Remembers Kovach: "For quite a long period Jesse became my morning alarm clock. I'd get a 5:30 A.M. call at least three or four times a week so he could complain about Priscilla's questions."

Many other reporters covering Jackson were well aware of at least some background on Jackson's private life but chose to tiptoe around it. Even the normally fearless Mike Wallace of *60 Minutes* nearly avoided the subject entirely in a featured interview with Jackson and his wife.[11] Journalists who did ask Jackson blunt questions seemed willing to accept answers that would not have been so easily swallowed coming from other candidates. For example, in the wake of Gary Hart's 1987 withdrawal, Jackson announced he had no "obligation to answer" queries about adultery because there was "not such activity" on his part, and regardless, it was only "a legitimate question . . . if national security is involved."[12] Later Jackson insisted "the second floor of the White House is off limits to the press."[13] Weighing the contrast between the treatment received by Jackson and that meted out to his competitors, Bill Kovach says bluntly, "Had he been a white candidate, there would have been considerably more effort devoted by more organizations to looking into [the allegations of womanizing]. There was a kind of self-censorship going on; it was fear of being attacked for piling on the black candidate."

Many of our interviewees made comments similar to that of ABC's Jim Wooten when he observed that "the media didn't do a very good job covering Jackson." Reporters cited many reasons for the "kid gloves" treatment Jackson usually received. As already mentioned, the press dreaded the charge of racism, a common allegation leveled by black politicians who are under fire. "The fear of being called racist led the press — and his Democratic opponents as well — to treat Jackson like he had fenders," columnist Jack Germond observes. Related to this is the ideological devotion of most journalists to the ideals of the civil rights movement and its practical application by means of affirmative action. PBS's Paul Duke sees Jackson's status as the first major black candidate for president as the reason why "the press was sheepish about doing anything that would diminish him." Jackson's position as a role model for young inner-city blacks and the candidate's reverential reception at most African-American gatherings probably reinforced the traveling media's instincts. Less praiseworthy was another assessment by many journalists: that Jackson was unelectable, and therefore close scrutiny of his character and positions was unnecessary. On occasion, Jackson's inaccurate claims on the campaign trail went unexamined because of this sentiment, but just as important, Jackson was not taken as seriously as his competitors merely on account of his color. The truly racist question of the 1984 and 1988 campaigns was "What does Jesse really want?" when Jackson had made it abundantly clear that the presidency was his objective.

Other nonracial explanations for the special handling of Jackson are also apparent. Candidates who consistently provide good, colorful copy and who are by nature blunt and straightforward frequently receive favorable treatment from a grateful press. Jackson's clever tactics deserve credit as well. On his alleged extramarital sex life, Jackson and his wife launched a preemptive strike, aggressively staking out their privacy and warning reporters about invading it. Mrs. Jackson, for example, told Mike Wallace she would permit no "vulgar questions" in the 60 Minutes interview, and on other occasions she admonished reporters not to "go digging" in an attempt to "destroy my family."[14] As for Jackson himself, "There's a disinclination to want to deal too harshly with Jesse," surmises columnist Robert Novak. "He's a tough fighter; you're not dealing with Michael Dukakis there." Certainly Jackson's supporters' methods in dealing with Barbara Reynolds after publication of her (partly) unflattering biography of him might have warned off potential press challengers. After an enraged Jackson claimed the book had been ghostwritten by white editors,

Reynolds was harassed by threatening telephone calls and pickets outside her apartment house.[15] Jackson has also been known to ask probing reporters an intimidating question or two, such as, How many blacks do you have on your staff? (Jackson's query may well have introduced some not entirely inappropriate white guilt from time to time; American newsroom personnel are 91 percent white, and just 6 percent of newspaper executives are members of minority groups.[16])

Jesse Jackson notwithstanding, exercising too much discretion is usually the least of the press's worries. The excesses identified earlier are of far greater concern, foremost among them the publication or broadcast of rumor, gossip, and innuendo without reasonably strong evidence.

CHAPTER SEVEN

Consequences

HAVING EXAMINED some of the truths about feeding frenzies, we now turn to their consequences. Frenzies have major repercussions on the institution that spawns them — the press — including how it operates, what the public thinks of it, and whether it helps or hurts the development of productive public discourse. The candidates and their campaigns are obviously directly affected by the ways and means of frenzies; which politicians win and which lose, and the manner of their running, are affected by the rules of frenzy coverage. How the voters view politics at any given time — whether the electorate is optimistic or pessimistic, idealistic or cynical — is partly a by-product of what they learn about the subject from the news media. And above all, the dozens of feeding frenzies in recent times have had substantial and cumulative effects on the American political system, from determining the kinds of issues discussed in campaigns to influencing the sorts of people attracted to the electoral arena.

Consequences for the Press

We have already discussed some of the immediate consequences of the decline of press standards and the increase in competition: lowest-common-denominator journalism, the publication and broadcast of unproved rumor, the invasion of legitimate areas of privacy, and the strengthening of pack journalism. The focus in this section will be on two practical results of the press's own modern aggressiveness — its reduced access to elected officials and the growing hostility toward the press on the part of the general public.

One of the great ironies of contemporary journalism is that the effort to report more about candidates means that the news media often learn less than ever before about them. Wise politicians today consider everything they say to a reporter to be on the record, if not immediately, then eventually — perhaps of use the next time the newsperson writes a profile. Thus the pols are much more guarded around journalists than they used to be, much more careful to apply polish and project the proper image at all times. The dissolution of trust between the two groups has meant that "journalists are kept at arm's length by fearful politicians, and to some degree, the public's knowledge suffers because reporters have a less-well-rounded view of these guys," surmises veteran newsman Jerry terHorst. NBC News commentator John Chancellor agrees and believes his young colleagues have paid a steep price for "junkyard dog" journalism:

When the politicians realized they couldn't unbutton themselves in front of the press anymore they all got careful. And what we saw then was the closing of the candidate — his character, his inner thoughts, his feelings about a lot of things — he closed that off to us. And where it stands now, even with candidates you know pretty well, it's almost impossible to get beyond the facade. . . . Reporters work a hell of a lot harder these days to try to get some meaningful information about the candidates' characters and personalities. It's much harder now than it used to be.

The results are seen in the way in which presidential elections are conducted. Ever since Richard Nixon's 1968 presidential campaign, the press's access to most candidates has been tightly controlled, with journalists kept at a distance on and off the trail. And as 1988 demonstrated, the less accessible candidate (Bush) was better able to communicate his message than the more accessible one (Dukakis); the kinder and gentler rewards of victory went to the nominee who was able to keep the pesky media at bay. Harsh scrutiny — the current penalty for openness — reinforces the determination of campaign staffers to spin an impenetrable cocoon around their candidate. The positive aspect of this development is that the press is no longer coopted by the pols the way it was in the all-too-chummy days of the Rooseveltian rule, when many of the insights gleaned by access-rich reporters were self-censored and withheld from readers. But the loss of all sense of camaraderie between journalists and politicians also means that reporters do not see the "real" candidate easily, that their dispatches accordingly will be impoverished and lack the perception afforded by proximity.

However, it is by no means certain that the public *wants* the press to be proximate to candidates anymore. In recent years "there has been a significant erosion of public confidence in the press," concluded the Times–Mirror Center for the People and the Press.[1] Consider these findings from the Times–Mirror studies and other surveys:

- In 1985, 55 percent of Americans believed that news organizations generally "get the facts straight," while 34 percent thought reports were often "inaccurate." By 1988 the proportions had shifted decisively away from "get the facts straight" (40 percent) and toward inaccuracy (50 percent).
- By a two-to-one margin, Americans said that, "in covering stories about the personal and ethical behavior of politicians, news organizations are driving the controversy" rather than "only reporting the news."
- Asked to grade the candidates, the parties, the voters, the pollsters, the campaign consultants, and the press "for the way they conducted themselves in the 1988 campaign," respondents gave the press by far the lowest average score.[2]
- The proportion of voters who felt the press had "too much influence on which candidates became president" climbed over the course of the 1988 election season from 47 percent in May to 58 percent by November.
- When asked to judge "who was most responsible for the negative aspects of the 1988 campaign," 17 percent blamed the candidates, 32 percent the campaign managers, and 40 percent the news media.[3]
- When a random sample of Americans chose the professional group with "the lowest ethical standards," journalists placed second, just a percentage point below lawyers. Even those in Congress were judged less harshly.[4]
- In addition to survey findings demonstrating public concern about press intrusiveness into politicians' private lives, the citizenry also overwhelmingly wants a public official to have the same right as a nonpublic person to sue the news media for libel. Fully three-quarters believe the libel laws ought to be the same for public officials and private citizens alike, and two-thirds think a news organization ought to have to pay damages to an official for a false report *even if* the organization thought the report was true at the time of publication.[5]

Unquestionably, the press spectacle during feeding frenzies has contributed mightily to the decline in public support for the news media. The polls almost always show a considerable uptick in public criticism of journalistic practices during and after a frenzy. The cumulative effect produced over time by many frenzies translates into lessened support for the press. Many journalists do not need surveys to tell them antipress sentiment is on the rise; they see it in their mail and telephone calls and they sense it on the road. The *Wall Street Journal's* Jill Abramson fielded some angry calls from the public after her focus on Dan Quayle's college academic record: "One guy wanted to know if I was going to tackle his kindergarten performance next." The pro-Quayle, press-bashing mob at Huntington, Indiana, in late August 1988 gave many journalists a taste of ancient Rome's Colosseum. The crowd chanted, "Sam Donaldson, go home," with particular gusto, even though, says Donaldson, "I wasn't within a thousand miles of Indiana; thanks a lot, folks." Ellen Hume of the *Wall Street Journal* was in the thick of it, however, and CNN's live broadcast featured her grilling of Quayle in a tight close-up. "The *Journal* was flooded with angry phone calls demanding my firing, and my editors took enormous heat," recalls Hume.

Of course, journalists who thirst for popularity are in the wrong business. Frequently, voters are incorrectly blaming the messenger for delivering a disagreeable truth about a well-liked politician, and the press's special mission is to point out that a naked emperor is wearing no clothes even to a people determined to believe otherwise. Yet reporters would be foolhardy to ignore emphatic signs of the public's growing displeasure with them. In a 1989 *Los Angeles Times* poll, one-third of the Americans surveyed refused to back the First Amendment.[6] In another study, as many respondents said that "the government should *require* that news organizations give coverage to all sides of a controversial issue" as preferred that "the government should not be involved" in allocating coverage.[7] The press's First Amendment rights ought to be unassailable, whatever the media's shortcomings — but in a freewheeling democracy, privileges cannot always be guaranteed. Thoughtful journalists see their profession's own excesses as partly responsible for the citizenry's often lackluster support for press freedoms. "Our behavior definitely contributes to this," observes the *Washington Post's* Richard Harwood. His *New York Times* colleague, executive editor A. M. Rosenthal, made a similar case in a passionate exposition after the stakeout of Gary Hart, and his argument applies more generally to his frenzy-addicted profession:

We are begging the nation to treat us as unworthy of respect. In time, without any question, we will lose the support of the American people in our constant struggles against those who would erode the First Amendment. We cannot claim it was designed for voyeurs.[8]

Consequences for the Candidates

One glance down the list of case studies used for this book gives a reliable indication of a frenzy's consequences for a politician. All the candidate-victims were damaged by their controversies, most of them severely, and some were eliminated outright from competition for high office. The Eagletons, Harts, and Bidens on the list comprehend fully that a frenzy's penalty can be the political equivalent of capital punishment. Even the less serious frenzies disrupt a campaign, take a candidate off his or her stride, and send the polls plummeting, as we saw with Gerald Ford's "free Poland" gaffe and Michael Dukakis's mental health crisis. Undoubtedly frenzies also cause the politicians, as well as their families and supporters, emotional pain and agony. In some cases the pols' constituencies are damaged, too; fairly or not, the image of Washington, D.C., was badly tarnished by the scandals swirling around Mayor Marion Barry. While it may be difficult to work up sympathy for an electorate that chose Barry, compassion is easily extended in cases of rumor-wronged innocents, such as "mentally ill" Michael Dukakis and "gay" Jack Kemp. In Kemp's case, for example, the consequences of calumny were as serious as they were unjust. John Buckley, Kemp's former campaign press secretary, explained:

I know for a fact that a number of influential people who wanted to endorse Kemp did not because they were worried a "scandal" was going to break. The rumor was one of the reasons the influential *Manchester Union Leader* in New Hampshire was hostile to Kemp. There were people that could have raised money for Kemp who didn't raise money for him because they were moral Christian people who were convinced that he was immoral.

For Kemp and many others, a frenzy problem becomes a hindrance but not necessarily a fatal handicap. Kemp did not capture the presidency for many reasons, but he was able to gain a spot in the Bush cabinet. Edward Kennedy recovered sufficiently from Chappaquiddick to win several reelections to the U.S. Senate and achieve exceptional prominence in that body, though a successful White House bid is now probably well out of his reach. Other politicians with a strong base like Kennedy's in Massachusetts can also survive a frenzy and regroup. Some of Marion Barry's African-American constituency stuck by him to the bitter end and would have worked enthusiastically to reelect him had he chosen to run for mayor in 1990. As longtime Barry-watcher Tom Sherwood of WRC-TV comments, "People were always waiting for the other shoe to drop with Barry, and it always did; then people would say, 'now the mayor's finished' — but they ignored the fact that he was a centipede who had more shoes left to drop than Imelda Marcos."

Not just the candidates and officeholders caught up in a frenzy are affected by it, of course. The consequences of each case are felt beyond its borders, and the behavior of public officials is often modified. After Dukakis and Eagleton, not many pols were patronizing their friendly neighborhood psychiatrists. After Biden, they carefully checked the accuracy of their résumés and meticulously attributed borrowed passages in their speeches. After Hart, they employed extra discretion in their illicit affairs.

Any megafrenzy such as the one that engulfed Dan Quayle is a somewhat different animal, with the complexity of the creature producing contradictory consequences. On the one hand, Quayle himself was badly battered and bruised. Of the four candidates on the two major-party tickets, he received by far the most negative coverage.[9] The residue of his campaign shellacking was visible after the election as well, with Americans consistently expressing doubts about his qualifications to assume the presidency should that become necessary. Quayle's vice presidential spokesman, David Beckwith, sees little chance that Quayle can overcome the frenzy-generated image burdens anytime soon: "For the indefinite future there will be lingering questions about Quayle based on what people saw or thought they saw in the campaign, and it's going to be with him for a number of years." It would be difficult for a vice president to get the public's attention long enough to change an impression formed by a large dose of unfavorable coverage in the campaign. And in his next campaign, Quayle can be certain that remnants of his past frenzy will resurface and redevelop.

Oddly enough, though, in some ways Quayle's campaign woes helped the man who chose him, George Bush. Voter concern about Quayle probably cost Bush enough votes in November to deny the GOP ticket a popular-vote landslide. Yet Quayle served as a lightning rod for Democratic and press criticism, deflecting fire from Bush himself—and in the end, most people vote for president, not vice president. "If the media and the Dukakis campaign had spent nearly as much time trying to strike up a populist theme or trying to develop some real issues instead of going on a rabbit chase after Dan Quayle, they might have drawn blood," said Bush manager Lee Atwater. Moreover, Bush's "wimp" image was transformed into a "take-charge" one overnight as he forcefully defended his running mate and steadfastly refused to give in to pressure to dump him. The controversy also caused the Bush camp to focus its effort early, while an overconfident Dukakis retreated to Massachusetts apparently convinced that adverse reaction to Quayle would do the Democratic party's work for him. The news media also became spooked by the wave of public hostility generated by their Quayle coverage, and this aided the Republicans at a later stage of the autumn campaign. After Quayle's

mechanical, remarkably poor performance in the October 5 vice presidential candidates' debate in Omaha — indelibly remembered on account of
Democrat Lloyd Bentsen's "You're no Jack Kennedy" remark — television
news commentators tumbled over one another to declare Quayle's showing
a fine one.[10] And most attempts to probe Quayle's character and record
fizzled after the initial period of overkill. "We became obsessively and
excessively concerned with Quayle's military record, and after the understandable public backlash occurred, we backed off pursuing legitimate
elements of his background," observes *Los Angeles Times* media reporter
Tom Rosenstiel. *Washington Monthly* editor Charles Peters adds, "It's a
crazy thing that happens with the press. It does an overkill on a story,
then in reaction to the public reaction, it pulls back and the story disappears
almost entirely." The search for the golden mean is not restricted to
philosophers, and it proves as elusive in press coverage as in every other
sector of life.

Consequences for the Voters

What seems to gall the voters most about frenzies is not the indignities
and unfairnesses inflicted on candidates in the process, however bothersome they may be. Rather, people often appear to be irate that candidates
are eliminated before the electorate speaks, that irreversible political ver-
dicts are rendered by journalists instead of by the rightful jury of citizens
at the polls. The press sometimes seems akin to the Queen of Hearts in
Alice's Adventures in Wonderland, who declares, "Sentence first — verdict
afterwards."

The denial of electoral choice is an obvious consequence of some
frenzies, yet the news media's greatest impact upon voters is not in the
winnowing of candidates but in the encouragement of cynicism. There
is no doubt that the media, particularly television, have the power to
influence people's political attitudes. With the decline of political parties,
news publications and broadcasts have become the dominant means by
which citizens learn about public officials, and while news slant and
content cannot change most individuals' basic views and orientation, they
can dramatically affect *what* people think about and *how* they approach a
given subject. The massive press focus during many frenzies guarantees
that even casual news consumers will find out about the controversy; the
media's agenda-setting function for society is never more in evidence.
Since redundant media concentration is usually essential in order to capture
the attention of a distracted public, this intensity is not necessarily bad,
assuming the frenzy does not center on a trivial, irrelevant event. However,

the approach taken by the media — the way in which a frenzy is framed and the context into which it is put — is critical to the public's view of politics. And the approach usually taken by journalists is clear: a repetitive, disproportionate stress on scandal; a "more of the same" theme; a "what can you expect from politicians" tone that deepens, extends, and reinforces the enduring public suspicion of all things political. Post-Watergate reporting about government has been unrelentingly negative, scandal giving way to scandal, so that Americans not unreasonably conclude that all politicians must indeed be crooked even if only a few get caught. The substantial majority of public officials who do their jobs honestly and well are not nearly as newsworthy under the old maxim, "Bad news is news, good news is unreported."

Consequences for the Political System

The enhanced — some would say inordinate — influence possessed by the modern press is pushing the American political system in certain unmistakable directions. On the positive side are the increased openness and accountability visible in government and campaigns, which have been achieved during the past two decades. But this is balanced by two disturbing consequences of frenzied press coverage: the trivialization of political discourse and the dissuasion of promising political candidacies.

As to the former, the news media have had plenty of company in impoverishing the debate, most notably politicians and their television consultants. Nonetheless, journalists cannot escape some of the responsibility. First, the press itself has aided and abetted the lowering of the evidentiary standard held necessary to make a charge stick. In addition to the publication of rumor and the insinuation of guilt by means of innuendo, news outlets are willing to target indiscriminately not just real ethical problems, but possible problems and the perception of possible problems. Second, the media often treat venial sins and mortal sins as equals, rushing to make every garden-variety scandal another Watergate. Not only does such behavior engender cynicism in readers and viewers, but it cheapens and dulls the collective national sense of moral outrage that ought to be husbanded for the real thing. Third, the press often devotes far more resources to the insignificant gaffe than to issues of profound national and global impact; on many occasions, titillation has replaced transportation on the country's agenda, sex has substituted for serious debate, and peccadilloes have supplanted policy on the front pages. T. R. Reid of the *Washington Post* supplied a fitting anecdote about his attempt to get a substantive story into his newspaper ahead of a sensationalized one. Shortly after Gary Hart announced his candidacy for president in 1987, Reid and other reporters secured a comment from Hart on the subject of taxes that was remarkable in light of Walter Mondale's experience in 1984, to say nothing of the Republican party's strongly antitax rhetoric. Mondale had announced in his Democratic National Convention acceptance speech that, if elected, he would raise taxes—a declaration that most analysts came to deem politically foolish. While quibbling with Mondale's semantical approach, Hart told Reid that it would be "irresponsible" for any presidential candidate to rule out a tax increase, given the size of the federal budget deficit, and that he was leaning toward a combination of tax increases on imported oil, luxuries, and high-income Americans. "This was a fairly daring thing for any candidate to say, and I considered it big news," says Reid, and when he telephoned his editors, they agreed. But on the same day came the manufactured, inconsequential story of Hart's reaction to the possibility that rival candidates were spreading rumors about his womanizing. Back to the telephone went Reid, who argued that the gossip "was bullshit, not nearly as important as the tax story, plus we'd pledged to stay away from those rumors unless they were proven." Excited editors huddled, then gave Reid his writing orders: The gossip was the headline, and the breakthrough tax statement would be buried deep in the article.[11] "They just couldn't resist," concluded Reid. Louis D. Brandeis, later a distinguished justice of the United States Supreme Court, well expressed the dangers inherent in such editorial decisions in a seminal 1890 law review article with his colleague Samuel D. Warren:

[Gossip] belittles by inverting the relative importance of things, thus dwarfing the thoughts and aspirations of a people. When personal gossip attains the dignity of print, and crowds the space available for matters of real interest to the community, what wonder that the ignorant and thoughtless mistake its relative importance. Easy of comprehension, appealing to that weak side of human nature which is never wholly cast down by the misfortunes and frailties of our neighbors, no one can be surprised that it usurps the place of interest in brains capable of other things. Triviality destroys at once robustness of thought and delicacy of feeling.[12]

Simultaneously, reporters have become inclined to ask narrowly drawn, unrevealing questions rather than broad ones that assist voters in making their election day choices. For example, newspeople were more interested in telling their audiences whether Joe Biden and Dan Quayle had plagiarized college term papers than whether Biden and Quayle were intelligent and understood government. The answer to the first query was not only basically unenlightening but may very well have provided a misleading clue to the candidates' overall capacities and aptitudes. Yet it is the realization that the press will pursue the narrow rather than the broad aspects of their pasts and characters that fills candidates with fear and prevents them from letting down their guard. Instead of giving extended insight into their real thoughts and personalities, the ultracautious pols will deliver only sanitized, programmed, prefabricated sound bites spiced with pabulum. "Did you ever wonder why we have these highly structured debates with no spontaneous give-and-take between the nominees?" asks ABC's Brit Hume. "Because these candidates don't think they can afford to make any kind of honest mistake, since we'll just go wild over it. If we ever want to get candidates to be more forthright, news organizations are going to have to rethink their approach to gaffes and other such stories."

The second troubling consequence of modern media coverage for the political system has to do with the recruitment of candidates and public servants. Simply put, the price of power has been raised dramatically, far too high for many outstanding potential officeholders. An individual contemplating a run for office must now accept the possibility of almost unlimited intrusion into his or her financial and personal life. Every investment made, every affair conducted, every private sin committed from college years to the present may one day wind up in a headline or on television. For a reasonably sane and moderately sensitive person, this is a daunting realization, with potentially hurtful results not just for the candidate but for his or her immediate family and friends. To have achieved a nongovernmental position of respect and honor in one's community is a source of pride and security, and the risk that it could all be destroyed by an unremitting and distorted assault on one's faults and foibles cannot be taken lightly. American society today is losing the services of many exceptionally talented individuals who could make outstanding contributions to the commonweal, but who understandably will not subject themselves and their loved ones to abusive, intrusive press coverage. Of course, this problem stems as much from the attitudes of the public as from those of the press; the strain of moral absolutism in portions of the American people merely finds expression in the relentless press frenzies and ethicsgate hunts. In addition, the absurdities of modern standards of public purity are everywhere. For instance, a candidate with marital difficulties would do well to get a divorce rather than reach an accommodation with his or her spouse because divorce is deemed acceptable while extramarital relationships, even past ones in a surviving marriage, are potential grist for the press mill. All this leads not just to the discouragement of candidates who possess a mixture of great virtue and hidden vice but the encouragement of other kinds of politicians: those with a naive, saintly image; ideologically driven crusaders; psychologically unbalanced individuals whose lust for power and craving for impersonal affection overcome fear of the risks of public unmasking; and comprehensively conventional, uncreative contenders whose lack of vision is matched only by their dullness. Qualities of shrewdness, worldliness, balance, and pragmatism— which are essential to success in governing—are sadly missing here.

Some journalists argue that concern about the deterrence of good candidates is overdrawn and outweighed by the advantages of close scrutiny. "A lot of the people that that is said about couldn't get elected in a hundred years [while press scrutiny] maybe keeps a lot of the fuckers out of government," as *Washington Post* executive editor Ben Bradlee indelicately puts it. And, notes *Time*'s Ted Gup, "If people don't want to undergo profound scrutiny, then perhaps they have something to hide or have onion-thin skin and shouldn't be in public office." Adds *Post* ombudsman Richard Harwood, "Some people may be discouraged from running, but we've never had to call off an election for a lack of candidates." Other reporters see frenzies not as deterrents but as opportunities to test how a politician deals with stress and unexpected pressure. "Campaigns are supposed to confront candidates with tough choices, because once in office they will have to cope with crises that come from nowhere," asserts CBS's Eric Engberg. These arguments are indisputable in part: Frenzies have indeed eliminated some unworthy potential officeholders, and they certainly have measured crisis-managing skills. Yet a long campaign is fraught with enough revealing tests of a politician's mettle; it is wholly unnecessary to manufacture any on tangential matters. And while no ballot will ever be devoid of names, some may well be lacking good ones if the price of power continues inflating. It comes down again to the sorts of persons our society wishes to nudge toward and away from public service. *New York Times* columnist Anthony Lewis is surely correct when he suggests, "If we tell people there's to be absolutely nothing private left to them, then we will tend to attract to public office only those most brazen, least sensitive personalities. Is that what we want to do?"

If these are the unfortunate consequences, then what remedies can counteract them by preventing the excesses of frenzy coverage?

CHAPTER EIGHT

Remedies

I have lent myself willingly as the subject of a great experiment, . . . to demonstrate the falsehood of the pretext that freedom of the press is incompatible with orderly government. — THOMAS JEFFERSON[1]

MR. JEFFERSON'S experiment is still our own — a continuing challenge to citizens, politicians, and journalists alike. Unfettered freedom of the press is cherished by every American who values robust democracy, and few would seriously suggest tampering with the principle. Yet the extraordinary degree of constitutional protection afforded the news media (matched by no other national institution or private enterprise) carries with it corresponding and weighty obligations: to inform the citizenry as fully and accurately as possible, to check governmental power responsibly, and to report with fairness and balance. Feeding frenzies are not representative of day-to-day journalism in every respect; nonetheless the coverage of them is indicative of serious problems and excesses that cast into doubt the press's fulfillment of its side of the implied constitutional bargain. There is no question of what the press, under the First Amendment, has the right to do. Rather, the question is: What is the right thing for the press to do; what news is truly fit to print and how should it be presented?

The Dividing Line between Public and Private

Whatever one's view of journalism in the 1950s and early 1960s, it *was* an easier, tidier enterprise. Public life was public life, and private life was private life, and never (or rarely) did the twain meet. Now the line between the two seems blurred and fuzzed and in constant motion. The disputed no-man's-land is a gray area that "has become a large red zone of press–politics combat," observes Marvin Kalb, former CBS newsman and director of the Joan Shorenstein Barone Center on the Press, Politics, and Public Policy at Harvard University.

On one side of the line are those who defend some or all aspects of the modern press's closer examination of public officials' private lives. They say that the voters need the information to judge character, and that the press has no business withholding it; if anything, assert a few, the press is still not being forthcoming enough. On the opposing side are mainly candidates but also some reporters who believe that the news media are too intrusive today, that not enough privacy is reserved for public servants. There is no direct relationship between private behavior and public performance, they insist, so why report it?

In discussions with many dozens of journalists on this subject, the only clear aspect of the debate is the division and uncertainty that surround it. But two boundaries are accepted by most reporters. First, a large majority reject the old Rooseveltian rule as too permissive. No longer does anyone want, as columnist Robert Novak put it, "to grow up believing that a crippled president like Roosevelt can walk or a terribly ill president like FDR in his last years is healthy." And newspeople certainly do not yearn for the good old days when a U.S. senator could stagger around drunk during floor debate and no one would report it. Virtually no one defends the press cover-up for John F. Kennedy, either. "The press helped to sell a lie, and we have the obligation to tell the truth," says *Washington Post* columnist Richard Cohen. "JFK's narrow margin of victory might well have been the number of people who were attracted to this handsome, loving couple enjoying the greatest marriage ever seen; if we had told the truth and people had known he was screwing everything that moved, would he have won the presidency?" The press's shame during Camelot has generated a silent but powerful mantra in the current generation of journalists: "No more JFKs." To their credit, newspeople today would never even consider overlooking a candidate's or president's personal recklessness and compulsive sexual behavior, much less willingly act as propagandists by projecting a false image of domestic harmony and perfection such as the one that benefited Kennedy. The second boundary on personal-life investigation embraced by most people in the contemporary news business is the belief that the "anything goes" rule that replaced the Rooseveltian one has taken coverage too far, exposing many private lives too fully and including wholly unacceptable aspects such as the airing of unproven rumors. Thus, the press — at least during thoughtful periods — rejects both extremes in private-life coverage, the "tell almost nothing" of the Rooseveltian rule and the "tell just about everything" of the anything-goes substitute, despite the rules' appealing purity and simplicity. However, in most news organizations no specific guidelines exist to enable journalists to navigate successfully between these extremes when a frenzy storm hits, thereby increasing the chances that the almost irresistible competitive dynamics of the frenzy will determine the rules of coverage. (In our interviews, many journalists complained about their organizations' tendency to make up the rules on a case-by-case basis with no attempt at standardization.) Every newspaper and broadcast outlet needs a relatively precise and clear set of guidelines to govern private-life frenzies. Based on the lessons learned from recent frenzies, as well as the opinions and preferences of our interviewees, we would suggest a kind of "fairness doctrine." It is designed to be fair to voters by giving them appropriate and sufficient information they can use in judging candidates and officeholders; fair to candidates by ceding them some reasonable reservoir of privacy while articulating the rules which the press appears to expect them to live under; and fair to journalists and editors by spelling out areas of legitimate and illegitimate investigation, freeing them from some uncertainty and confusion about their undertakings. A "fairness doctrine" that is sensible and can be widely accepted among the press, politicians, and public might include the following provisions:

PRIVATE LIFE SUBJECT TO PUBLICATION AND BROADCAST
1. All money matters (investments, transactions, earnings, taxes, and so on) of the candidate and, to the extent that they directly bear on the financial well-being of the candidate, the financial arrangements of his or her spouse and immediate family.
2. All health matters that may affect the candidate's performance in office.
3. Any incident or charge that reaches the police blotter or a civil or criminal court.
4. Sexual activity where there is a clear intersection between an official's public and private roles; for example, relationships with staff members or lobbyists, where elements of coercion or conflict of interest inherently exist.
5. Sexual activity that is compulsive and/or manifestly indiscreet, and therefore potentially dangerous.
6. Any ongoing private behavior that is potentially or actually debilitating, such as alcohol or drug abuse.
7. Any illegal drug use (whether ongoing or not) that has occurred as an

adult within perhaps the decade prior to candidacy, and any incident over the same period in which the candidate has condoned the use of illegal drugs in his or her presence, whether participating or not.

8. Any private behavior (whether or not included in the above categories) that involves the use of public funds or taxpayer-subsidized facilities in a substantial way.

PRIVATE LIFE SHIELDED FROM PUBLICATION AND BROADCAST

1. Nonlegal matters involving the candidate's underage children and also other family members, except to the extent that the relatives seek the limelight or influence the official.

2. Current extramarital sexual activity as long as it is discreet, noncompulsive, and the official's partner(s) are not connected to his or her public responsibilities and are not minors; in addition, all past sexual activity and personal relationships that occurred many years earlier should *not* be examined. (Offenses older than a decade might be exempted from scrutiny as a reasonable statute of limitations.)

3. Sexual orientation per se, unless compulsive behavior or minors are involved.

4. Drug or alcohol abuse that was a youthful indulgence or experimentation; also adult abuse at least a decade old, when the individual has fully recovered and clearly abandoned the harmful practices.

5. Internal family matters, such as child rearing and nonfinancial relationships with relatives and nonpolitical friends.

ADDITIONAL PROVISIONS AND QUALIFIERS

1. Every charge printed or aired by the news media must either be proven or be accompanied by a substantial body of evidence. Excluded from publication and broadcast under this provision: rumors and sizable chunks of most FBI reports. Also discouraged: fishing expeditions.

2. Situational ethics inevitably apply to each case. Scrutiny ought to be greatest, with the fewest exceptions concerning candidates for president and vice president, and correspondingly less intense for lower-level elective and nonelective offices. (As *U.S. News & World Report's* Michael Barone puts it, "There's no equal opportunity clause that applies to the presidency; it's not important that every person get an opportunity to be president, but it's important that we get a good president.") Similarly, job-specific exceptions can be made. For example, *any* past drug offense may be relevant to the appointment of the federal drug czar. Also, offenses committed after a politician's declaration of candidacy, when any prudent individual will be on his or her best behavior, are justifiably subject to added emphasis.

3. A candidate's degree of hypocrisy and lying can also rachet coverage up or down. For instance, a bold philanderer who avidly uses family issues and his own loved ones to gain political advantage begs to have his lies and hypocrisy exposed.
4. Since no one is sure what, if any, implications much of a person's private life has on his or her public performance, private-life incidents that reach print ought to be interpreted cautiously by the media. After all, some faithful husbands produced flawed presidencies (Calvin Coolidge, Richard Nixon) and others did creditable jobs (Harry Truman, Gerald Ford); some philandering presidents (such as Warren Harding) were failures and others (Franklin Roosevelt) historically towering.

A strong case can be made that under these standards, voters are given all the information about a candidate's private character they need to make a responsible choice, while facts that invade an official's legitimate privacy and add little but prurient, gossipy titillation are withheld. Granted, these guidelines are not airtight, will not end the debate about privacy, and do not pretend to be a rote substitution for considered editorial judgment when a new frenzy arises. But they are an improvement over the inconsistent, ad hoc seat-of-the-pants decision making existing in many news organizations today. The current lack of clearly articulated standard leads inexorably to increasing intrusiveness, more lowest-common-denominator journalism, and additional instances of unproven rumors reaching print. The standards suggested here are the result of a mental exercise that ought to take place in media outlets across America before the frenzy-spawning pressures build in the next presidential election cycle. Of course, the precise standards separately agreed upon by the various print and broadcast outlets will differ from organization to organization; it could not be otherwise in such a diverse, competitive industry. But the opinion leaders in journalism — the networks, the prestigious newspapers, the major weekly newsmagazines — can individually and collectively set the standards that matter for their profession. If they publicize those standards and hold to them, whatever the provocation from sources or left-wing weeklies or rebel competitors, they can effectively reduce the impact of frenzies, rumormongering, and junkyard dog journalism.

Whether or not the "fairness doctrine" becomes widely adopted in whole or in part, there is another way for the media to provide voters with invaluable glimpses into the souls of candidates and public officials while reducing the spotlight's intensity on purely private lives. Journalists ought to put more emphasis on *public* character than *private* character, for the former is at least as revealing of an individual's makeup as bedroom behavior. Part of the public side of character is on the record and easily accessible, such as courage demonstrated by taking issue stands that may be unpopular with the public at large or special interest groups. Other aspects, less frequently commented on, include a finely developed sense of humor or irony, the ability to rebound from setbacks and frustrations, the degree to which a person tends to shade the truth or deny reality, and an individual's general openness or secretiveness. The two most telltale indicators of public character are surprisingly little explored: how the candidate relates to his or her working associates and peers, and how he or she deals with staff. Concerning the former, columnist David Broder points out that Gary Hart's determination to go it alone and play by his own set of rules was shown just as convincingly by his public life as his private one:

What frustrates me about the Gary Hart thing was we should not have had to wait for a Donna Rice incident to raise large questions in people's minds about the character of Gary Hart. Here was a man who had served in the United States Senate for twelve years, and yet it was hard to find another senator who said, "I know Gary very well, know him inside out, feel very comfortable with the idea of his being president." This was a job where if you're going to be a success at all, you have to be able to build relationships with other political players. This guy had never demonstrated the slightest inclination or capacity to build any kind of relationship with any other politician. Now that was something that we should have been able to write about.

If anything, the exploration of a candidate's relationships with his or her staff is even more eye opening—and it is a completely aboveboard, legitimate topic for press commentary and analysis. Already, journalists extensively cover *who* a politician's key subordinates are, but rarely do they write about *how* staff are treated. Personality traits that include bad temper, pettiness, laziness, and stupidity as well as hints of underlying racist or sexist attitudes can all be on display here. Several 1988 presidential candidates had reputations for browbeating staff members, and none more so than Jesse Jackson.[2] Yet a search through all the major 1988 profiles and feature articles on Jackson turned up only one in which the subject was given any serious attention.[3] If the press is willing, the staff room can substitute for the bedroom in investigating the nature of candidates' characters, and it can add a political dimension not found in the boudoir. As the *Wall Street Journal's* Al Hunt asserts, "Political character ought to be much more important to us than the personal character revealed by who's screwing whom."

If reporters need some additional incentive to set aside a reservoir of privacy for public officials, the privacy-threatening celebrity trend in journalism itself might provide it. A number of our well-known interviewees complained about recent encroachments on their own personal lives, and this is certain to continue. Angry politicians and consultants, such as strategist Stuart Spencer, are demanding the same privacy standards be applied to "the powerful public figures in the media": "Let's have a level playing field and see how they like it." And interestingly, some in journalism are not ruling out such fair play. *Washington Post* managing editor Len Downie was asked whether his stated goal of increasing the scrutiny of the behavior of influential leaders in government, business, and religion[4] applied to prominent reporters, even his own: "I include the news media in that, sure." It may be time to modify the "anything goes" rule before the press is hoist by its own petard.

On Reporting Rumors

Rumor thrives on motion, stronger for the running.[5]
Aeneid, 4

The single most disturbing development in modern journalism is the loosening of standards that permits the publication or broadcast of unproven rumor. Responsible news veterans are deeply concerned about this trend. "It's just the shabbiest journalism to go with rumors. If you can't pin it down, you shouldn't put it in the paper or on the air," declares NBC News commentator John Chancellor. Columnist David Broder emphatically agrees: "It's not a close question for me. If you can't make the distinction between rumors and journalism, between gossip and journalism, then you're in the wrong business." Adds his *Washington Post* colleague, media-beat reporter Eleanor Randolph, "We print enough things as it is that turn out not to be true, without adding rumors to the mix."

Several excuses are offered to explain the regrettable deterioration in standards. Skillful political consultants who plant and carefully nurture rumors receive some blame, though it is difficult to believe the current crop are any more adept at manipulating the press than their predecessors. The consultants may be no different today, but the rules of journalism have indeed changed. Earlier generations of political operatives were frequently unable to convince reporters to print the goods on candidates even when proof was available, thanks to the prevailing Rooseveltian rule. Some current reporters suggest that they have an obligation to the public to discuss all the factors affecting a political campaign, including the rumors that regularly sweep the electoral caravan. "That's too easy an out, just a way of breaking into some juicy gossip," says Broder. Moreover, any news attention to unproved rumor multiplies whatever effect the rumor may be having on a candidate, so media intervention is not simply a matter of passive, neutral reporting. "There is a false sense among reporters that, 'Oh, everybody's already talking about it anyway so it doesn't hurt to print it.' But they don't realize that everyone *isn't* talking about it — at least not until they publish it," notes former *Wall Street Journal* staffer Ellen Hume. The political rumor mill churns in a tiny, enclosed echo chamber, but when its mutterings are broadcast, they can become a deafening roar, reverberating around the networks' Grand Canyon and drowning out all other campaign dialogue.

Rationalizations aside, the real reason for the new attractiveness of rumor is the spread of lowest-common-denominator journalism. "The range of standards acceptable to individual reporters and their outlets has become enormous, and stories produced under the lowest standards are now sometimes getting the widest circulation," says Dan Howard, who experienced the phenomenon as John Tower's spokesman. Responsible media organizations must fight back by adopting strict rules about the use of "rumor news" broken by other outfits. First, a story from another organization ought to be independently verified by a media outlet's own reporters before the subject is given prominence on its pages or airwaves. Publication or broadcast by a single organization should not automatically open the floodgates to publication and broadcast everywhere. "Something shouldn't become part of the public debate simply because one newspaper has printed something," argues the *New York Times's* Andrew Rosenthal. "You always have to ask whether the story meets the standards set by *your* newspaper." Adds *Time's* Ted Gup, "There's no shame in being scooped on a story that shouldn't be published."

Under certain conditions, journalists might also want to debunk a persistent and debilitating rumor that may be unfairly inflicting great damage on a political figure. This suggestion is a "back to the future" idea, since Ben Bradlee (then of *Newsweek*) did precisely this in demolishing the 1962 rumor about John F. Kennedy's "prior marriage" to a twice-divorced socialite. However, there are distinct dangers in this kind of media rebuttal. "The trouble with setting up a straw man and knocking him down is that sometimes people only see the straw man and fail to notice you've dispatched him, and this is especially true on television," warns ABC News's Peter Jennings. This in extremis remedy should be reserved for the truly insidious rumors that will not subside on their own.

Of course, from time to time rumors do break into print through no fault of the media, as with President Reagan's "invalid" pronouncement concerning Michael Dukakis's mental health or Jack Kemp's own strategic choice to kick his "gay" rumor out of the campaign closet. But the news media still have clear obligations in these instances. The most obvious is to downplay the rumors and not to sensationalize. "Run stories like that deep inside the paper or way down inside another story," advises the *Detroit News*'s Jim Gannon. "In effect, you signal the readers not to take it too seriously." Second, once the amassed evidence is enough to convince even Perry Mason that a rumor is false, news organizations have the duty not to keep raising dead-and-buried tales from the crypt. Some outlets were nothing short of irresponsible in their unrelenting rehashing of the Kemp "gay" gossip, for instance. Third, when a perfidious rumor comes out in the open thanks to the efforts of rumormongers, the press ought to go after the evildoers. "We ought to devote just as much energy to trying to trace down who's responsible as we do in investigating the original tip," declares Hal Bruno.

Unfortunately, the same favor was not extended to Michael Dukakis after the classic dirty trick played on his campaign in the form of the mental health controversy. Not only should the press have criticized President Reagan more severely for his churlish effort to undermine Dukakis, but the rumor should have been forthrightly labeled as the lie and the smear it was, rather than timidly described in many places as merely "unproved," suggesting to between-the-lines readers that there might be a kernel of truth to a malicious falsehood. Moreover, greater investigative resources should have been devoted to uncovering the LaRouche and Republican origins of the gossip and those groups' efforts to spread it. "We should have tried much harder to nail the sources of that rumor because it did Dukakis a lot of damage," asserts Jeff Greenfield of ABC News.

None of this is to suggest that journalists should be at all limited in the subjects they can explore and check out, so long as a high standard for publication or broadcast is maintained. As ABC's Chris Wallace notes: "I feel comfortable asking all kinds of impertinent, personal, or sensitive questions while not on live [television], but what I decide to put on the air has to pass a much higher and more serious threshold." CBS's Bob Schieffer agrees: "We're obligated to check out all kinds of distasteful things, but unless we're absolutely certain something personally damaging is true, we have the obligation to put it away and say nothing about it." Alas, there are perils even in checking out rumors. Gossip can be spread more widely in the political community, and on good authority, when reporters call well-connected sources to verify such tips. And one suspects that media organizations have occasionally worked oblique rumor references into stories as a way to justify the substantial resources invested in chasing rumors down. But these are relatively minor concerns compared with the brazen practices criticized earlier, which lead inescapably to one conclusion: Professional journalists must report facts, not rumors, and responsible editors must only publish the news that is fit to print—gossip and rumors being most definitely excluded from the mix.

Internal Checks and Balances

No one and no institution outside the press can or should limit what the press does, but those in the profession who care about its standards and want to fend off threats to its liberty ought to try to temper the excesses associated with feeding frenzies. The best solution is old-fashioned leadership and determination to cure the ills within each media organization. For instance, at CBS News, Dan Rather says he has learned from the problems exhibited in past frenzies and that now his "goal for this outfit is to be less a part of the frenzy, less a part of the herd, more difficult to stampede, more willing to set higher standards and go our own way on these stories." Ideally, every editor would insist on the same, killing investigative stories that fail to make a real case, refusing to give in to lowest-common-denominator journalism, resisting competitive pressures, and providing voluntary accountability when mistakes are made. A frenzy of good editing alone could counteract many bad effects of feeding frenzies. But, in truth, not enough editors are able to do this because, as David Broder notes, "It's very hard to be both the person who is goading your staff to 'go get the story' and the one who is saying in a very detached and skeptical way, 'Is this story really there?'" "In my experience many editors don't really perform the editing function; instead of canning bad stories, they make excuses for getting them into print," suggests the *Baltimore Sun's* veteran columnist Jack Germond. "We don't have nearly enough accountability in this profession. Reporters who go too far on a story or screw up are rarely disciplined in a significant way by their editors," says CNN's Frank Sesno.

Besides editors, prominent journalists also have a responsibility to provide leadership for their profession and to call a halt to the excesses seen in many frenzies. Occasionally, senior reporters and columnists have indeed helped to restore civility and balance to coverage. For instance, James J. Kilpatrick's well-reasoned criticism of the press's Billygate antics (concerning the dubious antics of President Carter's brother, Billy) is credited with ending the out-of-control spiral of competitive "wiggle" stories. "He basically said, 'What is all this shit? I've been reading it and reading it, and I can't see that you've got anything that matters.' And he clearly had the effect of toning down the coverage," remembers an approving David Broder. Broder himself has often served as an ethicist in the press corps, never hesitating to criticize press practices or inadequacies. Several syndicated columnists, including Ellen Goodman of the *Boston Globe* and Mike Royko of the *Chicago Tribune*, lambasted the *New York Times* for its intrusive 1988 candidate questionnaire, encouraging the newspaper to take a second look and eventually withdraw it. But these internal circuit breakers occur all too seldom during political seasons, partly because of the intensity of the competition but also because journalism is a special animal. In just about all professions the individuals generally acknowledged to be the leading lights are E. F. Huttons — when they speak, others listen and usually follow their precepts and heed their warnings. But in journalism, most scribes and correspondents pride themselves on their independence and contrariness. "No one is the keeper of the conscience of journalism," insists the *Washington Post*'s Bob Woodward, and, adds PBS's Paul Duke, "Reporters tend to say 'screw you' to anyone who tries to set standards for the whole business." Appearance also matters: "It can look like sour grapes, that because you got beaten you're whining about 'excesses' and trying to knock down the other guy's story," explains CNN's Brooks Jackson.

Raising Standards

Much of this study has focused on the need to raise standards in many specific respects: resisting the reporting of rumors; preserving areas of legitimate privacy for public officials; treating all candidates alike; decreasing sensationalism, wiggle disclosures, and lowest-common-denominator journalism; and so on. But the job of elevating press standards is a broader mission than these items suggest, encompassing journalists' attitudes, their methods of operation, and the substance of their coverage.

Newspeople could probably induce officials to give better answers to legitimate questions, and preserve more public tolerance in the process, if their cynicism could be dampened and their civility augmented. First of all, as ABC's Brit Hume observes, "We need to be unyieldingly skeptical but ought to draw back from the relentless cynicism we've engaged in recently." Mark Twain may have been correct when he opined, "The only way for a newspaperman to look at a politician is down," but a journalist also needs to acknowledge that not everything a politician does is completely self-interested and manipulative; politicians, like the rest of us, are mainly destined for purgatory, not heaven or hell. David Broder has even proposed that the press balance its attacks on officeholders by regularly saluting those who serve well.[6] Few reporters will probably ever share Cokie Roberts's generosity of spirit toward politicians ("I see most of them as hardworking, underpaid public servants"), but then both Roberts's father and mother have served in Congress. And not many in the new school of journalism seem to share the sentiments of the gregarious Jack Germond, who admits that he enjoys the social company of carousing pols and who declares: "I like most politicians and I'm willing to forgive them the things they do, just as they forgive us." But all journalists might want to take to heart the delightful slogan of one of their most marvelous institutions, the Gridiron Club: "Singe but never burn." Since 1885 the annual Gridiron dinner has good-naturedly roasted presidents and press alike, relaxing the tensions that inevitably exist between reporters and politicians. A little of the Gridiron spirit of tolerance, and its underlying premise that government and press are wary adversaries but not bitter enemies, could be usefully applied to coverage the year round. So could an effort to restore more of a "sense of decorum and propriety in reporting — not stuffiness but civility," as Howell Raines of the *New York Times* described the goal. Civility means not asking whether Gary and Lee Hart kissed on the lips, not calling individuals involved in a frenzy at 2 A.M. (as one DePauw University professor experienced in the midst of Dan Quayle's plagiarism controversy), and not screaming impertinent questions at a beleaguered official. Granted, many reporters shout because they are frustrated and lack access, but the *Los Angeles Times*'s Jack Nelson still sees this kind of behavior as counterproductive: "I've always felt that members of the press who shout and make asses of themselves . . . don't do themselves any good, don't elicit information, and make the public weary and leery of the press." And one other old-fashioned but preferable standard to which modern journalists might return is a more rigid separation and labeling of commentary and straight, factual reporting. "There's too much spinning of stories to one side or the other, too great a selectivity in the presentation of the facts in this post-Watergate group," insists veteran Jerry terHorst. "Many of these young journalists want to change the world by starting on page one, which is supposed to be straight news." NBC News's John Chancellor agreed and recalled a recent conversation with former NBC News executive Tom Pettit "about why our correspondents following the presidential campaign always had to end their pieces with some snippy little piece of criticism":

I said, "Pettit, why the hell can't they just come on and say, 'Tomorrow the candidate goes to Cleveland,'" and Pettit replied, "Because with this generation, it would come out, 'Tomorrow the candidate goes to Cleveland — and no one knows why.'"

When standards fall, viewers are treated to a larger dose of soft news and even "recreations" of real-life events. The titillating topics that form the core of many feeding frenzies also move to center stage. Unlike the complex issues that require sophistication and study to report, most frenzies are a news entertainer's delight, featuring the sensationalistic simplicity on which trash TV thrives. When likability matters more than sound journalism, young television reporters are given the wrong message and encouraged to embrace the wrong values. "The danger is in the signals sent to journalism school graduates, that what matters is not an agile brain but a pretty face, not straight-ahead, hardnosed reporting, but getting onscreen and making people sweat like Diane Sawyer or Connie Chung," says Wyatt Andrews. When form matters more than substance, big-salary personalities substitute for streetwise reporters and foreign bureaus. One "deeply worried" longtime CBS correspondent rightly bemoans the loss of fourteen of twenty-eight CBS Washington bureau positions over the decades of his employment, while the news division's money was drained to "support multimillion dollar salaries and find vehicles [that is, shows] for the news 'stars' we hired." When the Q-rating—the networks' polling measurement of the popularity of on-air personalities—is king and news personnel become the focus of public relations management, the First Amendment becomes a shell, its raison d'être destroyed since reporters fear to raise unpleasant hard news subjects. "The main problem with star journalism is that it leads to timidity in reporters," admits CBS News executive producer Tom Bettag. "The stars have to avoid controversy, which is usually bad for ratings."

There may be no quick fix to "star journalism" in the age of tight corporate control and fierce competition for a dwindling audience market share. But there are some acceptable stopgap solutions, the most effective of which is self-denial and a simple stiffening of spines among concerned anchors and reporters. CNN's Bernard Shaw has shown the way, actively rejecting "the cult of personality," as he describes it, that surrounds many of his competitors. Shaw politely refuses autograph requests and late-night show invitations alike because, "I'm not an entertainer, I'm not a star, and I greatly resent what's happening to this profession." Roger Mudd, formerly of CBS and now of PBS, is even more emphatic about "the responsibility of well placed journalists to say no":

I'm bewildered, disheartened and crushed that men and women with great talent and integrity would find it necessary to demean the profession to the extent of participating in a comedy show. The idea that being on the air several nights a week in this marvelous six-thirty P.M. position is not enough, that you must match wits with David Letterman and Johnny Carson, that you must reveal a warm side of yourself, a nonprofessional side—it's everything I believe in upside down.

Another positive step to raise standards and counteract celebrity journalism would be to curtail some journalists' propensity to cash in on
their stardom. News organizations ought to forbid their employees from
receiving honoraria (speaking fees) over a set amount. Currently, some
of the networks' and newspapers' hottest properties are receiving ten
thousand to twenty-five thousand dollars, and occasionally up to an incredible fifty thousand dollars per appearance. Given the enormous potential
for conflict of interest here — reporters may cover many of the interests
represented by the sponsoring groups — and in order to build public confidence in their public-service profession, superstar journalists ought to
be willing to make this sacrifice; with their regular take-home pay, few
will need to apply for public assistance. And there is also the question of
hypocrisy, the human foible that newspeople use to justify so many feeding
frenzies. Like most media outlets, the *Washington Post* has strongly attacked
public officials' acceptance of honoraria. Comments *Post* ombudsman
Richard Harwood:

We run a chart . . . once a week in the paper about the honoraria that congressmen
get. If you ever ran a chart about the honoraria that is being collected in this
newsroom, it would knock your eyes out. And there are a lot of people in
Washington who make so much money talking to these lobbies and special interest
groups that they would quit their jobs before they would give up their speaking
fees.

At the very least, and whether or not large fees are banned, every news
organization should regularly require its reporters to disclose fully their
speaking fees and sources of income, and the disclosures should be available
for public inspection.

Remedies from the Candidate's Perspective

While the remedies suggested here for press excesses would no doubt
delight most politicians, candidates and officeholders can make their own
contributions toward ending the worst aspects of feeding frenzies. Naturally, realistic remedies on the candidate's side of the equation must make
political sense. In nature some animals avoid becoming frenzy victims by
fleeing or freezing, options not practical for pols fixed clearly in the sights
of deadly aimed television cameras. Equally impractical today is an attempt
to ignore whatever charges have been made. This used to be the standard
political advice doled out by grizzled veterans: For example, in 1962
Richard Nixon wrote, "The man in political life must come to expect
the smear and to know that, generally, the best thing to do about it is

ignore it — and hope that it will fade away."[7] But in the modern age of negative attack politics, to make no defense when charges fly is a ticket to political oblivion. As Gary Hart discovered in 1984 about his name change, age, and so on, the questions cannot be brushed off and will be raised continuously until credible answers are given. Of course, Hart suffered from a poor relationship with many in the traveling press corps, but even when most journalists personally like a candidate (Gerald Ford and Geraldine Ferraro are examples), good press relations no longer carry a candidate very far when a frenzy hits. The press is determined not to be coopted, as in the days of FDR and JFK, and appeals for mercy generally (and often appropriately) fall on deaf ears. Building up chits with the press through favors and good relations used to provide some insulation when disaster struck. "You built up deposits in a press bank account so you could draw down in times of trouble; now you can never make enough deposits because at any time a mega-withdrawal, a frenzy, can take place," said Lee Atwater.

The most rational, logical solution for candidates is to avoid the sins and circumstances that spawn frenzies. "When one of my congressional candidates asks me about the rules today, I tell him that if he's married and is going to have his wife and six-year-old daughter sitting on his knee in the brochure, he'd better not be fucking his secretary," explains Republican operative John Buckley. *U.S. News & World Report*'s Michael Barone goes beyond advising the avoidance of hypocrisy: "If you want sex, get married and stick to your wife. If you're unmarried, don't have sex." These are excellent suggestions, as are the Ten Commandments, but history suggests that such perfection is also a bit contrary to human nature. Given the nearly certain assumption that flesh-and-blood candidates will falter on the way to the Promised Land, the next-best option is to be prepared for the inevitable stumbles. Democrat Bruce Babbitt's 1988 campaign was certainly ready for the drug frenzy that briefly enveloped the presidential field. More than a year earlier, during a long bicycle trip with the candidate and his wife across Iowa, Babbitt's press secretary, Michael McCurry, sounded out his boss on all potential past foibles. Says McCurry: "In this new age the first thing the press secretary to a presidential candidate should do is to have a long, exhaustive, up-close and personal interview with the candidate." Babbitt frankly confessed his 1960s marijuana experimentation, saving time and preventing mixed signals when the real onslaught began many months later. As it happened, after discussions with his campaign advisers, Babbitt took a direct but offhand approach. While on an airplane, Babbitt approached a *Washington Post* reporter, Maralee Schwartz, and teased, "I hear the subject of the day is marijuana. What about it, Maralee, have you ever used it?" Schwartz said yes, then logically turned the question on Babbitt, who casually admitted his past. This matter-of-fact method of revelation helped to reinforce the press corps' belief that it was "no big deal," as McCurry suggested.

Most candidates and their staffs try to prepare for conceivable eventualities, especially when they have some hint of a future crisis. As reviewed, the Bush-Quayle camp went into high gear when the first rumblings of prisoner Brett Kimberlin's allegations of Quayle's marijuana use reached them. Former Reagan White House counsel Fred Fielding interviewed, Quayle extensively about the matter, and staff aide Mark Goodin compiled a thick file on Kimberlin's sordid criminal record to share with inquiring reporters. "I wanted to appeal to reporters' better instincts, to make sure they understood what kind of source they actually had here," explained Goodin. When a campaign team has more leisure — between election cycles — it often tries to short-circuit the bad aspects of the candidate's subtext or to clean up worrisome remnants of past frenzies, although such efforts can backfire. Senator Joe Biden, running for reelection in 1990, insisted during a C-SPAN interview that he had "never plagiarized in law school," a conclusion seemingly supported by the *Wilmington* (Delaware) *News Journal*'s widely circulated account of a probe into the Biden matter by the Delaware Supreme Court's Board of Professional Responsibility. As it turned out, however, the board had not judged the act of plagiarism at all; rather, it had merely exonerated Biden's decision not to disclose the incident on his application to practice law, an important distinction the *News Journal* had failed to make clear. To Biden's renewed embarrassment, the plagiarism controversy again found its way into the headlines.[8]

What is often surprising is how frequently candidates do not learn the plainest lessons taught by past frenzies. After Spiro Agnew, Thomas Eagleton, and Geraldine Ferraro, one might have thought a presidential nominee would not have selected a little-known, nationally untested running mate, but George Bush picked Dan Quayle anyway. At least Bush avoided McGovern's compounding error; when Quayle looked his shakiest in the hours after his nomination, Bush specifically refused to back him "1,000 percent," as McGovern had done for Eagleton. Instead, Bush said only that he was "comfortable" with Quayle "at this point," but if "evidence of wrongdoing" were presented, "I'd be happy to consider it."[9] By contrast, Gary Hart apparently drew no lessons at all from his own 1984 frenzy. A wise politician is always acutely aware of the press's subtext about him and wary of taking actions that confirm the undesirable elements of it; Hart ignored many warnings and recklessly validated his own womanizing subtext by means of Donna Rice in 1987. Moreover, to this day he denies that the subtext even existed. In a letter to this author, Hart wrote: "Clearly I disagree with your . . . suggestion that in my case there was something 'strange' about me, or that I was 'a playboy.' If these were such well known facts in the minds of the press, they seem[ed] to neglect them over the better part of fifteen years of public life."[10]

Whatever the degree of preparation, when a frenzy commences, disclosure — complete and quick — is usually the best policy. Any delay in a campaign should be only for purposes of gathering the facts and double-checking to ensure accuracy, since wiggle disclosures are sometimes generated by later corrections of the record; here again, adequate preparation can be critical. The most difficult aspect of this rational remedy, at least for the campaign staff, is getting the candidate to embrace it. For instance, Michael Dukakis abruptly refused to discuss his medical records at first, despite his advisers' recommendation to the contrary, a costly error that fueled press speculation about his mental history. Often hurt and angry, a politician is more inclined to lash out or hunker down, or when actually guilty, to cover up. Yet after Watergate and Chappaquiddick, the best assumption for a campaign is the worst-case scenario: that all the relevant information will eventually come to light, that obstinacy and subterfuge can convert a two-day story into a weeks-long water-torture frenzy, and that any attempt at cover-up will be potentially disastrous.

By contrast, full and even excessive disclosures helped to end frenzies as diverse as Ferraro's finances and Nixon's secret fund. Granted, disclosure does not always work, especially if the root problems are too serious (as with Eagleton) or too juicy (Jack Kemp's "gay" rumor). And disclosure can come too late to be of much assistance.

Sometimes an apology is attached to full disclosure, and contrition — as an act of uncharacteristic humility — usually assists a pol in the effort to move beyond a problem. It is a more effective tactic when coupled with plausible efforts to duck full responsibility for the controversy. Thus Michael Dukakis expressed sorrow for the "attack video" but shifted blame to his staff; many candidates have ascribed drug use to the foolhardiness of youth; and after his cocaine bust Mayor Marion Barry portrayed himself the victim of entrapment and disease, attributing his many mistakes to an uncontrollable passion that deprived him of free will. Throughout his frenzy-dotted career, Barry perfected a new type of apology: He insisted on his innocence after each new incident but simultaneously promised never to do it again, in the process turning over enough new leaves to defoliate a forest. At least Barry recognized that some sort of contrived repentance was necessary. Gerald Ford let his pride and stubbornness prevent him from acknowledging any error after his "free Poland" gaffe in 1976.

Most politicians are "take charge" individuals by nature, so they tend to judge the remedies suggested so far as too defensive. Candidates prefer to seize the offensive, as Richard Nixon did in the famed "Checkers" televised address on September 23, 1952. Ted Kennedy employed a similar appeal to Massachusetts voters a week after Chappaquiddick, on July 25, 1969, and a study by Professors Michael J. Robinson and Philip M. Burgess demonstrated that it was indeed effective in regaining support lost on account of the accident.[11] Other recent candidates, including Thomas Eagleton, Gary Hart, and Dan Quayle, considered but rejected such an approach, in part because of the press's increased (and warranted) propensity to analyze such dramatic appeals instantly and critically. Imagine, for instance, what journalists would do today with Nixon's "Checkers" fib that his wife Pat "was born on St. Patrick's Day" — part of a passage in which Nixon argued that he and his wife were not quitters because "the Irish never quit."

Politicians can take the offensive in other ways today. Their consultants and advisers go on "spin patrol," trying to focus the press and public opinion on aspects of a frenzy that are most favorable to their candidate. Thus, instead of asking why Dan Quayle avoided Vietnam combat, his camp framed the debate as one where Quayle's critics were questioning the patriotism of those who honorably served in the National Guard instead of fleeing to Canada or burning their draft cards. Surrogates can add spark to a candidate's counteroffensive, particularly spouses when a husband's fidelity is under attack.

The most satisfying form of counteroffensive for a politician caught in a frenzy is a direct assault on the news media even though any attempt to make the press the issue is fraught with peril. It does not work if you have already alienated the voters. More important, earning the enmity of people who buy ink by the barrel and normally have the last word is rash. "The only time it is truly safe to bash the media is if you are visibly wronged," said Lee Atwater, "and even then you ought to shoot back in as general a way as possible, never going after journalists by name."

The Voter's Contribution

It is entirely appropriate that we conclude our discussion of feeding frenzies by turning to the foundation of any representative democracy, the electorate. For in any system such as ours, the standards under which the political players and reporters operate are ultimately set by the voters collectively. Just as citizens are legitimately entitled to claim credit for the accomplishments of the society they sustain, they also must bear responsibility for the problems that exist in it. Concerning feeding frenzies, the predispositions and preferences of voters directly and indirectly influence frenzy development and denouement in three ways:

1. *Public interest or disinterest*[12]: Public opinion plays a role in regulating the fate of frenzies. If the public chooses to tune out the controversy, or expresses anger about the press's conduct, then the story will gradually be buried deeper in the back pages and new revelations will have less impact. After all, news delivery is a business that depends on public subscription, and however much they take to heart their First Amendment obligations, media organizations will generally not seek to alienate their viewers and readers for a lengthy period.

2. *Choice of outlets and information*: In any given frenzy, and in many respects overall, some media outlets will be more responsible and less excessive than others. To the extent that people choose to watch broadcasts and read publications with higher standards, the best in journalism is encouraged — and the reverse is also true. CBS's Dan Rather, in a radio tribute to his late, respected colleague Robert Schakne, noted that, "The feel-good alleged news correspondents, the good-news pretenders, are a dime a dozen and on every station. They're everywhere now. . . . One of the reasons, dear listener, is that not enough of you care."[13] This is not unrelated to the crisis of citizen education in the United States. One of the century's most outstanding political scientists, V. O. Key, was surely correct when he wrote, "voters are not fools"[14]; they understand their basic interests and generally vote accordingly, and therefore rationally, at the polls. But if not foolish, the electorate is ill informed. The knowledge by which voters determine their interests is paltry, their attention to political subjects is generally scant, and their devotion to quality newspapers — especially among the young — has declined sharply.

3. *Public attitudes about politics*: The voters' cynicism about politics is at least equal to, and reinforces, journalists' similar malady. All too ready to believe any charge of corruption or moral turpitude against a politician, the public is often as unwilling as the press to view candidates and office-holders in a balanced way, with vices weighed against virtues. Perhaps it is also a matter of hypocrisy, that maligned transgression that both press and public seem so unwilling to overlook in politicians. The public refuses to take Jesus's advice — "judge not that ye be not judged" — because they apparently do not fear judgment, and believe themselves to be far superior to the equally human class of politicians. One of the most humorous bits

of public opinion data ever gathered was the response to the following question: "Is there anything in your past that you think might prevent you from holding a high government office?" Even after preceding queries had made clear that disqualifying offenses included drug use, alcohol abuse, extramarital affairs, cheating on taxes, and so on, 80 percent answered "no."[15] Heaven must be a far larger place than anyone has imagined.

It follows, then, that the remedies from the voters' perspective for the excesses of frenzies must emphasize a dramatic improvement in the quantity and quality of civic knowledge. While individuals can accomplish this on their own, the schools must take the lead, stressing from kindergarten through college the study of current events, American government, and political history. A better informed citizenry will more wisely evaluate and select media outlets, and care more about issue substance and less about frenzy sensationalism. A little more trust and tolerance and a bit less cynicism and hypocrisy about politics and politicians is also warranted. The public would also do well to support strengthening the political party system in the United States since one root cause of frenzies has been the decline of the parties. The press has attempted to substitute its "character issue" screening for the peer review once provided by party leaders, but it is poorly suited for the task. Journalist Walter Lippmann understood as few seem to do today that the press is *not* the equivalent of parties — the former being a disjointed mass of separately run businesses collectively charged with checking power, the latter being the fundamental building blocks of democracy with the responsibility for organizing power and mobilizing public opinion. As Lippmann explained it in 1922:

The press is no substitute for institutions. It is like the beam of a searchlight that moves restlessly about, bringing one episode and then another out of darkness into vision. Men cannot do the work of the world by this light alone. They cannot govern society by episodes, incidents, and interruptions.[16]

When all is said and done on this subject, it is a good bet that more will be said than done. "The press is a business, and it is almost never going to do things purely out of altruism," noted Bill Plante of CBS News. Nor can the news-gathering process, chaotic by nature, become fully orderly, nor should any measure of press freedom be sacrificed to tame or prevent the excesses that have concerned us in this volume. "As long as America continues to be a free country, you will have a lot of bad journalists writing a lot of garbage," declares Ted Koppel. But it would be tragic to see the prediction of Koppel's ABC colleague, Brit Hume, come true: "My guess is that it will take some monstrous episode which is so bad and so obviously excessive that the press is forced to step back."

As I have learned in the course of interviewing, good journalists do not shrink from examining their profession's weaknesses; to the contrary, they welcome it as an opportunity to improve the quality of reporting as well as to bolster public confidence in their craft. It is toward the fulfillment of these vital twin goals that the suggestions offered in this study have been made. "The duty of the press is to print the news and to raise hell," says Tom Brokaw, and that will never change. But Roger Mudd added an essential qualifier: "We are not in the business to protect public officials, but we are in the business to be fair to them." Feeding frenzies have included substantial elements of unfairness not just to candidates but to the general public and to the high standards good journalists hold dear. Alexis de Tocqueville celebrated news organizations because "they maintain civilization."[17] As press conduct during feeding frenzies has proved repeatedly, they can also decivilize politics. The legions of responsible and dedicated newsmen and -women must work to moderate the excesses that destroy confidence in their profession and threaten support for press freedoms. Journalists and journalism must feed less at frenzies and more at the table of fairness and civility.

NOTES

CHAPTER ONE Inquisition, American Style

1. Quoted by Richard E. Cohen, "Fall from Power," *National Journal* 21 (August 19, 1989): 2086.

2. Quoted by Eleanor Randolph, "'Quayle Hunt' Turns News Media Into Target for Angry Public," *Washington Post*, August 25, 1988, A10.

3. From a random-sample telephone survey of 1,000 adults nationwide conducted by Yankelovich Clancy Shulman for *Time* and CNN, October 15–17, 1990. The exact wording of the question was, "Do you think that the media focus on the most important issues or do they spend too much time focusing on things that are irrelevant, like candidates' personal lives?" About 17 percent responded "the most important issues" while 5 percent were undecided.

4. William Safire, "Stop Keyhole Journalism," *New York Times*, May 11, 1987, A17.

5. Russell Baker, "All Shall Be Disclosed," *New York Times*, May 12, 1987, A31.

6. The "Saturday Night Live" television show concocted just such a skit at the height of the 1988 presidential campaign's preseason preliminaries, with Democratic candidate Bruce Babbitt playing the role.

7. Quoted in Michael Wines, "In Bed With the Press," *Washington Journalism Review* 9 (September 1987): 17.

8. From a speech delivered at Yale University on November 11, 1987.

9. Quoted by Carol Matlack, "Crossing the Line?" *National Journal* 21 (March 25, 1989): 724–29.

10. The word *frenzy* is derived from the Greek *phrenitis*, meaning a temporary madness or delirium.

11. Michael J. Robinson, "The Media in 1980: Was the Message the Message?", in Austin Ranney, ed., *The American Elections of 1980* (Washington, D.C.: American Enterprise Institute, 1981), p. 191.

CHAPTER TWO   The Press of Yesteryear

1. From *Democracy in America*, vol. 1 (New York: Vintage, 1945), p. 194.

2. See Mitchell Stephens, *A History of News: From the Drum to the Satellite* (New York: Viking, 1989), p. 2.

3. Charles Press and Kenneth VerBurg, *American Politicians and Journalists* (Glenview, Ill.: Scott, Foresman, 1988), pp. 8–10.

4. Press and VerBurg, *American Politicians*, pp. 36–39.

5. Doris A. Graber, *Mass Media and American Politics*, 3rd ed. (Washington, D.C.: Congressional Quarterly Press, 1989), p. 12.

6. See Thomas C. Leonard, *The Power of the Press: The Birth of American Political Reporting* (New York: Oxford University Press, 1986), chap. 7.

7. Louis D. Brandeis and Samuel D. Warren, "The Right to Privacy," *Harvard Law Review* 4 (December 15, 1890): 196.

8. Nan Britton, *The President's Daughter* (New York: Elizabeth Ann Guild, Inc., 1927).

9. Press and VerBurg, *American Politicians*, p. 24.

10. Stephen Bates, *If No News, Send Rumors* (New York: St. Martin's, 1989), p. 98.

11. Gary Wills, *The Kennedy Imprisonment* (Boston: Atlantic Monthly, Little Brown, 1981), p. 54.

12. Stern is now deceased; this is based on the reminiscence of Lardner alone. The original article by Stern was subtly entitled "Probers Doubt Kennedy Knew of Poison Plot Against Castro," *Washington Post*, November 16, 1975, A6.

13. William Safire, "The President's Friend," *New York Times*, December 15, 1975, A31.

14. See Judith Campbell Exner, *My Story* (as told to Ovid Demaris) (New York: Grove, 1977).

15. C. David Heymann, *A Woman Named Jackie* (New York: Lyle Stuart, 1989), pp. 278–89. See also pp. 231–35.

16. Ibid., pp. 290–92.

17. Bates, *If No News*, p. 146.

18. Both of these incidents were related by John Mashek of the *Boston Globe*.

19. J. F. terHorst et al., *The Flying White House: The Story of Air Force One* (New York: Bantam, 1979), pp. 206–8.

20. Bates, *If No News*, pp. 101–2.

21. See Shelley Ross, *Fall from Grace: Sex, Scandal, and Corruption in American Politics from 1702 to the Present* (New York: Ballantine, 1988), pp. 191–93.

22. This was the fundamental conclusion of Shanto Iyengar and Donald R. Kinder, *News That Matters* (Chicago: University of Chicago Press, 1987).

CHAPTER THREE   The Boys in the Bush

1. John and Mary R. Markle Foundation, *Report of the Commission on the Media and the Electorate: Key Findings* (New York: Markle Foundation, May 1990), pp. 16–18.

2. S. Robert Lichter, Stanley Rothman, and Linda S. Lichter, *The Media Elite* (Bethesda, Md.: Adler and Adler, 1986).

3. Quoted in "Dagmar Celeste Calls Governor Good Mate," Cleveland *Plain Dealer* (AP dispatch), June 10, 1987, B10.

4. Quoted in John Stacks and David Beckwith, "More Hurt Than Angry," *Time* 124 (September 3, 1984): 21.

5. Timothy Crouse, *The Boys on the Bus* (New York: Ballantine Books, 1972), p. 7.

6. Michael Cornfield and David Yalof, "Innocent by Reason of Analogy: How the Watergate Analogy Served Both Reagan and the Press During the Iran-Contra Affair," *Corruption and Reform* 3 (1988): 185–206.

7. Gary Hart, "Why Our Media Miss the Message," *Washington Post*, December 20, 1987, C4.

8. American Society of Newspaper Editors, *The Changing Face of the Newsroom*, (Washington, D.C.: ASNE, May 1989) pp. 27–28; and figures supplied by the Gannett Foundation drawn from ongoing research conducted by Jean Gaddy Wilson of the University of Missouri.

9. Suzannah Lessard, "The Issue Was Women," *Newsweek* 109 (May 18, 1987): 32, 34.

10. The author wishes to acknowledge the invaluable counsel and editorial assistance provided by Professor Scott Matheson of the University of Utah School of Law in preparing this section.

11. Randall Bezanson, Gilbert Cranberg, and John Soloski, *Libel Law and the Press* (New York: Free Press, 1987), p. 122, 201.

12. Rodney Smolla, *Suing the Press* (New York: Oxford University Press, 1986), p. 16.

13. Bezanson, Cranberg, and Soloski, *Libel Law and the Press*, p. 8.

14. Laurence I. Barrett, "Orator for the Next Generation: Does Joe Biden Talk Too Much?" *Time* 129 (June 22, 1987): 24–25.

15. Douglas A. Harbrecht, "Is Joe Biden More Than 'Just A Speech'?" *Business Week* 2991 (March 30, 1987): 59–60.

16. "More Urge Than Surge," *The Economist* 303 (June 13, 1987): 41–42.

17. This anecdote was related by CBS News's Eric Engberg.

18. Howard Fineman, "Gary Hart: A Candidate In Search of Himself," *Newsweek* 109 (April 13, 1987): 25–27. McEvoy later claimed the quote was "hypothetical" and off the record; Fineman insists it was an on-the-record remark.

19. Quoted in David R. Runkel, *Campaign for President: The Managers Look at '88* (Dover, Mass.: Auburn House, 1988), p. 207.

20. Times-Mirror Center for the People and the Press, "The People and the Press, Part 5: Public Attitudes Toward News Organizations," (Washington, D.C.: Times-Mirror Corporation, 1986–89) based on an in-person random-sample survey of 1,507 adult Americans, conducted by the Gallup organization between August 9–28, 1989 (margin of error: plus or minus 3 percent).

21. See Sig Mickelson, *The Electric Mirror: Politics in an Age of Network Television* (New York: Dodd, Mead, 1972), pp. 4–5, 164–67.

22. Patrick J. Buchanan, "Pundit vs. 'Re-Pundit' on Writers' Rights and Reasons," *Richmond Times-Dispatch*, December 29, 1988, A14.

23. See Mark Hertsgaard, *On Bended Knee: The Press and the Reagan Presidency* (New York: Farrar, Straus, & Giroux, 1988).

24. Quoted in *Hotline* 2 (January 16, 1989): 1.

25. Jody Powell, *The Other Side of the Story* (New York: William Morrow, 1984), p. 108.

26. As quoted in Howard Kurtz, "Networks Stressed the Negative in Comments About Bush, Study Finds," *Washington Post*, November 15, 1992, A7.

27. As quoted in *National Journal* 24 (October 3, 1992): 2247.

28. Joann Byrd, "73 Days of Tilt," *Washington Post*, November 8, 1992, C6.

29. Center for Media and Public Affairs, "The Boom in Gloom," *Media Monitor* 6 (October 1992): 1–3. The time period covered by the study was July through September 1992.

30. David Weaver and G. Cleveland Wilhoit, *The American Journalist in the 1990s* (New York: The Freedom Forum, 1992), pp. 6–7.

31. As quoted in The Freedom Forum Media Studies Center, *The Homestretch: New Politics, New Media. New Voters?* (New York: The Freedom Forum, Columbia University, October 1992): 49–50.

CHAPTER FOUR   A Thousand Points of Gossip

1. E. J. Dionne, "Gary Hart: The Elusive Front Runner," *New York Times Magazine*, May 3, 1987, p. 28.

2. LBJ biographer Doris Kearns Goodwin discovered the discrepancy and discusses it in the American Press Institute, *Covering the Candidates: Roles and Responsibilities of the Press* (Reston, Va.: American Press Institute, 1987), pp. 47–48.

3. Andrew Rosenthal, "Dukakis Releases Medical Details to Stop Rumors on Mental Health," *New York Times*, August 4, 1988, A1, D20.

4. Times-Mirror Center for the People and the Press, "The People and the Press, Parts 1 through 5" (Washington, D.C.: Times-Mirror Corporation, 1986–89).

5. From the Harris poll, a telephone random-sample survey of 1,253 adults conducted nationwide from April 19–23, 1989, with a margin of error of plus or minus 3 percent.

6. CBS News/*New York Times* telephone random-sample survey of 589 adults nationwide conducted on November 8, 1987.

7. Random-sample telephone survey of 589 adults conducted November 8, 1987, with a margin of error of plus or minus 4 percent.

8. Bill Peterson, "Hart Falls Into a Cross-Country Campaign Trap," *Washington Post*, May 27, 1984, A5.

9. Center for Media and Public Affairs, "Clinton's the One," *Media Monitor* 6 (November 1992): 2. The average sound bite was 9.8 seconds in 1988, and 42.3 seconds in 1968.

10. Voters and pundits accounted for the remaining 17 percent of the time. Center for Media and Public Affairs, "Clinton's the One," p.2.

11. The source of each quotation is as follows: Margaret Warner (CNN's "The Capital Gang," February 29, 1992), John McLaughlin ("The McLaughlin Group," April 12, 1992), Ed Rollins ("Nightline," January 27, 1992), and Robert Novak ("The Capital Gang," February 15, 1992 and March 3, 1992).

12. Center for Media and Public Affairs, "Clinton's the One," pp. 2–3.

13. *Ibid.* In the 1992 general election there were 258 horserace stories and 233 issue segments; in 1988, 145 horserace stories and 232 issue segments.

14. The Freedom Forum, *The Finish Line*, pp. 13–16, 55–59, 129–30, 147–48.

CHAPTER FIVE   Rumor and Excess

1. From the "700 Club" of June 27, 1989, Christian Broadcasting Network, as quoted in *Hotline* 2 (June 28, 1989): 1.

2. Eleanor Randolph, "Ferraro Emerges From 'Full-Court Press' in Media's Good Graces," *Washington Post*, August 23, 1984, A4.

3. As quoted in W. Lance Bennett, *News: The Politics of Illusion* (New York: Longman, 1983), p. 64.

4. Mark Stencel originally wrote a first draft of parts of this section on Kemp.

5. Lou Cannon, *Reagan* (New York: G. P. Putnam's Sons, 1982), pp. 132–38.

6. Martin Tolchin, "Jack Kemp's Bootleg Run to the Right," *Esquire* (October 24, 1978), pp. 58–69 at p. 67.

7. Rowland Evans and Robert Novak, "Ugly Political Rumors," *Washington Post*, December 29, 1978, A15.

8. Myron S. Waldman, "Kemp, Asked Again, Says No Again," New York *Newsday*, March 14, 1986, 31.

9. Paul Taylor, "Asking Gary Hart the Question He Asked For," *New York Times* (letter to the editor), May 22, 1987, A30.

10. William Dixon, as quoted in an AP dispatch from Boston on July 14, 1987.

11. Rowland Evans and Robert Novak, "Behind Those Dukakis Rumors," *Washington Post*, August 8, 1988, A13.

12. Gerald M. Boyd, "Doctor Describes Bush As 'Active and Healthy,'" *New York Times*, August 6, 1988, A7.

13. The network Quayle coverage on evening news shows, August 18–27, 1988, was compiled by Leslie Greenwald from Vanderbilt University's *Television News Index and Abstracts* (Nashville, Tenn.: Vanderbilt Television News Archive, August 1988).

14. David Rogers and Jeffrey H. Birnbaum, "Quayle Family Contacts Helped Him Avoid Draft," *Wall Street Journal*, August 19, 1988, 38.

15. Jill Abramson and James B. Stewart, "Quayle Initially Failed a Major Exam at DePauw, Former School Official Says," *Wall Street Journal*, August 23, 1988, 54.

16. The interview was conducted on Wednesday evening, August 17, 1989.

17. Douglas Frantz, "Hypnosis: 'Parlor trick' Entrances the Courts," *Chicago Tribune*, February 7, 1982, A6.

18. Carried in an Associated Press dispatch and published in many newspapers on May 22, 1992.

19. Barbara Dafoe Whitehead, "Dan Quayle Was Right," *The Atlantic* 271 (April 1993): 47–84.

20. The school principal later insisted that the flash card had been prepared not by one of his teachers but by another Trentonite who participated in an after-school program.

21. Evelyn Nieves, "Spelling by Quayle (That's With an E)," *New York Times*, June 17, 1992, A23.

22. Thomas C. Palmer, Jr., "Reputation for bias seems well earned," p. 68.

23. Christopher Lydon, "Sex, War, and Death," *Columbia Journalism Review* 29 (May/June 1992): 58.

24. See data and discussion in Martha FitzSimon, "What the Polls Say About Campaign Coverage," *Covering the Presidential Primaries* (New York: The Freedom Forum Media Studies Center, June 1992), pp. 51–61, especially pp. 53–55, 58.

25. See data in "Politicians and Privacy," *The CQ Researcher* 2 (April 17, 1992): 341.

26. See the *Hotline* 5 (July 14, 1992): 19.

27. Michael Isikoff, "Clinton Team Works to Deflect Allegations on Nominee's Private Life," *Washington Post*, July 26, 1992, A18. Also see the *Hotline* 5 (July 20, 1992): 15.

28. Carried in an Associated Press dispatch and printed widely on October 17, 1992.

29. Dan Balz, "Miscalculations Mark Clinton's Attempt to Settle Draft Record Issue," *Washington Post*, September 8, 1992, A12.

30. Comment by Nelson on CNN's "Reliable Sources," September 19, 1992.

31. Quoted in Balz, "Miscalculations."

32. Published Monday, October 5, 1992 on A1.

33. *Hotline* 6 (October 8, 1992): 5.

34. The following article summarizes what was known about the Clinton passport search *prior* to the election: Bill Turque, "The Clinton File Mystery Grows," *Newsweek* 119 (November 2, 1992): 49. After the election the improper nature of the search became fully apparent, and two high-ranking Bush administration staffers in the State Department were dismissed or demoted. See Eric Schmitt, "Passport Search Brings Dismissal," *New York Times*, November 11, 1992, A1, D19; and David Johnston, "Prosecutor Named to Review Search of Files on Clinton," *New York Times*, December 18, 1992, A1, 34.

35. From the 1992 Christmas letter of Anthony Kenny, the Warden of Rhodes House.

36. See "Jackson Takes High Road in Open-Mike Flap," *Washington Post*, February 29, 1992, A20. CNN, NBC, and Fox networks used the videotape in news broadcasts.

37. The show, entitled, "One Day in New York," aired on April 2, 1992.

38. *Hotline* 6 (November 9, 1992): 10.

39. See *Hotline* 6 (February 17, 1993): 9.

40. Jeffrey H. Birnbaum, "President's Temper Unsettles Staffers Unused to His Ways," *Wall Street Journal*, February 17, 1993, A16.

41. David Rogers and Jill Abramson, "Under Cover: Ross Perot Takes Surveillance Tactics to Unusual Lengths," *Wall Street Journal*, June 12, 1992, A1, 6.

42. David Remnick, "H. Ross Perot — the Strengths and the Strangeness," *Washington Post*, March 29, 1992, C7.

43. Bob Woodward and John Mintz, "Perot Launched Investigations of Bush," *Washington Post*, June 21, 1992, A1, 18.

44. See William Safire, "Deep Ross," *New York Times*, June 29, 1992, A15.

45. See Steven A. Holmes, "Federal Contracts Gave Perot His Big Break," *New York Times*, May 5, 1992, A1, 28; and Michael Kelly, "Perot Under Fire: Sifting Facts and Motives," *New York Times*, June 25, 1992, A1, 27.

46. William Safire, "Old Pro Perot," *New York Times*, May 7, 1992, A27; "Perot's Plea of Hardship," May 28, 1992, A23; "Perot 'Hardship' Mystery Deepens," June 1, 1992, A17; "Perot Versus Social Security," June 15, 1992, A19; "Deep Ross," June 29, 1992, A15.

47. Marie Brenner, "Perot's Final Days," *Vanity Fair* 55 (October 1992): 74–104.

48. The segment was broadcast on September 29, 1992. See also the follow-up on September 30.

49. Thomas Toch, "All in the Perot Family," *U.S. News & World Report* 113 (October 5, 1992): 22–23; and Sidney Blumenthal, "He's Ba-a-ck!" *The New Republic* 207 (October 19, 1992): 12–15.

50. Laurence I. Barrett, "Perot-noia," *Time* 140 (November 9, 1992): 28–29. For more background see Sidney Blumenthal, "Brother Ray," *The New Republic* 207 (November 16, 1992): 18–22.

51. See survey results in *Newsweek* 119 (November 9, 1992): 23.

52. *Hotline* 6 (October 2, 1992): 5.

CHAPTER SIX   Frenzies That Weren't

1. Doris A. Graber, "Press and TV as Opinion Resources in Presidential Campaigns," *Public Opinion Quarterly* 40 (Fall 1976): 285–303, especially table 6, p. 298.

2. Quoted in American Press Institute, *Covering the Candidates: Role and Responsibilities of the Press* (Reston, Va.: American Press Institute, 1987), pp. 50–51.

3. Norman Mailer, "The Search for Carter," *Sunday Times Magazine*, September 26, 1976, 19.

4. James M. Perry, "Senator's Start," *Wall Street Journal*, March 13, 1984, A1, 20.

5. See *Hotline* 3 (June 6, 1990): 6–7 and (June 7, 1990): 7. The candidate chose not to comment, citing privacy rights.

6. S. Robert Lichter, Daniel Amundson, and Richard Noyes, *The Video Campaign: Network Coverage of the 1988 Primaries* (Washington: American Enterprise Institute, 1988).

7. See David S. Broder, *Behind the Front Page*, pp. 247–50.

8. Barbara A. Reynolds, *Jesse Jackson: The Man, the Movement, the Myth* (Chicago: Nelson-Hall, 1975) pp. 418–19.

9. See Elizabeth O. Colton, *The Jackson Phenomenon* (Garden City, N.Y.: Doubleday, 1989), pp. 82, 125–26.

10. See Priscilla Painton, "Jackson's Charisma, Principles Winning Converts, But Contradictions Linger," *Atlanta Constitution*, October 19, 1987, A1, 6.

11. The program was aired Sunday, October 11, 1987.

12. As quoted in Julia Malone, "Jackson Queried on 'Gary Hart Problem,'" *Atlanta Constitution*, June 6, 1987, A16.

13. As quoted in Colton, *The Jackson Phenomenon*, p. 126.

14. Quoted in Monica Langley, "Hart Campaign Debacle Prompts Media Debate About Whether a Politician's Sex Life Is News," *Wall Street Journal*, July 27, 1987, 44.

15. David Maraniss, "Jackson: Playing to the Camera," *Washington Post*, December 27, 1987, A8–9.

16. The American Society of Newspaper Editors compiled these figures on minority employment in 1990.

CHAPTER SEVEN   Consequences

1. Times-Mirror Center for the People and the Press, "The People and the Press, Part 5: Attitudes Toward News Organizations," conducted by the Gallup Organization in August to October, 1989. Unless otherwise noted, the survey findings cited below are from the Times-Mirror study.

2. The panelback Gallup telephone survey of 2,022 registered voters was taken November 9–10, 1988 (margin of error: plus or minus 2.5 percent).

3. Eleven percent gave another answer; Gallup random-sample telephone poll for *Newsweek* taken October 20–21, 1988, with 1,013 registered voters in the sample (margin of error: plus or minus 3 percent).

4. Random-sample telephone survey of 506 adults conducted June 1, 1989 by Yankelovich Clancy Shulman for *Time* and CNN (margin of error: plus or minus 4.5 percent).

5. Times-Mirror Center for the People and the Press, "The People and the Press, part 1: Attitudes Toward the News Media," conducted by the Gallup Organization in January 1986. See especially pp. 35–36.

6. This was a random-sample telephone survey of 2,217 adults conducted nationwide from September 14–19, 1989 (margin of error: 2.5 percent).

7. Times-Mirror Center, "The People and the Press, part 5." About 48 percent chose each contrasting statement, with 4 percent expressing no opinion.

8. A. M. Rosenthal, "Special to the Miami Herald," *New York Times*, May 7, 1987, A35.

9. Thomas E. Patterson, "The Press and Its Missed Assignment," in Michael Nelson, ed., *The Elections of 1988* (Washington, D.C.: Congressional Quarterly Press, 1989), p. 103.

10. William Boot, "Campaign '88: TV Overdoses on the Inside Dope," *Columbia Journalism Review* 27 (January/February 1989): 23.

11. T. R. Reid, "Hart Creates Mini-Flap on Campaign Day 2: Reporters Seize on Rumor-Monger Comment," *Washington Post*, April 15, 1987, A11.

12. Louis D. Brandeis and Samuel D. Warren, "The Right to Privacy," *Harvard Law Review* 4 (December 15, 1890): 196.

CHAPTER EIGHT   Remedies

1. In a letter to Thomas Seymour dated February 11, 1807.

2. See Elizabeth O. Colton, *The Jackson Phenomenon* (Garden City, N.Y.: Doubleday, 1989), pp. 23, 95, 98, 108, 143–45, 166, 173–77; and Donna Britt, "The Organizer, Up From the Chaos," *Washington Post*, October 7, 1989, C4.

3. See Priscilla Painton, "Jackson's Charisma, Principles Winning Converts, but Contradictions Linger," *Atlanta Constitution*, October 19, 1987, A1, 6.

4. Laura Sessions Stepp and Bill Dedman, "Priest Urges Boycott of Post Advertisers," *Washington Post*, September 11, 1989, E3.

5. Virgil, *Aeneid* 4.175 (New York: St. Martin's Press, 1967), p. 72.

6. Davie Broder, "Democracy and the Press," *Washington Post*, January 3, 1990, A15.

7. Richard M. Nixon, *Six Crises* (Garden City, N.Y.: Doubleday, 1962), p. 129.

8. The C-SPAN interview with Biden aired on August 19, 1990. The Wilmington newspaper article that boosted Biden was by Robin Brown, "Biden Cleared, Sets Sights on White House," *Wilmington Sunday News Journal*, May 28, 1989, A1, 8. The story was picked up by the *Washington Post* and UPI, among others, giving Biden a favorable burst of publicity as he made early preparations for his 1990 reelection campaign. The plagiarism issue first reemerged in a front-page article by George Archibald, "Biden Changes His Story, Insists 'I Never Plagiarized in Law,'" *Washington Times*, August 23, 1990, A1, 9.

9. Interview with Bush by correspondent David Beckwith in *Time* 132 (August 29, 1988): 20. Beckwith became Quayle's press secretary.

10. Letter to me dated May 1, 1989.

11. Michael J. Robinson and Philip M. Burgess, "The Edward M. Kennedy Speech: The Impact of a Prime-Time Television Appeal," *Television Quarterly* 9 (Winter 1970): 29–39.

12. I am grateful to my colleague Steven E. Finkel for his thoughts on this subject, which have influenced my own as expressed here.

13. Quoted in "Dan Rather's Lament," *Washington Journalism Review* 11 (November 1989): 52.

14. V. O. Key, Jr., *The Responsible Electorate* (Cambridge, Mass.: Harvard University Press, 1966), p. 7.

15. Random-sample telephone survey by Yankelovich Clancy Shulman for *Time* and CNN; the sample was 504 adults nationwide, taken March 2, 1989, with a margin of error of plus or minus 5 percent.

16. Walter Lippmann, *Public Opinion* (New York: Free Press, 1965), p. 19.

17. Alexis de Tocqueville, *Democracy in America*, vol. 2 (New York: Vintage, 1945), p. 119.

APPENDIX: Interviews

IN ALL, 208 individuals were interviewed during the course of research for the original volume. Following is a list of the 182 on-the-record interviews. Of the 182, 84 were conducted in person and 98 by telephone. (An asterisk denotes telephone interview). The length of the interviews varied greatly, with in-person sessions generally lasting one to three hours and telephone interviews fifteen minutes to one and one-half hours; 25 of the interviewees were interviewed more than once. Unless otherwise noted, only each individual's affiliation at the time of the interview is listed. Please see the preface to the 1991 edition for additional comments and details about the interviews. The names of off-the-record interviewees (about two dozen overall) do not appear in this listing. They provided background information only, and no direct quotations from these interviews are used in the text of this volume.

JILL ABRAMSON, *Wall Street Journal*, Washington, D.C., August 4, 1989.
*WYATT ANDREWS, CBS News, January 11, 1990.
*GEORGE ARCHIBALD, *Washington Times*, May 23, 1989.
LEE ATWATER, chairman, Republican National Committee, Front Royal, Va., January 6, 1990.
DAN BALZ, *Washington Post*, Washington, D.C., November 21, 1989.

JAN W. BARAN, general counsel, George Bush for President (1988 campaign), Washington, D.C., February 22, 1990.

FRED BARNES, *The New Republic*, Washington, D.C., August 4, 1989.

JAMES A. BARNES, *National Journal*, Washington, D.C., August 18, 1989.

MICHAEL BARONE, senior writer, *U.S. News & World Report*, Washington, D.C., September 7, 1989.

LAURENCE I. BARRETT, formerly national political correspondent and currently deputy bureau chief, *Time*, Washington, D.C., August 11, 1989, and *July 6, 1990.

*ROBERT BECKEL, Democratic political consultant, December 28, 1989.

*DAVID BECKWITH, press secretary to Vice President Dan Quayle, December 27, 1989.

TOM BETTAG, "CBS Evening News" executive producer, New York, N.Y., January 19, 1990.

CHARLES BIERBAUER, CNN, Charlottesville, Va., September 27, 1989.

*PAUL BLUSTEIN, *Washington Post*, June 5, 1989.

*KEN BODE, formerly of NBC News and currently director of the Center for Contemporary Media, DePauw University, January 12, 1990.

BENJAMIN BRADLEE, executive editor, *Washington Post*, Washington, D.C., September 15, 1989.

*MAX BRENTLEY, managing editor, *Arkansas Gazette*, September 25, 1989.

DAVID S. BRODER, *Washington Post*, Washington, D.C., August 25, 1989.

*TOM BROKAW, anchor, "NBC Nightly News," January 22, 1990.

HAL BRUNO, ABC News, Charlottesville, Va., September 28, 1989; *January 31, 1990; and *June 27, 1990.

JOHN BUCKLEY, National Republican Congressional Committee, Washington, D.C., July 7, 1989.

*KATHRYN A. BUSHKIN, 1984 press secretary to Gary Hart and currently with *U.S. News & World Report*, March 20, 1989.

*ROBERT E. CALVERT, DePauw University political science professor, August 9, 1989, and July 2, 1990.

*JOHN CHANCELLOR, NBC News, January 29, 1990.

*GARRY CLIFFORD, *People* magazine, December 29, 1989.

JOHN COCHRAN, NBC News, Charlottesville, Va., September 28, 1989.

*RICHARD COHEN, columnist, *Washington Post*, December 5, 1989, and January 2, 1990.

MILTON COLEMAN, *Washington Post*, Washington, D.C., September 22, 1989.

ANN COMPTON, ABC News, Charlottesville, Va., September 28, 1989.

*JIM CONNOR, formerly of NBC News, January 9, 1990.

*ALFREDO CORCHADO, *Wall Street Journal*, February 7, 1990.

*CONGRESSMAN PHIL CRANE (R., Ill.), 1980 Republican presidential candidate, October 25, 1989.

*BILL DEDMAN, *Washington Post*, January 16, 1990.

ANN DEVROY, *Washington Post*, Washington, D.C., October 5, 1989, and *June 15, 1990.

E. J. DIONNE, formerly *New York Times* and currently *Washington Post*, Charlottesville, Va., November 1, 1989.

SAM DONALDSON, ABC News, Washington, D.C., October 5, 1989.

LEONARD DOWNIE, managing editor, *Washington Post*, Washington, D.C., September 15, 1989.

*BOB DRUMMOND, *Dallas Times Herald*, October 31, 1989.

PAUL DUKE, host of "Washington Week in Review," Washington, D.C., August 17, 1989.

*THOMAS B. EDSALL, author and political reporter, *Washington Post*, July 16, 1990.

ALAN EHRENHALT, *Congressional Quarterly*, Washington, D.C., August 24, 1989.

ERIC ENGBERG, CBS News, Washington, D.C., January 5, 1990.

*TOM FIEDLER, political editor, *Miami Herald*, April 10, 1989; January 3, 1990; and January 29, 1990.

HOWARD FINEMAN, *Newsweek* chief political correspondent, *March 29, 1989, and Washington, D.C., August 24, 1989.

*WARREN FISKE, *Virginian-Pilot*, August 7, 1990.

*DON FOLEY, 1988 press secretary to the Richard Gephardt presidential campaign, January 8, 1990.

*BEN FRANKLIN, formerly of the *New York Times*, January 22, 1990.

*DOUGLAS FRANTZ, *Los Angeles Times*, September 1, 1989.

*AARON FREIWALD, *Legal Times*, October 6, 1989.

*BARBARA GAMAREKIAN, *New York Times*, February 24, 1989.

JAMES GANNON, bureau chief, *Detroit News*, Charlottesville, Va., September 28, 1989.

DAVID GERGEN, *U.S. News & World Report*, Washington, D.C., January 5, 1990.

JACK GERMOND, columnist, *Baltimore Sun*, Washington, D.C., August 18, 1989.

*STEVE GOLDBERG, Media General, November 20, 1989.

*MARK GOODIN, former Republican National Committee official, January 10, 1990.

*NORMAN GORIN, producer, "60 Minutes," March 16, 1990.

*JEFF GREENFIELD, ABC News, October 13, 1989.

TED GUP, *Time*, Washington bureau, Washington, D.C., July 10, 1989.

*JOHN HALL, visiting professor of journalism, University of Michigan, and freelance investigative journalist, March 8, 1990, and March 13, 1990.

STEVEN HANER, executive director, Virginia Republican Joint Legislative Caucus, Williamsburg, Va., September 28, 1990.

MICHAEL HARDY, *Richmond Times-Dispatch*, Richmond, Va., August 10, 1989.

RICHARD HARWOOD, *Washington Post* ombudsman, Washington, D.C., July 10, 1989.

*BRIAN HEALY, CBS News, September 8, 1989.

*GEORGE HERMAN, CBS News (retired), October 30, 1989.

KEN HIGHBERGER, CONUS Communications, Charlottesville Va., September 25, 1989.

*DAVID HOFFMAN, *Washington Post*, Washington, D.C., October 5, 1989.

*JOHN HOLLAND, "NBC Nightly News," March 8, 1990.

JERALD TERHORST, President Ford's first press secretary and formerly *Detroit News* reporter, Washington, D.C., August 4, 1990.

*DAN HOWARD, former spokesman for Senator John Tower, January 11, 1990, and February 15, 1990.

BRIT HUME, ABC News, Charlottesville, Va., September 28, 1989, and *June 27, 1990.

ELLEN HUME, executive director, Joan Shorenstein Barone Center, Kennedy School of Government, Harvard University, Boston, Mass., December 18, 1989.

ALBERT HUNT, D.C. bureau chief, *Wall Street Journal*, Washington, D.C., August 11, 1989.

TERRY HUNT, Associated Press, Charlottesville, Va., September 28, 1989.

*MICHAEL ISIKOFF, *Washington Post*, July 5, 1990.

BROOKS JACKSON, *Wall Street Journal*, *May 23, 1989; Milwaukee, Wis., February 24, 1989; and Washington, D.C., August 4, 1989.

*KENT JENKINS, JR., *Washington Post*, August 8, 1990.

PETER JENNINGS, ABC News, September 28, 1989.

*MARK JOHNSON, former press secretary to 1988 Democratic presidential candidate Richard Gephardt and press secretary to U.S. House Speaker Jim Wright, July 23, 1990.

*DAVID JOHNSTON, *New York Times*, January 31, 1990.

*PHIL JONES, CBS News, September 8, 1989.

MARVIN KALB, director, Joan Shorenstein Barone Center, Kennedy School of Government, Harvard University, Boston, Mass., December 18, 1989.

*MARIANNE KEELY, reportorial producer, ABC News, January 30 and June 27, 1990.

DOUGLAS KIKER, NBC News, Washington, D.C., October 5, 1989.

JAMES J. KILPATRICK, syndicated columnist, Washington, D.C., September 7, 1989.

*BRETT KIMBERLIN, federal prisoner, October 12, 1989.

SUSAN KING, WJLA-TV (Washington, D.C.), Charlottesville, Va., September 27, 1989.

*WAYNE KING, *New York Times*, January 2, 1990.

TED KOPPEL, ABC News, and host of "Nightline," Washington, D.C., January 5, 1990.

*BILL KOVACH, curator, the Nieman Foundation, March 6, 1990, and July 25, 1990.

*ANDREW LACK, CBS News, January 9, 1990.

GEORGE LARDNER, *Washington Post*, Washington, D.C., August 25, 1989.

JAMES LATIMER, *Richmond Times-Dispatch* (retired), September 26, 1989.

MICHAEL LAWRENCE, former DePauw University professor, August 10, 1989.

ANTHONY LEWIS, columnist, *New York Times*, November 20, 1989.

BILL LIVINGOOD, executive assistant to the director, U.S. Secret Service, February 2, 1990.

MRS. NACKEY LOEB, publisher and president, *Manchester Union-Leader*, Goffstown, N.H., June 23, 1989.

MARY LUKENS, aide to pollster Robert Teeter, March 17 and 21, 1989.

JOHN MASHEK, *Boston Globe*, Charlottesville, Va., September 28, 1989.

BARBARA MATUSOW, *Washingtonian* magazine, Washington, D.C., September 22, 1989.

BILL MCALLISTER, *Washington Post*, March 27, 1990.

SARAH MCCLENDON, independent Washington, D.C. news correspondent, March 5, 1990.

DAVID MCCLOUD, administrative assistant to U.S. Senator Charles Robb, Washington, D.C., July 3, 1990.

MICHAEL MCCURRY, Democratic Congressional Campaign Committee, Washington, D.C., August 28, 1989.

CHARLES MCDOWELL, *Richmond Times-Dispatch*, Washington, D.C., August 22, 1989.

MARY MCGRORY, *Washington Post*, Washington, D.C., November 21, 1989.

*DICK MEYER, CBS News producer, July 9, 1990.

ANDREA MITCHELL, NBC News, Washington, D.C., December 21, 1989.

*DAN MORANO, Brett Kimberlin's lawyer, October 4, 1989.

*G. C. MORSE, press secretary to Governor Gaston Caperton, March 26, 1990.

BRUCE MORTON, CBS News, Washington, D.C., October 16, 1989.

ROGER MUDD, PBS and "MacNeil/Lehrer NewsHour," Arlington, Va., January 5, 1990.

JACK NELSON, D.C. bureau chief, *Los Angeles Times*, Washington, D.C., August 24, 1989.

ROBERT NOVAK, syndicated columnist, Washington, D.C., August 25, 1989.

*ROSE ELLEN O'CONNOR, *Virginian-Pilot* and *Los Angeles Times*, November 14, 1989; November 20, 1989; December 28, 1989; and March 6, 1990.

*KIRK O'DONNELL, senior adviser to 1988 Dukakis presidential campaign, June 29, 1990.

MICHAEL ORESKES, *New York Times*, Washington, D.C., November 21, 1989.

*PRISCILLA PAINTON, *Time*, January 29, 1990.

*JAMES PERRY, *Wall Street Journal*, September 8, 1989.

CHARLES PETERS, editor, *Washington Monthly*, Washington, D.C., September 22, 1989.

*BILL PETERSON, *Washington Post*, April 5, 1989 and July 13, 1990.

*ROBERT PIERPOINT, CBS News, October 26, 1989.

*WALTER PINCUS, *Washington Post*, May 26, 1989.

BILL PLANTE, CBS News, Washington, D.C., November 21, 1989.

MARTIN PLISSNER, CBS News, Washington, D.C., September 7, 1989.

JIM POLK, NBC News, Washington, D.C., October 5, 1989.

HOWELL RAINES, D.C. bureau chief, *New York Times*, Washington, D.C., November 21, 1989.

*ELEANOR RANDOLPH, *Washington Post*, Washington, D.C., July 10, 1989.

JIM RAPER, managing editor, *Virginian-Pilot and Ledger Star*, Norfolk, Virginia, December 26, 1989, and *July 5, 1990.

*LARRY RASKY, former press secretary, Joseph Biden presidential campaign, January 2, 1990.

DAN RATHER, CBS News, New York, N.Y., January 19, 1990.

*T. R. REID, *Washington Post*, March 5, 1990.

CHARLES S. ROBB, U.S. senator (D., Va.), Washington, D.C., July 3, 1990.

COKIE ROBERTS, National Public Radio and ABC News, Washington, D.C., October 5, 1989.

STEVEN V. ROBERTS, *U.S. News & World Report*, Washington, D.C., August 18, 1989.

*CARL ROCHELLE, CNN, January 9, 1990.

*GLEN ROCHKIND, producer, NBC News, January 11, 1990.

*LOIS ROMANO, *Washington Post*, Washington, D.C., July 31, 1989.

*ANDREW ROSENTHAL, *New York Times*, January 11, 1990.

*TOM ROSENSTIEL, media reporter, *Los Angeles Times*, October 30, 1989.

*KNUTE ROYCE, *Newsday*, April 16, 1990.

TIM RUSSERT, D.C. bureau chief, NBC News, Washington, D.C., January 4, 1990.

JIM SAVAGE, *Miami Herald*, Washington, D.C., November 11, 1989, and December 28, 1989.

JEFF SCHAPIRO, *Richmond Times-Dispatch*, Richmond, Va., August 10, 1989.

*CODY SCHEARER, freelance reporter, March 8, 1990, and March 14, 1990.

*BOB SCHIEFFER, CBS News, November 22, 1989.

*MARALEE SCHWARTZ, *Washington Post*, July 20, 1990.

FRANK SESNO, CNN, Charlottesville, Va., September 27, 1989.

*MICHAEL SHANAHAN, McClatchy Newspapers, July 23, 1990.

WALTER SHAPIRO, *Time*, New York, N.Y., December 19, 1990.

*TOM SHERWOOD, WRC-TV (Washington, D.C.), and formerly of the *Washington Post*, November 24, 1989, and January 18, 1990.

MARK SHIELDS, columnist and television commentator, Washington, D.C., September 22, 1989.

ROBERT SHOGAN, *Los Angeles Times*, Washington, D.C., September 22, 1989.

*ROBERT SHRUM, Democratic political consultant, July 3, 1990.

*WILLIAM SLOAT, Cleveland *Plain Dealer*, September 8, 1989.

LARRY SPEAKES, spokesman for President Reagan, Washington, D.C., August 24, 1989.

*STUART SPENCER, Republican political consultant, November 21, 1989.

*JOHN ROBERT STARR, *Arkansas Democrat*, March 15, 1990.

*STEVEN STOCKMEYER, Washington, D.C. consultant, August 10, 1990.

*KEVIN SWEENEY, 1987 press secretary to Gary Hart, March 22, 1989.

*PAUL TAYLOR, *Washington Post*, April 5, 1989, and March 14, 1990.

STEPHEN TAYLOR, Unistar Radio Network, Charlottesville, Va., September 28, 1989.

*PETER TEELEY, formerly Vice President George Bush's communications director, May 30, 1989.

BILL THOMAS, *Roll Call*, Washington, D.C., August 24, 1989.

*CHARLIE THOMPSON, ABC News "20/20" and CBS News "60 Minutes," December 27, 1989, and March 14, 1990.

*NINA TOTENBERG, National Public Radio, October 4, 1989.

*JOHN G. TOWER, former U.S. senator (R., Tex.), January 12, 1990.

*KAREN TUMULTY, *Los Angeles Times*, March 13, 1989 and January 3, 1990.

*TOM TURNIPSEED, South Carolina Democratic politician, August 21, 1989.

*CHRIS WALLACE, ABC News, November 22, 1989.

*EDWARD WALSH, *Washington Post*, March 13, 1989.

KENNETH T. WALSH, *U.S. News & World Report*, Washington, D.C., August 11, 1989.

O. T. WATKINS, Director of Advertising, *Washington Times*, May 30, 1989.

*BERNIE WEINTRAUB, *New York Times*, January 9, 1990.

*BENJAMIN WEISER, *Washington Post*, June 14, 1989.

*TOM WESTBROOK, president, Tell-Back Inc., Spokane, Wash., March 21, 1989.

*PAUL WEYRICH, president, Free Congress Foundation, January 5, 1990.

*HAL WINGO, *People* magazine, December 29, 1989.

BILL WOOD, editorial editor, *Virginian-Pilot and Ledger Star*, Charlottesville, Va., September 28, 1989, and Norfolk, Virginia, December 26, 1989.

JUDY WOODRUFF, PBS and "MacNeil/Lehrer NewsHour," Washington, D.C., October 17, 1989.

BOB WOODWARD, *Washington Post*, Washington, D.C., December 21, 1989.

JAMES WOOTEN, ABC News, Washington, D.C., September 15, 1989.

*BOB ZELNICK, ABC News, January 9, 1990.

SELECTED BIBLIOGRAPHY

Books

ABRAMSON, JEFFREY B., F. CHRISTOPHER ARTERTON, and GARY R. ORREN. *The Electronic Commonwealth*. New York: Basic Books, 1988.

ALTHEIDE, DAVID L. *Creating Reality: How TV News Distorts Events*. Beverly Hills: Sage, 1976.

American Press Institute. *Covering the Candidates: Role and Responsibilities of the Press*. Reston, Va.: American Press Institute, 1987.

ARTERTON, F. CHRISTOPHER. *Media Politics: The News Strategies of Presidential Campaigns*. Lexington, Mass.: Lexington Books, 1984.

BATES, STEPHEN. *If No News, Send Rumors*. New York: St. Martin's, 1989.

BENNETT, LANCE. *News: The Politics of Illusion*. 2nd ed. New York: Longman, 1988.

BERKMAN, RONALD, and LAURA W. KITCH. *Politics in the Media Age*. New York: McGraw-Hill, 1986.

BLACK, CHRISTINE M., and THOMAS OLIPHANT. *All By Myself: The Unmaking of a Presidential Campaign*. Boston: Globe Pequot, 1989.

BRODER, DAVID S. *Behind the Front Page*. New York: Simon & Schuster, 1987.

COOK, TIMOTHY E. *Making Laws and Making News: Media Strategies in the U.S. House of Representatives*. Washington, D.C.: Brookings, 1989.

COSE, ELLIS. *The Press*. New York: William Morrow and Co., Inc., 1989.

CROUSE, TIMOTHY. *The Boys on the Bus*. New York: Ballantine, 1973.

DIAMOND, EDWIN. *The Tin Kazoo: Television, Politics, and the News*. Cambridge, Mass.: MIT Press, 1975.

EFRON, EDITH. *The News Twisters*. Los Angeles: Nash, 1971.

ENTMAN, ROBERT M. *Democracy Without Citizens: Media and the Decay of American Politics.* New York: Oxford University Press, 1989.

EPSTEIN, EDWARD JAY. *Between Fact and Fiction.* New York: Random House, 1975.

———. *News from Nowhere: Television and the News.* New York: Random House, 1973.

GANS, HERBERT J. *Deciding What's News.* New York: Vintage, 1980.

GINSBERG, BENJAMIN, and MARTIN SHEFTER. *Politics by Other Means: The Declining Importance of Elections in America.* New York: Basic Books, 1990.

GOLDBERG, ROBERT, and GERALD JAY GOLDBERG. *Anchors: Brokaw, Jennings, Rather and the Evening News.* New York: Birch Lane, 1990.

GOLDSTEIN, TOM. *The News at Any Cost.* New York: Simon & Schuster, 1985.

GRABER, DORIS A. *Mass Media and American Politics.* 3rd ed. Washington, D.C.: Congressional Quarterly Press, 1989.

———. *Media Power in Politics.* 2nd ed. Washington, D.C.: Congressional Quarterly Press, 1989.

GRAHAM, FRED. *Happy Talk: Confessions of a TV Newsman.* New York: W. W. Norton, 1990.

GREENFIELD, JEFF. *The Real Campaign: How the Media Missed the Story of the 1980 Campaign.* New York: Summit, 1982.

HESS, STEPHEN. *The Ultimate Insiders: U.S. Senators in the National Media.* Washington, D.C.: The Brookings Institution, 1986.

HIRSCH, ALAN. *Talking Heads: Television's Political Talk Shows and Pundits.* New York: St. Martin's, 1991.

ISAACS, NORMAN E. *Untended Gates: The Mismanaged Press.* New York: Columbia University Press, 1986.

IYENGAR, SHANTO, and DONALD R. KINDER. *News That Matters.* Chicago: University of Chicago Press, 1987.

LEE, MARTIN A., and NORMAN SOLOMON. *Unreliable Sources: A Guide to Detecting Bias in the News Media.* New York: Lyle Stuart, 1990.

LEONARD, THOMAS C., *The Power of the Press: The Birth of American Political Reporting.* New York: Oxford University Press, 1986.

LICHTER, S. ROBERT, STANLEY ROTHMAN, and LINDA S. LICHTER. *The Media Elite.* Bethesda, Md.: Adler and Adler, 1986.

LICHTER, S. ROBERT, DANIEL AMUNDSON, and RICHARD NOYES. *The Video Campaign: Network Coverage of the 1988 Primaries.* Washington, D.C.: American Enterprise Institute, 1988.

MATUSOW, BARBARA. *The Evening Stars: The Making of the Network News Anchor.* Boston: Houghton Mifflin, 1983.

MITROFF, IAN, and WARREN BENNIS. *The Unreality Industry.* New York: Birch Lane Press, 1989.

MICKELSON, SIG. *The Electric Mirror: Politics in an Age of Network Television.* New York: Dodd, Mead, 1972.

NIMMO, DAN, and JAMES E. COMBS. *Mediated Political Realities.* 2nd ed. New York: Longman, 1988.

ORREN, GARY R., and NELSON W. POLSBY, eds. *Media and Momentum: The New Hampshire Primary and Nomination Politics.* Chatham, N.J.: Chatham House, 1987.

PALETZ, DAVID L., and ROBERT M. ENTMAN. *Media Power Politics.* New York: Free Press, 1981.

PATTERSON, THOMAS E. *The Mass Media Election.* New York: Praeger, 1980.

PATTERSON, THOMAS E., and ROBERT D. MCCLURE. *The Unseeing Eye: The Myth of Television Power in National Elections.* New York: G. P. Putnam's Sons, 1976.

PERRY, JAMES A. *Us and Them: How the Press Covered the 1972 Election.* New York: Clarkson Potter, 1973.

PRESS, CHARLES, and KENNETH VERBURG. *American Politicians and Journalists.* Glenview, Ill.: Scott, Foresman, 1988.

RANNEY, AUSTIN. *Channels of Power: The Impact of Television on American Politics.* New York: Basic Books, 1983.

ROSS, SHELLEY. *Fall from Grace: Sex, Scandal, and Corruption in American Politics from 1702 to the Present.* New York: Ballantine, 1988.

RUSHER, WILLIAM A. *The Coming Battle for the Media: Curbing the Power of the Media Elite.* New York: William Morrow, 1988.

SCHRAM, MARTIN. *The Great American Video Game: Presidential Politics in the Television Age.* New York: William Morrow, 1987.

SIMON, ROGER. *Road Show.* New York: Farrar, Straus & Giroux, 1990.

STEPHENS, MITCHELL. *A History of News: From the Drum to the Satellite.* New York: Viking, 1989.

TAYLOR, PAUL. *See How They Run: Electing the President in an Age of Mediaocracy.* New York: Alfred A. Knopf, 1990.

WATTENBERG, BEN J. *The Good News Is the Bad News Is Wrong.* New York: Simon & Schuster, 1985.

Articles

ADAMS, WILLIAM C. "'84 Convention Coverage." *Public Opinion* 7 (December/January 1985): 43–48.

———. "Media Coverage of Campaign '84: A Preliminary Report." *Public Opinion* 7 (April\May 1984): 9–13.

ADATTO, KIKU. "The Shrinking Sound Bite," *The New Republic* 202 (May 28, 1990): 20–23.

ALTER, JONATHAN. "How the Media Blew It." *Newsweek* 112 (November 21, 1988): 24–26.

AMUNDSON, DANIEL, and ROBERT S. LICHTER. "Heeere's Politics." *Public Opinion* 11 (July/August 1988): 46–47.

BAGDIKIAN, BEN H. "The Fruits of Agnewism." *Columbia Journalism Review* 11 (January/February 1973): 9–21.

BALZ, DAN. "Capitol Hill Stuck in Ethics Quagmire." *Washington Post,* May 28, 1989, A1, A20.

———. "The Public Politics of Rumors." *Washington Post,* June 8, 1989, A1, A10.

BARBER, JAMES DAVID. "Candidate Reagan and the Sucker Generation." *Columbia Journalism Review* 25 (November/December 1987): 33–36.

BARNES, JAMES A. "Changing Company Town." *National Journal* 21 (February 4, 1989): 278–80.

BARRETT, LAURENCE I. "The Dark Side of Competition . . . Woodward, Bernstein." *Columbia Journalism Review* 12 (July/August 1974): 14–15.

———. "Rethinking the Fair Games Rules." *Time* 130 (November 30, 1987): 76, 78.

BONAFEDE, DOM. "Blame the Scribes." *National Journal* 20 (July 9, 1988): 1803–6.

———. "Crossing Over." *National Journal* 21 (January 14, 1989): 102.

———. "Go Away." *National Journal* 21 (February 11, 1989): 378.

———. "Scoop or Snoop?" *National Journal* 20 (November 5, 1988): 2791–94.

———. "Taking On the Press." *National Journal* 21 (April 8, 1989): 856–60.

BOOT, WILLIAM. "Campaign '88: TV Overdoses on the Inside Dope." *Columbia Journalism Review* 27 (January/February 1989): 23–29.

———. "Iranscam: When the Cheering Stopped." *Columbia Journalism Review* 25 (March/April 1987): 25–30.

BOYD, JAMES. "The Ritual of Wiggle: From Ruin to Reelection." *Washington Monthly* 2 (September 1970): 28–43.

BRAMEN, SANDRA. "Public Expectations of Media Versus Standards in Codes of Ethics." *Journalism Quarterly* 65 (Spring 1988): 71–77, 240.

BRANDEIS, LOUIS D., and SAMUEL D. WARREN. "The Right to Privacy." *Harvard Law Review* 4 (December 15, 1890): 193–220.

BRODER, DAVID S. "Beware the 'Insider' Syndrome: Why News Makers and News Reporters Shouldn't Get Too Cozy." *Washington Post*, December 4, 1988, L2.

Center for Media and Public Affairs. "Quayle Hunt: TV News Coverage of the Quayle Nomination," *Media Monitor* 2 (September 1988): 1–4.

CLANCEY, MAURA, and MICHAEL J. ROBINSON. "General Election Coverage in Campaign '84: Part 1." *Public Opinion* 7 (December/January 1985): 49–54, 59.

COOPER, THOMAS W. "Ethics, Journalism and Television: Bibliographic Constellations, Black Holes." *Journalism Quarterly* 65 (Spring 1988): 450–55, 496.

DEWAR, HELEN. "Defeat of Tower Reflects Dramatic Changes in Senate." *Washington Post*, March 13, 1989, A1, A6–7.

DIAMOND, EDWIN. "Fairness and Balance in the Evening News." *Columbia Journalism Review* 11 (January/February, 1973): 22–23.

———. "Gotcha: The Media's Frenzied Patrol of the Candidates." *New York*, October 26, 1987, pp. 50–53.

———. "New Wrinkles on the Permanent Press." *Public Opinion* 7 (April/May 1984): 2–4, 58.

EASTLAND, TERRY. "Ethicshock." *The Washingtonian* 23 (August 1989): 77–80.

FUNKHOUSER, G. RAY. "The Issues of the Sixties: An Exploratory Study in the Dynamics of Public Opinion." *Public Opinion Quarterly* 37 (Spring 1973): 62–75.

GARMENT, SUZANNE. "Political Imperfections: Scandal Time in Washington." *Public Opinion* 10 (May/June 1987): 10–12, 60.

———. "Sleaze, Scandal, and Successful Elections." *Public Opinion* 11 (September/October 1988): 15–17.

GERGEN, DAVID. "The Message to the Media." *Public Opinion* 7 (April/May 1984): 5–8.

GLASSMAN, JAMES K. "The 'Ethics' Frenzy." *Washington Post*, May 28, 1989, B1–2.

GUP, TED. "Identifying Homosexuals: What Are the Rules?" *Washington Journalism Review* 10 (October 1988): 30–33.

GUZZARDI, WALTER. "The Secret Love Affair Between the Press and Government." *Public Opinion* 8 (August/September 1985): 2–5.

HENRY, WILLIAM A., III. "Cover Story: Journalism Under Fire." *Time* 122 (December 12, 1983): 76–93.

HENTOFF, NAT. "Woodward, Bernstein and 'All the President's Men'." *Columbia Journalism Review* 12 (July/August 1974): 10–13.

HERSHEY, MARJORIE RANDON. "The Campaign and the Media." In *The Election of 1988: Reports and Interpretations*, edited by Gerald M. Pomper et al. chap. 3, pp. 73–102. Chatham, N.J.: Chatham House, 1989.

HERTZBERG, HENDRICK. "Sluicegate." *The New Republic* 196 (June 1, 1987): 11–12.

HOLLSTEIN, MILTON. "Congressman Howe in the Salt Lake Media: A Case Study of the Press as Pillory." *Journalism Quarterly* 54 (Autumn 1977): 454–58, 465.

HOSENBALL, MARK, and MICHAEL ISIKOFF. "Pssst: Inside Washington's Rumor Mill." *The New Republic* 200 (January 2, 1989): 16–19.

IVINS, MOLLY. "The Reporters Under the Bed." *Mirabella* 1 (June 1989): 120–21.

JOHNSTON, DAVID. "The Anonymous-Source Syndrome." *Columbia Journalism Review* 25 (November/December 1987): 54–58.

JUDIS, JOHN B. "The Hart Affair." *Columbia Journalism Review* 25 (July/August 1987): 21–25.

KING, ANTHONY. "Transatlantic Transgressions: A Comparison of British and American Scandals." *Public Opinion* 7 (December/January 1985): 20–22, 64.

LEEDEN, MICHAEL. "Public Opinion, Press Opinion, and Foreign Policy." *Public Opinion* 7 (August/September 1984): 5–7, 60.

LESSARD, SUZANNAH. "The Issue Was Women." *Newsweek* 109 (May 18, 1987): 32, 34.

LICHTER, S. ROBERT. "How the Press Covered the Primaries." *Public Opinion* 11 (July/August 1988): 45–49.

———. "Misreading Momentum." *Public Opinion* 11 (May/June 1988): 15–17, 57.

LICHTER, S. ROBERT., DANIEL AMUNDSON, and RICHARD E. NOYES. "Election '88 Media Coverage." *Public Opinion* 11 (January/February 1989): 18–19, 52.

LICHTER, S. ROBERT., and LINDA S. LICHTER. "Covering the Convention Coverage." *Public Opinion* 11 (September/October 1988): 41–44.

LICHTER, S. ROBERT., and STANLEY ROTHMAN. "Media and Business Elites." *Public Opinion* 4 (October/November 1981): 42–46, 59–60.

MCCARTNEY, JAMES. "What Really Happened in Manchester?" *Columbia Journalism Review* 10 (May/June 1972): 26–27.

MATLACK, CAROL. "Crossing the Line?" *National Journal* 21 (March 25, 1989): 724–29.

———. "Rules of the Game." *National Journal* 21 (June 3, 1989): 1386.

MATUSOW, BARBARA. "Washington's Journalism Establishment." *The Washingtonian* 23 (February 1989): 94–101, 265–70.

MOORE, DAVID. "The Legacy of William Loeb." *Public Opinion* 5 (December/January 1983): 43–44.

ORNSTEIN, NORMAN. "The Post's Campaign to Wreck Congress." *Washington Post*, May 29, 1989, A25.

PATTERSON, THOMAS E. "The Miscast Institution: The Press in Presidential Politics." *Public Opinion* 3 (June/July 1980): 46–51.

———. "The Press and its Missed Assignment," pp. 93–110. In *The Elections of 1988*, edited by Michael Nelson. Washington, D.C.: Congressional Quarterly Press, 1989.

PLISSNER, MARTIN. "Inkbites." *Washington Post*, March 20, 1989, A11.

RANDOLPH, ELEANOR. "Candidates Limit Media Access." *Washington Post*, September 21, 1988, A1, A14.

———. "Frustrated Reporters Add Megaphones, Binoculars to Notepads." *Washington Post*, November 2, 1988, A25.

———. "'Quayle Hunt' Turns News Media into Target for Angry Public." *Washington Post*, August 25, 1988, A10.

ROBINSON, MICHAEL J. "Just How Liberal Is the News? 1980 Revisited." *Public Opinion* 6 (February/March 1983): 55–60.

———. "Pressing Opinion." *Public Opinion* 9 (September/October 1986): 56–59.

ROBINSON, MICHAEL J., and MARGARET SHEEHAN. "Brief Encounters With the Fourth Kind: Reagan's Press Honeymoon." *Public Opinion* 3 (December/January 1981): 56–61.

ROBINSON, MICHAEL J., NANCY CONOVER, and MARGARET SHEEHAN. "The Media at Mid-Year: A Bad Year for McLuhanites." *Public Opinion* 3 (June/July 1980): 41–45.

ROSENSTIEL, THOMAS B., and PAUL HOUSTON. "Rumor Mill: The Media 'Try to Cope.'" *Los Angeles Times*, August 5, 1988, 1, 18.

SCHNEIDER, WILLIAM, and I. A. LEWIS. "Views on the News." *Public Opinion* 8 (August/September 1985): 6–11, 58–59.

SHAPIRO, WALTER. "Is It Right to Publish Rumors?" *Time* 132 (July 10, 1989): 53.

SMITH, TED J., III. "The Watchdog's Bite." *American Enterprise* 1 (January/February 1990): 62–70.

STANLEY, ALESSANDRA, and MAUREEN DOWD. "The Dweebs on the Bus." *Gentleman's Quarterly* 57 (September 1988): 430–33, 482–87.

STEIN, M. L. "How Editors View Ombudsmen." *Editor and Publisher* 122 (May 13, 1989): 15–16.

STEVENSON, ROBERT L., et al. "Untwisting *The News Twisters:* A Replication of Efron's Study." *Journalism Quarterly* 50 (Summer 1973): 211–19.

STOVALL, JAMES GLEN. "Coverage of the 1984 Presidential Campaign." *Journalism Quarterly* 65 (Summer 1968): 443–49, 484.

SWERDLOW, JOEL. "The Decline of the Boys on the Bus." *Washington Journalism Review* 3 (January/February 1981): 15–19.

THIMMESCH, NICK. "The Editorial Endorsement Game." *Public Opinion* 7 (October/November 1984): 10–13.

WHEELER, MICHAEL. "Reining in Horserace Journalism." *Public Opinion* 3 (February/March 1980): 41–45.

WILDAVSKY, AARON. "The Media's 'American Egalitarians.'" *Public Interest* 88 (Summer 1987): 94–104.

WILKIE, CURTIS, "Too Hot to Handle." *Washington Journalism Review* 6 (March 1984): 38–39, 58.

WINES, MICHAEL. "In Bed with the Press." *Washington Journalism Review* 9 (September 1987): 16–19.

WINSHIP, TOM. "Answering Hart and Kennedy." *Columbia Journalism Review* 25 (May 1988): 39–41.

WITCOVER, JULES. "The Trials of a One-Candidate Campaign." *Columbia Journalism Review* 11 (January/February 1973): 24–28.

———. "William Loeb and the New Hampshire Primary: A Question of Ethics." *Columbia Journalism Review* 10 (May/June 1972): 14–25.

WITT, EVANS. "Here, There, and Everywhere: Where Americans Get Their News." *Public Opinion* 6 (August/September 1983): 45–48.

YUM, JUNE O., and KATHLEEN E. KENDALL. "Sources of Political Information in a Presidential Primary Campaign." *Journalism Quarterly* 65 (Spring 1988): 148–51, 177.

INDEX